D1229920

BUS PLANNING AND OPERATION IN URBAN AREAS:
A PRACTICAL GUIDE

To all my colleagues
who encouraged me to keep working
on this book
and of course to the two persons
who make it worthwhile.

Bus Planning and Operation in Urban Areas: A Practical Guide

Technical Resource Center

HE
5611
.G52
1989

G. A. GIANNOPOULOS
Professor, Department of Civil Engineering,
Transportation Engineering Section,
University of Thessaloniki, Greece

Avebury

Aldershot · Brookfield USA · Hong Kong · Singapore · Sydney

© G.A.Giannopoulos, 1989

All rights reserved. No part of this publication may
be reproduced, stored in a retrieval system or transmitted in any form or by any means, electronic, mechanical, photocopying, recording, or otherwise without
the prior permission of Gower Publishing Company Limited.

Published by

Avebury

Gower Publishing Company Limited,
Gower House, Croft Road, Aldershot,
Hants. GU11 3HR, England

Gower Publishing Company,
Old Post Road, Brookfield, Vermont 05036
USA

British Library Cataloguing in Publication Data
Giannopoulos, G.A. 1946-
  Bus planning and operation in urban areas :
a practical guide.
  1. Urban regions. Bus services. Routes.
  Operation. Travel time
  I. Title
  388.4'1322

  ISBN 0-566-05673-9

Printed and Bound in Great Britain by
Athenaeum Press Ltd., Newcastle upon Tyne.

Contents

CHAPTER 5. GUIDELINES FOR THE NETWORK

BUS STOP SHELTERS

Preface

This book is intended to fill what appeared to me as an unmet need for a practical and easy to use guide (based on current practice) for bus transport planning and operations in urban areas. Bus transport managers all over the world feel increasingly the need to use their limited physical and financial resources more efficiently within the political and social constraints that are particularly evident in urban areas. The necessity of some guidelines that would permit this to be done in a more uniform and orderly way has been stressed by several authors.

The problems are even more acute in the developing countries, where the limited resources for planning and research, together with increased bureaucratic procedures in the decision making processes, severely hinder proper management and operation of public transport.

In this author's experience there are often cases of bus managers and supervising agencies, where the existence of a certain "standard" or guideline is desperately desirable, in order to proceed with actions that might otherwise be blocked as unwise or "unpopular", by the political and social environment, in which a bus undertaking has to operate.

By examining the major areas of bus operation

1

and by presenting the main characteristics and current practice for such operation, this book intends to provide a valuable help to planners and managers of bus transportation in urban areas.

It is also hoped that the book will prove equally interesting for the academics in this field, and especially for those doing courses on bus operation and planning. In fact the original intention was to create more of a reference book for educational purposes. However, later thoughts and a specific project assigned to the author's research team at the University of Thessaloniki, Greece, proved the importance of addressing also the more practical issues facing the day to day bus operations and planning of the network and service.

The material comes from two major sources. The first is the author's own experience in the field as well as the (rather limited) international bibliography, while the second is the specific project mentioned earlier. This project was an eighteen month-study dealing with the characteristics and proposed standards for Bus Operations in Urban areas in Greece, assigned by the Hellenic Organization for Local Government and Development (EETAA). The outcome of the study was a set of detailed guidelines for bus operations and planning in Greece, designed to provide an easy to follow and understand guide for bus operators.

In writing this book special emphasis was given to the problems faced by the operations in developing countries. Without ignoring the all too often cases, where these problems also exist in the so called developed countries, extremely limited resources and the lack of specialized personnel in developing countries call for special emphasis to be given for solutions easy to understand and implement. For example, I find it extremely difficult to see how the methodologies for transit capacity calculations in the new 1985 (US) Highway Capacity Manual can be followed and applied in practice by the generally non-specialized personnel of bus agencies (or even supervising bodies) in most countries (developed or developing). Even if that was possible, the numerical values and the results given there cannot be easily applicable to the situation in many countries.

All these considerations made me extremely cautious, when writing the various chapters, not to overlook the practical application side of the material, while maintaining a certain acceptable academic standard and justification for the various notions

2

and suggestions. I hope this has been achieved to a considerable degree.

The material has been divided into nine main Chapters and two Annexes. The first chapter contains an introduction to some general issues and presents some simple and easy to understand definitions and principles related to bus operations.

The second chapter addresses the problem of a proper organizational structure for a bus transport undertaking. This is an issue generally neglected in the literature, despite being of extreme importance to the generally less organized smaller bus operators, especially in developing countries. Apart from addressing the forms of Organization, this chapter also discusses the various types of ownership of the bus operators. This is an issue of considerable debate in several urban areas around the world, that has not been addressed adequately in the existing literature.

The third chapter contains guidelines for the Service and Operation Planning Processes that are recommended for bus operations. In doing so it gives some details on data collection and other tasks, that are associated with every day bus operation. Although the level of detail may not be the same as that in more specialized publications, it provides the reader with all the necessary information which will enable him to both understand and implement these procedures in practice. Again the procedures proposed have been adapted to the overall focus of this book, namely the medium to small operators, especially in developing countries.

The fourth chapter is devoted to what has been called the "Service Standards and Evaluation Process". This is a continuous procedure, that is recommended for medium and large agencies to provide a minimum of evaluation and testing of the service offered to the public. It also gives important guidelines for a process of "standards" application, which could help the agency towards a uniform assessment of the various requests for service extensions, new services or other suggestions.

The next three chapters, i.e chapters 5,6, and 7, contain material concerning the Network (i.e. lines, stops and terminals), the Rolling Stock and the whole Operation (or Exploitation) of the service. Each of these chapters has been written with emphasis on specific practical suggestions that have been found to provide a good result in practice. Adaptation to suit local conditions may, of course, be necessary before applying the suggestions in these chapters. However, in most cases an effort has been made to give ranges of values instead of single numbers, as well as to point out the advantages or disadvantages of the various alternative actions.

In Chapter 8 the various bus priority measures are discussed. This subject deserved special attention, because such measures are now a necessity in the usually congested urban areas. Besides, they form a crucial part of bus operation affecting its final outcome. The emphasis is on bus lanes although other priority measures are also treated.

The final chapter presents what I feel is the most neglected part in bus operation today, namely Marketing and Public Information. With the exception of the large operators in certain cities of Western Europe and North America, the majority of the other agencies do not apply the techniques of modern marketing, while their public information system is generally inadequate or non existent. It is hoped that the material in this chapter gives useful information on both of these subjects and provides the reader with a concise description of the techniques and possibilities available. Two annexes complete the material given in this book. Annex 1 contains a detailed presentation of the Organizational, Institutional and Financing arrangements for public transport in France, as an example of a successful structure with respect to our suggestions in Chapter 2.

Annex 2 contains the results of a questionnaire survey which the author made among major Bus Operators worldwide in order to assess current practices and the status in the formulation and application of guidelines or standards for bus operation in urban areas.

A word of caution when using the contents of this book is necessary. No book can be a text that will cover all possible aspects of the subject it treats, especially when dealing with a subject as large and "sensitive" in many aspects, as that of guidelines for Bus Planning and Operation. What has been attempted here is to provide the reader with as much information as possible about the current practice and state of the art in this field, so that he will be in a better position to understand and, if applicable, to take necessary actions. In each case the final application of the ideas expressed here will depend on the local conditions, i.e. the so called "operating environment".

4

I am indebted for the help given to me, at the various stages of writing this book, by my colleagues of the Laboratory of Transportation Engineering, Civil Engineering Department of the University of Thessaloniki. I particularly thank my colleagues who participated in the original research assigned to us by the Hellenic Organization for Local Government and Development (EETAA). These are Aristotle Naniopoulos, Magda Pitsiava, Spyros Vougias and Vasilis Demarelos. Many thanks are also due to Transportation Planner Eleni Giannitsopoulou who helped with corrections to the texts, the final hectic weeks of the preparation of the book. Her perspective and attention to detail are greatly appreciated.

My secretary Stella Christeli, who typed most of the texts patiently deciphering my indecipherable writing, and Niki Economou who did all the drawings, have my sincere gratitude for their dedicated work.

My deepest thanks are also due to two colleagues from the United States who have read and commented on different parts of the manuscript. These are Professor Wolf Homburger of the University of California's Institute of Transportation Studies at Berkeley and Professor Nigel Wilson of the Center for Transportation Studies of the M.I.T. Their comments, ideas, and constructive criticism substantially enhanced the manuscripts and have improved the quality of the various chapters they have seen.

Of course, full responsibility for any remaining errors or omissions is mine.

Thanks are finally due to all my friends and collaborators in Thessaloniki and Athens who put up with a certain moody professor at times when he was best left to himself and his deadline. Especially fond regards go to Diana for her cheer, thoughtfulness and continual understanding.

G.A.Giannopoulos

1 Introduction

World-wide the bus carries the main burden of collective public transport. Its application is, however, in many urban areas limited by inefficient organization and management, shortage of proper equipment, inadequate planning and by the fact that buses run on most routes of the public street network in the same space as the rest of the traffic while in addition stopping at more or less clearly marked points to enable passenger turnover to take place. Limiting the bus operation in this way means leaving considerable transport potential untouched and using capital and operational costs uneconomically. On the other hand, our cities are turning into ever more complex structures. The measure of their functional capability is determined by the effectiveness of their components and the integration thereof into the whole framework. Public passenger transport is a fundamental urban function, which can be fulfilled better, the more. system-oriented and systematic the planning and operation. The most neglected options and therefore also the largest potential for improvement and change in this respect is in the field of bus transport.

7

The greatest advantage of the bus is that, as a rule, it can use the whole of the public street network. This makes it extremely flexible in its application. However, when a certain degree of mutual hindrance is reached with the other types of street traffic, this advantage may turn into a disadvantage, i.e. the use of buses may become unattractive and their operation uneconomical. However, this is not a fault inherent to the system, it is a fault of laying out and planning the system.

A properly laid out and operated bus system requires an adequate design of all of its principal elements. These elements are: the network (roadway/stops/terminals), the vehicles and the operations. Whereas to start running a bus operation only vehicles and drivers are basically necessary, offering an effective transit system in towns and metropolitan areas requires much more than this. It requires efficient planning, proper management and innovative thinking in supplying attractive services to the public, able to form (together with the other modes of transit) a credible alternative to the use of private cars.

To give some examples of the various problem areas that need to be addressed and solved in this comprehensive approach, one could state the following:

From the passenger's point of view the following goals should be achieved:
- reduced journey times, increased journey speed
- better passenger transfers
- reduced waiting periods
- better protection from weather conditions
- improved punctuality and reliability
- improved "handiness"
- better interconnections
- more information
- improved ride comfort.

From the operator's point of view, besides being interested in safety and profitability, he also rates efficiency. Improvements in this respect can be achieved through:

- reducing hindrances at bus stops, crossroads and traffic lights
- priority right-of-way, e.g. influence on traffic flow for a better passing of buses at traffic light controlled intersections

8

- reducing passenger transfers and processing
  times
- reserved lanes

as well as through more sophisticated techniques
such as:

- automatic guidance systems
- adapting the transit network to changing
  traffic demands.

It would seem appropriate that we no longer
speak of the "bus" as a well known and taken "for
granted" mode of transit, but of modern " bus transit
systems" comprising a number of individual components
(see later section in this chapter). To achieve this,
there is need for proper planning and a new approach
towards co-ordinated measures aimed at improving the
entire system by acting simultaneously on all its
components. In other words by upgrading the bus to a
bus transit system .
Proper planning and operation can achieve this
and at the same time help exploit the two greatest
advantages of a bus system over other modes, i.e.
flexibility and adaptability.
The material in this book will help to clarify
many of the points in this respect and help planners
and managers to setup and operate bus systems efficiently and effectively in urban areas.

THE BUS IN URBAN TRANSIT AROUND THE WORLD

General

The bus represents today the most common means
of urban transit world-wide. It has universal application and, as a series-produced industrial product,
it is both reliable and economical. It can be used to
cover sprawling areas or can be operated in a linear
network, which can be quickly adapted at low cost to
meet changing demands. The costs of bus operation, of
special rights-of-way, of bus stops and of control
systems are known and readily calculable.
The bus has today many applications in local
transit which can be summed up in the following
three:
a. It can assume the sole Public Transport
service of an entire town.

9

b. It may be operated as a co-ordinated service in conjunction with rail vehicles
(providing feeder, tangential or intercon-
necting service).

c. It may provide transport connection between
city centres and peripheral communities, as
express or main trunk lines.

Historically the bus has steadily increased its
share of the urban transit market and has become the
major mode for urban transport in the majority of
towns and cities around the world.

As regards serving the entire town, the bus system fulfils the role of the only public transport
operator that has to serve all, or almost all, of the
population. Towns and cities around the world with
populations below 300,000 have almost invariably only
one mode of public transport and this is the bus. As
the population increases and according to the position and importance of the particular urban area in
the country (e.g. capital city or major port etc)
other modes of transport may be introduced in addition to buses. It is estimated that world-wide there
are between 8-10,000 towns and cities with a population between 10,000 and 200,000, in which there is an
organized system of (bus) public transport.

The larger-scale urban areas are obviously much
less, 784 according to one count (UITP, 1985), and in
any case less than 1,000. Thus, bus transportation
operating as the only mode of urban public transport
for the small to medium sized urban areas, dominates
the scene world-wide.

In its role as a complementary mode, bus transport is again a major element in any urban public
transport system. It offers flexibility to cover
wide areas that cannot be covered by any other mode.
Multimodal integrated systems of public transport
rely heavily on buses to supply feeder services as
well as main lines to areas with lesser densities of
development.

Some Statistical Evidence

Some statistics, taken from an analysis of the
results of a recent survey by the International Union
of Public Transport - UITP, will help to demonstrate
further the role of the bus in urban transport around
the world.

A 50-70% share of the bus in the total number of
passengers or passenger-kms carried within urban
areas is quite typical. In Athens, Greece, for ex-

10

ample, buses carry nearly 65% of the passengers and run more than 80% of the vehicle - kms in the area (average figures over a five-year period). In the Federal Republic of Germany as a whole, and for all urban transport, the relative share in 1984 was as follows (MAN, 1985):

	Bus	Subway Trains	Street cars-LRT	Other
Passengers	55.0%	21.4%	23.4%	0.2%
Pass-place miles	57.7%	19.8%	22.2%	0.3%
Vehicle - miles	72.0%	13.5%	14.2%	0.3%

Similar figures apply to other European countries. Urban areas in the developing world show invariably greater use of bus transport.

Of the 784 major urban areas included in the 1985 UITP survey over 70% have buses and one more mode of public transport, while the rest have buses and 2 other modes. The size of the bus transport undertakings in these urban areas is in the majority of the cases what one could call medium to small. In 22% of the cases the bus agencies have up to 100 buses, in 37% of the cases between 400-1,000 buses and in only 15% of the cases over 1,000 buses. Considering that the UITP survey usually includes only the major urban areas (both in terms of size and national importance), it follows that world-wide, medium to small-sized bus agencies dominate the scene of urban transport.

Of interest is also to see the ownership of the agencies that operate bus transport. This is interesting because it shows a situation where public ownership irrespective of its type dominates the scene and influences inevitably the scope and form of bus transport provision. Again, of the 784 agencies reported in the UITP survey, the distribution according to forms of ownership is as follows:

	No.of agencies	%
Privately owned	125	16%
Owned by central government	140	18%
Owned by local or regional government	439	56%
Mixed economy (public and private)	71	9%
Other	9	1%
Total	784	100%

11

So it can be said that the bulk of urban public transport agencies is owned by the central, local or regional governments, while a 25% is still in private or mixed economy companies. Again it is noted that these figures may be only representative of the major urban areas included in the UITP survey. In this author's experience, the bulk of the bus agencies operating in the smaller urban areas around the world are still in private hands and generally operate in a loose and disorganized way.

Overall it can be said that the bus forms the backbone of public transport in urban areas all over the world. In fact, for millions of people it is the only means of transportation. It seems also very probable that the bus will play the same role for many years to come.

BUS SYSTEM COMPONENTS

The success of a bus transportation system, in terms of meeting the user's needs in an efficient way, depends largely on how much it operates as a "system". In other words it depends on the quality of its components and how well these are combined into a workable overall system.

The principal "components" of a bus system may be distinguished in six categories (see Figure 1.1):

   a.   Service planning ("offer" of transportation services).
   b.   The actual operation (i.e. execution of the services planned).
   c.   The passenger information and other services (usually also referred to as demand management).
   d.   The Rolling Stock (vehicles).
   e.   The bus stops and terminals.
   f.   The rest of the "network", i.e. the roadway and tracks (including bus lanes).

The first two as well as the last two of the above components may sometimes be grouped together respectively. In the first case, we are referring to the "Operation" or "Exploitation" while in the second, generally, to the "network". In the following we will describe each of the above six components in somewhat greater detail.

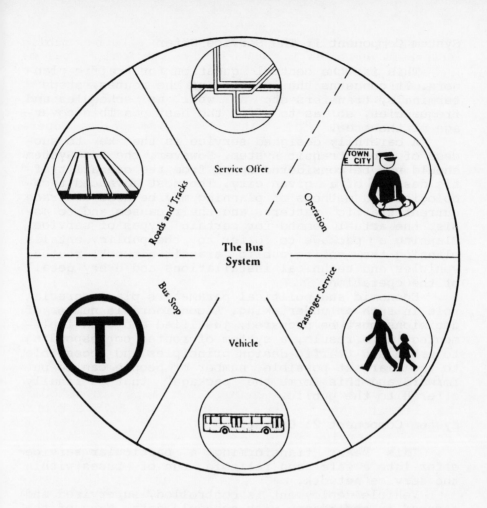

Figure 1.1: The principal "components" of a bus system.

13

System Component 1: The Service Offer

This is the central question for traffic planners. It concerns the location of the routes, stops terminals, transfers etc as well as schedules and frequencies, so as to offer the best possible coverage of the area.

A carefully designed service is the key to success of a bus transit system. However, the Bus System should not be considered apart from the overall traffic design of a given city. The most advanced technologies and methods of planning may be used to trace current traffic patterns and their causes and to assist the actual demand for certain types of service. Planning a package to offer to the public, entails planning the entire public transit network, routes, vehicles and technical installations and every detail of the operation.

Economic and political parameters play a crucial role in such an undertaking. A considerable number of decisions must be prepared, justified and then implemented. As a result, a system of routes corresponding to urban and traffic design principles and accessible to the largest possible number of people can be put forward and this forms the "package" that is finally offered to the public.

System Component 2: Operation

This means transforming a particular service offer into a safe and reliable run of buses within the service network.

Vehicle deployment is controlled, supervised and secured in accordance with schedule data. Many of the operational tasks are routine. Computerized Transit Control Systems (CTCS) may perform these standard tasks, organize operational sequences and relieve the personnel.

The principal objective of this component is to improve reliability and punctuality and ensure that passengers catch their connection to other transit modes. Any irregularities can be spotted and mended immediately. In addition, passengers receive faster and better information about their journeys, before and after them.

Operation is an area where a lot of improvements can be made mainly through modern techniques based on informatics and telecommunications applications.

System Component 3: Passenger Service

"Passenger Service" is aimed at facilitating and encouraging the use of public transportation. Such a service cannot be limited to just keeping people moving; rather, in a kind of concerted action, the service must create a positive overall image of the system in the eyes of the public. Passenger service is to motivate and to inform in a clear understandable manner. Finally, it is to help lower the operating expenses and to reduce administrative labour while maintaining the standards of operation.

Information sheets and route-maps accompany the passenger from start to finish. Fare schedules, easy to understand and to remember, and multiple use tickets, which can be paid without cash on hand, make public transit more attractive and will potentially increase its use. Public Relations campaigns and special offers tailored to particular needs will bring in new passengers and thus tend to fill the gap in times of low demand.

"Passenger service", however, as a concept and component of the bus system, goes further than that. It includes other components' performance. For example comfortable bus stops with safe and convenient access, with easy-to-read information displays and protective shelters reduce the subjective waiting time for the passenger. The bus ride must also be as comfortable as possible. For that purpose, entries and exits must be made comfortable, as well as individual seats; fresh air and heating systems and possible air conditioning are definitely contributing to passenger comfort and add to passenger service.

In the same sense, co-ordinating the various transportation systems permitting a unified fare and schedule integrated transfers, shorter travelling times etc are parts of "passenger service".

Finally, an indirect element affecting passenger service is the fare system used. Fares which are both attractive and cost effective are the best inducement to use the system. Also friendly and well trained personnel and a good management which sets up and efficiently organizes all of this, are essential parts of what is meant by "passenger service".

System Component 4: The Vehicle

The vehicle of the Bus system is continuously adapted to the latest technological standards. The goals here are to increase cost-effectiveness, on the one hand, and passenger comfort, on the other. Diverse vehicle types can be incorporated into an overall fleet, improving the system's flexibility. A wide range of sizes are available: minibus, medium-sized bus, standard bus, single or doubly articulated bus and double-decker. Also, new generations of buses are coming into the market with features such as:

- comprehensive, continuous and early detection of malfunctions
- standardized, precise and more comprehensive check on the various components without the need to dismantle them
- humane and functional working space for the driver to facilitate his task
- interior with components of proven design and aesthetical appearance
- reducing the noise level for passengers and others by encapsulating the engine
- safer driving due to advanced Anti-blocking Systems (ABS)
- energy savings up to 25% by re-using the energy stored during braking
- reducing dependence on mineral oils by using alternative forms of liquid fuels (such as methanol or hydrogen) or of electric power and finally
- increasing operational flexibility by combining electrical and diesel propulsion ("dual propulsion") and by joint operation of Bus and Light Rail System on the same track, or even in tunnels.

System Component 5: The Bus Stop

Location, installation, form and equipment of bus stops make access to public transit as easy and convenient as possible. Standardized components permit flexible adaptation to the needs of the particular area. Such standardized components increase cost-effectiveness and performance of the Bus System, while at the same time they improve the aesthetics of the city environment in general.

A convenient bus stop requires not only attractive and easy-to-maintain shelters but also:

- Short and safe access, exits and crossings.
- Advanced information technologies which help the passenger toward optimal use of the system.
- Facilities which help to make the inevita-

16

ble waiting time more agreeable, such as small sales stands, telephones, mailboxes and information displays.

System Component 6: Roads and Tracks

The modern Bus System uses a variety of roads or tracks in order to ensure a reliable, punctual and regular operation. Even for the conventional bus operation on public streets, there are several possibilities to avoid obstructions caused by private cars.
- Specially programmed traffic lights enable the bus to cross intersections without delays.
- Special bus lanes permit the vehicles to avoid obstacles and delays.
- Track guidance may combine the best features of two systems, i.e. the great flexibility of conventional buses and the capacity of track-bound systems to transport a great number of people in considerable comfort. At the same time the investments needed for the track are relatively low.

OBJECTIVES AND SCOPE OF THIS BOOK

This book has been written with a variety of potential readers in mind. It is primarily intended for the Transportation professional who is dealing in practice, in one way or another, with the planning or the operation of a bus system or its components. This can be the planner who will be called upon to study an actual system, or the operator himself (or his personnel) who will be involved in day to day management of a bus agency. It may finally be those involved in supervision of the bus operation at local, regional, or even national level.

However, an equally important number of readers will come from the academic world, either being students of Transportation Planning or Engineering courses or academic personnel interested in this subject.

The objectives of the book are therefore quite diverse, and this created considerable problems of balance and context in the various chapters. Perhaps the primary objective was to provide a text with practical information, ideas and concepts about the actual application aspects of bus operation and planning. It was felt in other words, that current literature on the subject fails to address the more prac-

17

tical and day to day problems that a bus undertaking is faced with. Examples of such problems are, for instance, the selection of the appropriate rolling stock, the configuration of the network of lines and bus stops, the public information system etc, as opposed to the more theoretical problems of bus scheduling, forecasting demand and so on.

Parallel to this primary objective, several secondary ones have been set. These can be identified as follows:

-    To provide a reference manual for certain aspects of bus operation in urban areas.
-    To establish some ranges of "reasonable" values for key indicators or configurations of the system.
-    To indicate the elements of good management and organization of the system based on modern techniques of marketing and planning.
-    To give specific guidelines for procedures to be followed in bus operation.
-    To provide the students of the subject with an easy to follow and understand material for their courses.

These objectives have inevitably influenced the material included in this book and the way of writing. On the one hand, considerable effort was directed towards avoiding theoretical texts and references and more emphasis was given to results presentation and actual experience discussion. On the other hand, since the material may be used by academics, it is not devoid of descriptions and sufficient justification of its proposals or concepts.

Particular attention was given to the problems and experiences in the so called developing countries. There, current experience indicates that the emphasis must be given to areas such as proper agency organization, establishing a proper planning process, developing viable structures of bus transport supervision and financing and so on. As already said, the bulk of public transport in urban areas throughout the world is undertaken by small to medium-sized bus operators, the majority of which are in developing countries. One can therefore easily understand why the problems faced by these operators must be looked at in some isolation from the others, and with the proper degree of emphasis put into them.

It is hoped that the text in this book meets to some extent these objectives.

2 Types of organization

INTRODUCTION

The organizational framework of bus operation in an urban area affects the productivity and overall operation of the system and determines, indirectly, the level of service provided to the travelling public. The term "organizational framework" or for simplicity "organization" is used here to include four main elements:

    a.   The supervisory and financing structure (including policy formulation).
    b.   The organization of the operating agencies.
    c.   The form of ownership of the operators.
    d.   The co-ordination between the various elements of public transport (including buses) that operate in the area.

All four of these elements are important for the efficiency and effectiveness of the system of bus transportation and they determine to a great extent its successful and economically independent operation. There is increasing evidence all over the world, that areas with a high degree of organization in the above sense are experiencing an operational and financial vitality that makes them successful

19

providers of public transportation.

While a lot of the details and particular elements of the specific organizational framework of a bus operation depend on the existing political and socioeconomic environment in each country as well as on the history of public transportation in the specific area, there are certainly some underlying principles that can be found and some general guidelines that can be given mainly based on existing experience. For instance, while the form of ownership may be mostly determined by the prevailing political and economic philosophy of the country concerned, and/or the historical development of the particular system, the general principles concerning the appropriate form of supervision and control as well as the co-ordination of the services, and even the organization of the operating agencies themselves, are found to be quite "universal".

The material in the following pages contains the principles and the basic elements of a successful "organizational structure" of urban transport as they have been formulated by existing experience mainly in European countries.

THE SUPERVISORY AND FINANCING STRUCTURE

If sound organizational structures of the operating agencies is a prerequisite for efficiency and maximum productivity of output, the existence of an efficient supervisory and financing structure is the prerequisite for the existence of the agencies themselves. This statement is not simply rhetoric, but it expresses the reality in this author's experience.

The bus operating agency is usually the last element in a long "chain" of intervening and decision making elements that have a very significant impact on the final outcome. These "intervening elements" may range from the supervising city department, to the regional, or central government competent services, and in many countries right up to Ministerial level in the central Government. Therefore it is important to deal with the role of these agencies and to try and define their proper position and interaction in an organizational structure.

The Organizational Structure for Supervising Bus Operation

Figure 2.1 shows two alternative organizational structures for the supervision of public transportation in an urban area (assuming that there will be other modes of public transport, besides buses). The main structure as suggested in figure 2.1 remains the same, although obviously more simplified, in the case of only one mode.

The first alternative (figure 2.1 (A)), applies more to situations where there is a strong central government, and a weak or no local government intervention. The urban "Transport Planning and Supervising Organization" is responsible for co-ordinating the service, setting the operating standards, and distributing the financial aid or compensation to the operating agencies. It is usually a publicly owned body with a governing board appointed by the central (or regional) government, in which there is representation of the various sides interested in the operation of public transport in the area. Typically, it contains representatives from:

- the central government (Ministry of Transport)
- the local government or governments
- the operating agencies
- the workers of the operating agencies
- experts or other prominent figures in the field.

The key element in this type of organization is a strong planning and supervising organization which ideally should also be responsible for the road traffic planning in the area. In the same time the operating agencies should be relatively "weak", responsible only for the day to day operation of their fleet in the most efficient and cost effective way.

An example of this type of structure is Athens, where the three public transport operators (buses, trolley buses, Metro) in the area are supervised and controlled by an overall Public Transport Planning Organization who is responsible for the general co-ordination, planning, and financial control of the three operators. This Organization is supervised by the Ministry of Transport.

The second type of structure is the one shown in figure 2.1B. Here, the local governments in the area under consideration, form an "Association" of local governments which plays the role of the central government in the previous structure. This Association

21

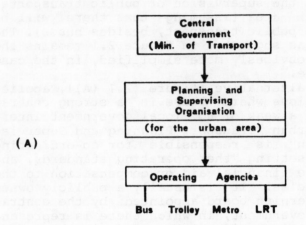

(A)

Central Government
(Min. of Transport)

↓

Planning and Supervising Organisation
(for the urban area)

↓

Operating Agencies

Bus   Trolley   Metro   LRT

Local Governments

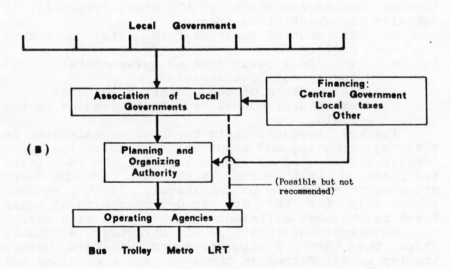

(B)

Association of Local Governments

Financing:
Central Government
Local taxes
Other

↓

Planning and Organizing Authority

(Possible but not recommended)

↓

Operating Agencies

Bus   Trolley   Metro   LRT

Figure 2.1: Possible Organizational Structures for supervising and financing urban transport operation. (A) Case with strong central government control (preferably with more than one operators. (B) Case with more decentralized control.

22

is accountable to the Local Government Councils that constitute it. The Planning and Organizing Authority in this case is formed by <u>elected</u> representatives from the areas that are represented in the Association, and has one or more specific responsibilities (e.g. public transport, housing, etc). The financing comes from a number of sources such as the central government, local taxes, etc. This type of organizational structure is to be found for example in France. The difference between this and the previous type of organization is the increased role of local governments and the fact that the body responsible for public transport planning consists of elected officials thus being more directly accountable to the local electorate of the area.

In all cases what is important is to have a coordinating body that will ensure the proper distribution of receipts (in the case of common fares), the co-ordination of the services through common short and long term planning and the distribution of the subsidies. Furthermore, such a body will undertake all types of control concerning the function of the operating agencies, the setting of standards for the service, etc.

Each case should of course be studied in its own particular characteristics and constraints (political, cultural, historical, etc) until the best form of organization can be defined. The above two cases provide a general framework of reference which has a reasonable potential for success, provided that some other factors or conditions, which are discussed in the following, apply.

Some Basic Conditions of Success

With regard to the supervisory and financing structure, experience has shown (Mitric, 1987)[a] that a successful organization depends on the existence of five basic elements or principles governing this structure. These are:
- coherence and stability of policy
- a contracting approach to the operations
- existence of competition
- decentralization of political power

---

[a]. This section and the one that follows about the experience in France draws several points from the work of S.Mitric presented in the 66th Annual meeting of the American TRB.

23

- stability of the source of finance.
These five "conditions" of a successful approach
to the supervision and financing of bus operation are
discussed in more detail in the following.

A.   Coherence and Stability of Policy

There must exist an explicit and coherent policy
concerning the urban public transportation in the
area. The term "coherent" is used to express the fact
that all important aspects of the systems operation
have been properly planned not only each one in itself but also in relation to each other and there is
no contradiction within the system's provisions.
Stability of policy is also necessary for some considerable time periods so as to give the system the
chance to settle and develop its full potential.
These two elements, which are also expressed to a
great extent with the term "systems approach", are
usually lacking from the public transport planning of
many areas especially in the developing countries.
The desired situation is one where there exists
an explicit policy, with basic principles expressed
in the form of laws which name all the key institutions, define the nature of their relationships,
state political preferences and provide means of
implementation (i.e. sources of finance and/or pro-
cedural tools). Decrees or advisory documents issued
by authorization of these laws, will provide further
details while leaving substantial maneuvering space
to individual actors (e.g operators, local supervising and planning bodies, etc) in line with the decentralization principle.
A necessary prerequisite for success is the
existence of a strong political consensus, in the
area and/or country politics on these matters. It is
not coincidental that such political consensus did
exist in successful stories such as the one in France
which is mentioned in more detail in Annex 1. For
example, in France the VT tax was instituted by the
political right-of-center (central) government, while
the key principles for its application were legislated later by the political left-of-center.

B.   Contracting Approach

The relationships among the principal actors are
definitely preferable to be in the form of contracts.
These contracts may be between the Planning and
Supervising Organizations and the transit operators,

24

or between these and the state, or between different Planning and Supervising Organizations (e.g. at urban and regional level), and so on. Although actual contracts will vary in degree of complexity and in terms of content and balance, they help in establishing measurable goals (thus permitting evaluation and correction) clarify relationships and mutual responsibilities, stress partnership and negotiation and delegate authority. In contrast to this suggested approach, there exists today the rather typical situation, especially in developing countries, where the relationships are murky and the style is that of "master to servant" (Mitric, 1987). This "master to servant" attitude unfortunately seems to be the usual way for technical Ministries to treat transit enterprises.

C.   Competition

For a service held to provide an essentially public good and thus departing from market rules, the preservation of competition and the private enterprise in bus transit provision in many countries has proved a worthwhile achievement. Though the private sector is usually excluded from capital ventures and plays the role of the operator, its competitiveness in the sphere of know-how and efficiency of operation has given very tangible and positive results both in the technical and the economic dimension. Potential benefits from further involvement of private enterprise in bus transportation are possible, provided there exists a sound organizational structure for supervision and planning, along the lines and principles discussed here.

There are examples in Europe today (e.g. in France as discussed in Annex 1, but also in Great Britain, Greece, etc) where the role given to private enterprises and competition in the field of bus transport, offers a model towards which publicly-owned transit operation in many other countries could evolve. Such evolution can (and should) be made without getting out of step with other social and political objectives and processes in the countries concerned.

D.   Decentralization of Political Power

Transit resurrection in many countries rode on the wave of the redistribution of political power and the fiscal means from the central towards the local

level. Leaving aside the arguments for decentralization as a means of increasing democracy, such development has permitted experimentation (at least in the
field of bus transport) and variety in technical matters, in tariff policies, in modes of organization
and, importantly, in amounts of transit investment
per capita. It may even have induced an element of
financial responsibility, notably absent when urban
wish-lists are submitted to central governments for
funding. Furthermore, one should not disregard the
benefits of matching local wishes to local resources,
and avoiding the politics of neglect of public transportation especially in provincial cities, practiced
by central governments in many countries.

The chances of success with decentralization
lie in the understanding of the need to achieve first
the necessary technical skills at local level and
prepare the ground, so to speak, before going ahead
with it. In this sense, developing countries should
not rush ahead with plans to decentralize, as the
successful examples from developed countries imply.
They should instead create first the necessary technical and managerial skills at local (or regional)
level, necessary to understand and manage the delicate problems related to the provision and maintenance of good public transport services in these
areas.

Given this point, it may well be advisable to
build up advisory units and regional offices of central institutions rather than full decentralization.

E.   Stability of the Source of Finance

For any bus (or public) transportation agency,
the stability of the source of finance is an essential prerequisite for sound and efficient planning.
The usual problem faced by such agencies is the uncertainty as to the coverage of their economic losses
which may be largely due to the imposed fare policies
by the supervising authorities. Leaving the question
of coverage of the deficits open creates a negative
outlook about the future of the agency which leads to
many negative results.

Permanent and sound means of financing the
transportation service in an area, must be sought.
The subject is of course a very delicate and complex
one and is dealt with in other more specialized publications (e.g. Giannopoulos (1985), Keefer (1984),
etc). However, some rather well established principles may be mentioned here.

26

First, the operating agency should be automatically compensated for the part of the lost revenue due to the wider social and other policies followed by the political authorities at central or local government level. Two typical examples of such policies are, on the one hand the non-approval of fares higher than what is considered by the supervising authorities as socially (or politically) acceptable, even though they may be far lower than the actual cost of operation, and on the other hand the compulsory (for the agency) acceptance of free or reduced fare passengers.

Other sources of finance, in addition to subsidies, may be the following:
- normal lending agencies
- exploitation of the agency's assets (e.g. building rights over terminals or stations, or exploitation of shops and advertising)
- central government subsidy
- local taxes, provided that these are well planned to be equitable and not having secondary negative impacts on the economy of the area (e.g. reducing employment opportunities).

ORGANIZATION OF THE OPERATING AGENCIES

General Principles

The principal aim of the organization in a bus operating agency, is to maximize the productivity of the personnel and equipment and thus increase the economic and operating efficiency of the organization. The main point is that individuals organized into a team have considerably more power than the same number of individuals operating independently. The major job to be done must be divided into relevant pieces, and the efforts of individuals must be channelled toward meeting the objectives of the agency.

Several forms of organization may be used. All of them involve dividing and fixing authority and responsibility, a matter that becomes more difficult and complex as an organization increases in size.

Probably the simplest and most usual type of organization is the "line" type, which is illustrated in Figures 2.2 and 2.3 for small, and 2.4 for medium to large bus transport agencies. In this "line" type of set-up, the chief executive directs his assistants, each of whom has responsibility for specific phases of the operation. They, in turn, direct others who are responsible to them and so on. The sections or departments are established on the basis of functions that must be accomplished. The chain of command is unquestionable and each person can understand exactly to whom he is responsible for the performance of his assigned duties (Institute for Urban Transportation, 1971).

The "line and staff" structure is similar to the line organization in that the line executives are still concerned with making all major decisions; they are those who issue the orders. As firms grow larger, however, the work becomes so complex that no one line executive or manager can become expert in all details of his (or her) particular function. Therefore, it is desirable to utilize the services of specialists. None of these people has direct line authority except within his own particular duties. For example, the director of marketing research or the advertising manager provides staff services for the vice president in charge of marketing. However, the market research team has no direct "command" relations with the sales force.

Regardless of the form chosen, all organizations involve at least four principles:

a. All the work of the agency must be split up among the employees into specific tasks.
b. Responsibility and authority must be fixed for each employee.
c. The chain of command must be established clearly, specifying the authority to whom each employee will report.
d. The activity of individuals must be co-ordinated so that desired goals can be met.

Discussion of the Suggested Organizational Structures

The ultimate goal of any bus transportation agency is to <u>produce and sell</u> acceptable transportation services to the travelling public in the area. The key words here are "produce" and "sell". Traditionally the first has been almost the sole point of concern of bus transportation managers with little or no regard to the second, especially if the operating agency was a publicly owned (and subsidized) monopoly. The second has been consistently underestimated

28

and neglected in the majority of cases at least until recently, when the techniques of modern marketing and market research have been successfully employed in the field of urban public transportation (see Chapter 9). The accumulating experience from efforts to revive the urban public transportation scene in many European and American countries, have made it clear that a good public transportation system must be complemented with a good public relations and marketing policy mainly through use of the techniques of modern marketing.

In suggesting therefore the forms of organization that are shown in figures 2.2 - 2.4, due account was taken of the above new realities. Especially in Figure 2.4 which refers to medium and large agencies, marketing and operations are combined as the major central function. Such a combination blends management's resources and other controllable factors in a way that best serves the desires and needs of transportation consumers. Of course the elements in the suggested organization charts are mainly "operational" tasks and can be seen to have as their additional function to support the marketing function. In this sense the suggested charts can be applicable even if the agency decides to give special emphasis to marketing.

In reviewing the structures shown in Figures 2.2 - 2.4 several things should be kept in mind.

First, the diagrams are intended to show organizational structure; they are not a personnel organization chart. In other words, the diagrams (especially those of Figures 2.2 and 2.3) illustrate jobs to be done and their relationships and not necessarily slots for individuals. Obviously, a relatively small transit firm could not possibly have separate individuals performing each function. There simply has to be much overlapping of jobs when firms are small. With larger firms, increasing complexity and the opportunity for increasing specialization makes it possible if not necessary for the functions shown, to be carried out by separate persons or even small departments.

Secondly, the organizational structures shown here are intended to be used as a guideline in drawing up individual organization charts for specific agencies. Because local conditions have to be taken into consideration, it is simply not possible to provide detailed and definitive organization charts tailored to specific situations.

Finally, some observations concerning the struc-

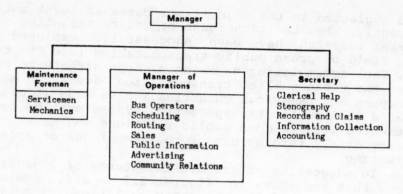

A. (Up to 10 buses)

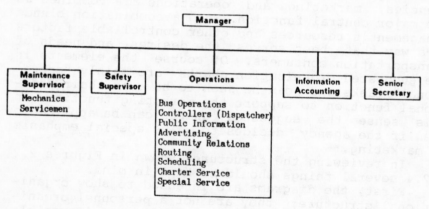

B. (10-30 or 40 buses)

Figure 2.2.: Organization diagrams for small agencies

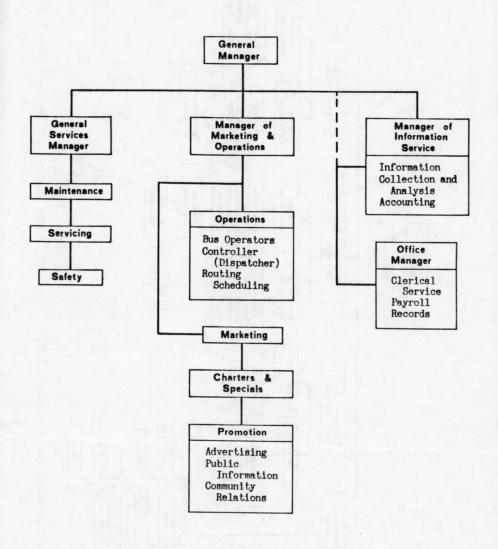

Figure 2.3.: Organization diagram for small to medium-scale agencies (up to 100 buses).

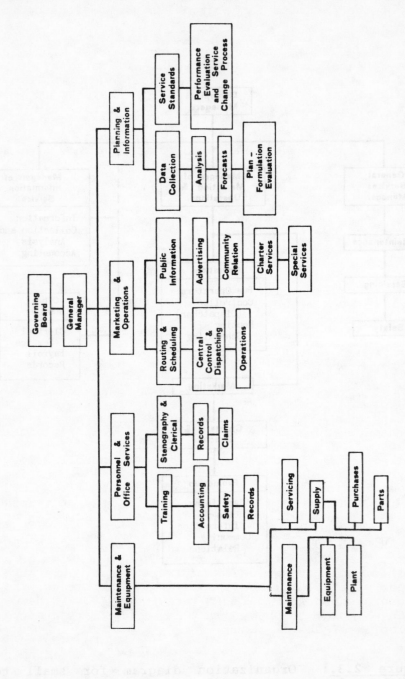

Figure 2.4: Organization diagram for medium to large agencies (more than 100 buses)

32

ture of the agencies in relation to their size should be made.

In the smallest type of operations (1 to say 20 or 30 buses) the general manager, a chief mechanic and a secretary can usually handle all matters. Figure 2.2 is a guideline for such small agencies (Figure 2.2A for very small agencies of say up to 10 buses, and Figure 2.2B for larger ones up to 30 or 40 buses). The whole of the operation and marketing function is under the direct supervision of the general manager. A maintenance foreman oversees repair and service work (which is usually done in independent garages and workshops) and the secretary oversees the information and records keeping work in the office, and, if the agency is very small, the payment of the personnel. Need determines the actual number of mechanics, drivers, and secretaries/clerks to be employed.

As the operation increases in size, for example, up to 100 buses, the chart shown in Figure 2.3 might be a useful guide. In this system, the manager of marketing and operations with the help of an operating supervisor directs the operations end of the business. He also handles the less routine marketing tasks and coordinates the marketing effort. An assistant manager or sales manager handles the more routine marketing program. A chief mechanic or maintenance supervisor oversees the maintenance and servicing of equipment. A safety supervisor takes care of training new employees and the safety program. The information and clerical services are under the direction of an information and office manager who personally handles much of the information collection, analysis and preparation of reports and accounting statements. Once again, the actual number of employees involved depends on need. As a rule of thumb, between 1.6 and 1.8 employees are needed for each bus in operation.

As the size increases further (more than 100 buses), the whole organization should be subject to a specific, and more specialized, study that would take account of the local conditions and constraints. The structure shown in Figure 2.4 provides, as said before, an example of how such an organization could develop in a general case.

OWNERSHIP OF THE OPERATING AGENCIES

Types of Ownership

The ownership of the operating agencies is of interest so far, as it may affect the efficiency and the service to the public, provided by the transport system. The question often asked is whether one or the other type of ownership would result in economic and service improvements.

Traditionally, when the provision of public transport was still the unchallenged form of transportation, almost all operators were private. Their operation was not subsidized and based on profit making, a task which could well be accomplished for a good many decades until perhaps the end of the fifties for most European countries. Then the increasing car ownership and usage as well as the increased level of income for most urban travellers brought about the well known "vicious circle" of the deterioration of the public transport services in urban areas. As car usage increased, public transport patronage dropped. At the same time traffic congestion on the streets increased, slowing down buses and other public transport vehicles and thus causing bus patronage to further drop in favour of private transport.

Very quickly, public transport operation became uneconomic for private operators and, in order to keep the services running, public authorities had to intervene. So the sixties and the seventies saw in almost all European countries, and many other countries of the world, the transformation of the majority of urban public transport operators from mostly privately owned, to mostly publicly or semi-publicly owned ones.

Today, of the 784 bus transport operators[a] listed in the last (1985-1986) UITP Handbook , UITP (1985), more than 17% are owned by Central Governments or Government owned Organizations, 56% are owned by municipalities or other forms of local government associations, 16% are privately owned and the rest are of mixed economy.

It can be said that trends are slowly changing towards more privately owned or mixed economy bus transport agencies. However, the bulk of the agencies

---

[a]. Paratransit, which in the great majority of cases is privately owned, is not included.

remains under public ownership and control.

The principal types of ownership can be categorized in the following three categories.

a. Publicly owned operators. These are fully owned by some public body which invariably is some form of local, regional, or central government authority or organization. The operator in these cases is the public authority itself or it may be a separate entity having the legal form of a private company (e.g. a Limited, or Societe Anonyme) but whose shares are wholly owned by the public authority who also appoints its management and supervises its operation.

b. Privately owned operators. These are privately owned bodies in both the legal and economic sense of the work, which can have a variety of forms. They can be a limited liability company, or a widely owned Limited whose shares belong to the public at large, and so on. Another form of private ownership is that of a co-operative where a number of private owners own the buses and form a co-operative to operate them in a certain area, under a licence or contract usually with the local government. This form of private ownership has been particularly successful in countries where the general business environment is not very advanced and the owners of the buses feel the need to have a more "tangible" form of ownership in the form of their own bus.

c. Finally, a relatively more recent type of ownership is that of "mixed economy" company where there is a publicly owned percentage of the shares and a private one. The management is appointed by the general assembly of the shareholders and is responsible to them for the results of the operation. The idea with this type of entity is to blend successfully the efficiency and effectiveness of a private company (ensured through the control of the private shareholders and their interests) with the satisfaction of the social requirements of the service (ensured through the publicly owned part of the shares).

The above types of ownership of the operators, although probably not entirely exhaustive of the various types to be found around the world, can be said to cover the great majority of cases. The important point to stress here, is that there are differences which can exist even between the same "type" of operators according to the specific legal status that exists in each particular case and which usually reflects the peculiarities (historical, cultural and economic) of each particular area.

An interesting example of a country where there exist several different types of operators with different legal status, is Greece. There are:

a. Three wholly publicly owned operators (one of which for buses) in the Greater Athens Area (population 4 million). The central government owns 100% of their shares, appoints their management and governing b oards, and "forms" the general assembly which by law are the Ministers of Transport, National Economy, Finance, and Commerce. It is a typical case of public ownership by the Central Government. Local governments, because of their great number in the area of operation, have not been directly involved, although they are represented in the governing board.

b. In the Greater Thessaloniki area, which is the second largest urban area of the country (population 800,000) the only public transport operator is a private company with some 1,000 shareholders. There is a special legal status provided for this company which allows her to secure a minimum amount of "profit" per year for the share-holders irrespective of whether the company is "profitable" or not. This "special" form of private company when conceived was justified on the grounds that since there is strong government intervention in the fares and general policy which prevents the company from operating under "normal" free market conditions, some form of compensation should have to be found.

c. In the city of Rhodes (population 80,000) the urban bus operator is a company owned and operated by the local municipality.

d. In the rest of the urban areas of the country (varying in population from 20,000 to 150,000) the bus operators are private co-operatives, one for each area, which operate under a generally very simple organizational structure. This structure has been, until very recently, successful in maintaining fairly adequate services despite the great difficulties and constraints put in their operation by the supervising (public) authorities, and the seasonal variations of the demand.

The experience from the operation of the different types of operators in Greece can be very useful for other countries, and forms the basis for the comments and suggestions in the following.

"Public" versus "Private" Operators

There can be no definitive answer as to which type of ownership is the most preferable and effective. Results vary according to a variety of influencing factors which obviously differ from one situation to another. There are advantages and disadvantages to be found in all of the previously mentioned types of ownership, and the best one for each particular case has to be determined in view of the historical, economic, and social environment of the area concerned. Some general remarks however, based on experience, can be made.

It can be said that publicly owned operators tend to experience a greater degree of intervention from their local or central government "owners", which is over and above the usual intervention experienced by all types of ownership. Intervention in the publicly owned agencies can usually be most identifiable in the following three areas:

- the long term as well as the day to day management and policy making
- relations with the labour force
- general attitudes and productivity of the personnel.

As regards the first of the above, the tendency for publicly owned agencies is to experience greater constraints on the manager's freedom to act and frequent changes on the objectives of the agency's operation as well as its immediate goals. A typical area of "constraints" on the manager's freedom to act, is in deciding the number of necessary personnel (the tendency usually being to employ more personnel than it is actually necessary for the service), or for the desired cuts in expenditure.

As regards relations with the labour force, when the "owning" public authority or political administration is sympathetic to the traditional trade union opposition to change, the manager's task to reduce costs is more difficult but his failure to do so may be excused leading to long delays in the adjustment of a transport enterprise to changes in cost. Where the "owning" authority is unsympathetic to trade unions, the management's task in reducing costs and effecting change is more acceptable by the authority, but the unions see it as an opportunity for confrontation, in theory with the management, but in essence with the governing authority which, nevertheless, in most cases appears to be politically resolute but comfortably one step removed from the conflict (Cameron, 1982).

Finally, as regards the general attitudes and productivity of the personnel, the influence in these cases of the public ownership may be so overwhelming that, like any other public organization, the transport agency is soon characterized by what has been called "the culture" of public enterprises.[a]

---

[a]   In his paper I.C.F. Cameron (Cameron, 1982) listed the main characteristics of this "culture" which I quote here as interesting, but with all due reservations:
- diminished authority at board level
- a self-perpetuating professional senior management whose influence exceeds that of the board
- high morale amongst these senior professional managers
- depressed initiative amongst the majority of middle and junior personnel
- a diminished sense of accountability for individual contributions to business objectives
- greater interest in professional achievement than in business performance
- personal emphasis on status and career progression
- sub-ordination of super-ordinate aims to professional standards
- a tendency for the number of professional functions to grow
- a tendency for the numbers of planners and engineers to grow
- an increasing centralization of authority and decision making
- ponderous decision-making shared in committees
- an increase in bureaucratic processes for the protection of managers from criticism
- business objectives confused by conflicting social, economic and political aims

Privately owned operators on the other hand, although theoretically free from the very close interventions of public authorities, are more aware of the restraints of economic viability of the services they offer. This, if kept at a socially acceptable level, is desirable and accounts for the generally better economic performance of private or semi-private operators. It is characteristic that, in cases where comparisons can be made, the differences in economic performance between public and privately owned operators are quite striking. In Greece, for example, the privately owned bus operator for the urban area of Thessaloniki consistently shows maintenance and operating costs 20-25% lower, and number of personnel per bus 20% lower than the publicly owned bus operator in the Greater Athens area, while similar experience has been reported for Finland and other countries.

The final decision, as to the type of ownership, rests with the responsible authorities at local level operating within the overall legislative framework established by the central government for the country as a whole. The study of the experience in this field, of countries with more advanced organizational set ups, can be of great value and this is done in the following for the case of France. Another interesting comparative study, based on the experience from Canada, can be found in Haritos (1987).

EXAMPLES OF ORGANIZATIONAL STRUCTURES

The Case of France

France succeeded in the last 15 years or so in carrying out a public transport renaissance on such a scale that makes it certainly an interesting case to study. The most striking side of French transit lies not so in its technical achievements, but in the institutional arrangements which were established over the last fifteen years and have contributed tremendously in this renaissance. These arrangements are of

- a blurring of distinctions between decisions of policy and rulings on practice
- commercial awareness replaced by theories of worthwhileness.

particular relevance to the topic of this chapter. The French system is a hybrid: it is animated and guided from the central government, but the decision-making and most of the finance are local; vehicles, equipment and facilities are in public ownership, but the operators are mainly private companies; the general framework of the sector is defined through laws and decrees issued in Paris, but the specific relationships among various public and private sectors are regulated through a system of renewable contracts, some of which are based on competitive bidding.

The French system of (public transport) organization and finance, is interesting enough to study as a case study and this is done in detail in Annex 1. The information in that Annex refers to the situation in France in 1985.

The Case of London, Great Britain

Urban Public Transport in Great Britain is undergoing profound changes in organization, ownership and the system of supervision. These changes are motivated by the philosophy of lesser government involvement (and financing) and greater private involvement. London Transport has undergone such a profound reorganization recently (with the creation of a new entity- London Regional Transport) and it is certainly an interesting case to examine. In the following we give details, based on Bayliss (1986), of this reorganization. At the time of writing this book, it is still early to evaluate the consequences of this reorganization.

The General Background

London Regional Transport (LRT) was established in 1984 by the London Regional Transport Act to provide or secure the provision of public passenger transport services for Greater London, in conjunction with British Railways, and to coordinate fares and services on those operations over which they have control. At the same time the LRT became the holding company for a new entity, London Bus Lines - LBL, created to own and operate the existing initial services in Greater London. Amongst the many duties imposed on LRT by the Act were those of forming distinct subsidiary companies to run bus services and Underground railway services and, where appropriate, to put activities out to competitive tender. The reformation of the previous London Transport Executive (LTE) into LRT, apart from passing policy and financial control from metropolitan to central government (because the Greater London Council i.e. the metropolitan authority was also abolished), was an important milestone in the process of decentralization of the management of public transport in London. Additionally it marked an important break with a tradition stretching back to 1933 by introducing competition in the provision of passenger services.

The new philosophy relies on the premise that, like most large public sector enterprises, LRT buys in goods and services from outside suppliers many of whom are in the private sector. However, in the past LRT's predecessors have provided many functions internally which, at least in theory, could be provided externally. Sometimes this was for good reasons such as the need for immediate availability, internal provision being the most cost effective. Sometimes it was for less good reasons such as tradition. Recently, because of changing market factors and legislative change the internal provision of a growing number of activities has been challenged and more and more of these are being tested, one way or another, within or against the market place. The result of this it is hoped to be the halting and reversal of a long established trend of rising unit costs thus improving LRT's ability to face external competition.

The Form of the Contracts

Within this general approach the London Regional Transport has issued a number of tenders giving out to private operators parts of the bus services.There are several variants of contract format possible but principally two are the most common: "cost contracts" and "revenue contracts". Cost contracts require the contractor to provide a specified level of service and collect cash fares and pass these on to the client. For this he receives an agreed payment irrespective of takings, provided he fulfills the terms of the contract. With revenue contracts the operator keeps the fares, and contract price is related to the losses on the route rather than the costs. The advantage of revenue contracts is that the revenue risk lies with the operator and this should provide the incentive to be efficient and to deliver a high quality of service. In several situations, however, this advantage may be more apparent than real. Firstly, to be truly commercial, the operator would have to be

41

able to vary his fares but if the London-wide integrated fare system is to be retained he cannot be given that freedom. Secondly, a substantial and growing proportion of fare revenue is from "pass income" (principally Travelcards and Old Age Pensioners passes) and does not therefore materialize as cash on the bus. Thirdly, in dense bus networks, operators, may well maximize their "on bus" receipts by deviating from the contract schedule in order to abstract custom and fares which would use other services if the planned schedules were run.

Contracts used for bus services in London have a specific provision related to the quantity and quality of service and the standard of fare collection. Contracted routes are monitored by LRT staff and vehicle operating records (using tachograph type equipment) have to be supplied to LRT. Failure to run the predetermined (in the schedules) quantity of service, results in a pro rata reduction in the contract fee. Failure to provide the contracted quality of service leads to formal warnings if the service falls below a prescribed threshold. Repeated failure leads to contract termination. In the event of termination LRT negotiates with another operator for a replacement service until the contract can be relet. There are similar monitoring arrangements for revenue collection. On contracted routes operators use ticket issuing equipment provided by LRT and this provides secure records of tickets issued and therefore revenue due. LRT revenue inspectors check ticket issuing levels on contracted services and any shortfalls detected lead to corresponding financial penalties. By these means contractors are subject to powerful performance incentives albeit by a different means than in revenue contracting.

The Tendering Process

The tendering process contains a number of discrete stages, starting with the selection of routes and formulation of the service specification. The simplest form of service specification would have been to put the existing timetable out to tender. To do this, however, could have favoured the LBL, as timetables are compiled in a way which reflects the customs, practices and resources of the incumbent operator and this may not be convenient for other operators. On the other hand, it was clear that some other operators did not have the skills and experience needed to design effective service schedules.

42

Therefore, a basic service specification was drawn up which:

a. outlined the minimum service level, regularity, vehicle capacity and the appropriateness of the current timetable

b. contained a schedule which indicated the minimum number of departures in each time period between the main points on the route, the required regularity and the times of the first and last buses

c. contained a schedule describing the streets to be used on the service.

The routings and service frequencies of the tendered routes were reappraised prior to the basic service specification being settled in the light of current needs and the anticipated lowering of costs. Whilst frequencies on a small minority of routes were reduced on a significant number of others they were increased resulting in a small increase in bus miles overall on the tendered bus routes. The basic service specification did not limit the types of vehicles to be used, although, if bidders are proposing lower capacity vehicles than those already operating on the routes, then this has to be agreed with LRT first and, if necessary, the service frequency increased to ensure that adequate capacity is included in the bid. The suitability of the vehicle type is a factor taken into account at the tender evaluation stage.

The second stage of the tendering process is the pre-tender publicity. Here the intention to invite tenders is announced and advertised and outline information is presented to interested operators. With the first round of tenders a seminar was held for the operators at which the whole process was described and they were able to ask questions, make suggestions and express any concerns they had.

This was followed by the third stage, the pre-qualification, in which interested operators submit information about their companies, including a company profile the licenses held, their experience and an indication of which of the routes the operator was interested in. Those companies which appeared to have an adequate financial base, resources and experience were added to the approved tender list. The pre-qualification stage has been dropped in later rounds of tendering as experience of the ability and standing of independent operators has been acquired.

The fourth stage is the invitation to tender on the basis of the service specification and draft contract followed by the tender evaluation. As a result of tender evaluation the preferred contractors and service specifications are determined for each route. In a number of instances invitations to put in variants of the basic service have been made in the tender documents and in others tenderers have made their own suggestions. Before the contracts can be signed, however, it is necessary to go through a process of consultation with the London Boroughs and Shire countries concerned and the London Regional Passengers Committee (LRPC), which is an appointed body representing users' interests. When this is completed the contracts are signed and the commencement date settled. After the choice of the package of routes the process initially took nine months to commencement and even then there were complaints that some stages of the process were too short.

In subsequent tendering rounds the process is being shortened, as operators become more familiar with what is required, but it seems unlikely that it can be reduced much if the exercise is to be conducted properly.

Some Conclusions on the London Experience

Under the new organization of bus services increased cost effectiveness, greater responsiveness to consumers needs and decentralization of public transport service management have been increasingly important in LRT's policy and operations over recent years. As part of this, a growing range of functions are being put to the test of competitiveness with outside suppliers. The tendering of bus services within a basically regulated regime is a logical, if somewhat traumatic, step in this process. The contracting scheme adopted by LRT is designed to fit with London's particular conditions and its duties under the 1984 London Regional Transport Act and may not be a very successful way to proceed elsewhere. Experience with these schemes is still very limited but a number of significant lessons can be drawn. Firstly, competitive tendering does appear to offer the prospect of significant savings whilst allowing coordinated fares and service levels to be maintained. Secondly, the capacity of the independent sector is presently restricted and can only offer limited competition in London. This means that the pace at which tendering is built up must not go too fast or the competition will be largely limited to public

44

sector operations. This problem has to be seriously studied before similar experiments are made elsewhere.

The build up of private sector capacity will probably require some transfer of capacity from the public sector if it is to occur quickly and this could be by privatization of operating units or more marginal switching of resources (e.g. disposal of buses from the public to the private sector). The attitude of public sector operators is of crucial importance to the scale and form of this capacity transfer. The need for such a transfer will depend on how competitively public operators can perform, on whether tendering affects the total size of the local bus market and on the extent to which new types of operations develop.

Finally it appears that fears about the preparedness of independent operators to provide the standards of quality and safety required for local bus services were, in the case of London at least, ill-founded. The majority of operators who have shown an interest in tendering for bus services in London have approached this venture in a professional and responsible fashion. However, the experience of London, as years pass, will need more in depth study and scrutiny before its example is taken up by other urban areas.

The Case of Greece

In Greece there exist three types of bus operators. The wholly publicly owned operator in the Greater Athens area. The privately owned operator in Thessaloniki (the second largest urban area) and the (private) bus co-operatives in all other urban areas except Rhodes which has an operator owned by the municipality. Of particular interest is the arrangement with the co-operatives which for nearly 40 years now have worked well and provided an adequate service with minimum of costs to the public. The experience with the co-operation is analysed in the following in greater detail as it may provide a useful example to several similar situations worldwide.

Structure and Organization of the Bus Co-operatives

The Bus co-operatives in Greece sprung out of the need to reconcile two basic requirements. On the one hand, to provide efficient and flexible service to all parts of the country with the minimum of pub-

45

lic investment and expenditure and on the other hand, to avoid a situation where there is in fierce competition by independent operators.

The co-operatives were formed by bus owners, originally (in 1952) one in each of the 52 prefectures of the country, and later for the 32 largest cities and towns (except Athens and Thessaloniki). The bus owners contribute the use of their buses to the co-operatives. Recently, however, some co-operatives have bought their own buses. The drivers of the buses are employed by the owners and not by the co-operative. The co-operative, on the other hand, employs all the ticket collectors and administrative personnel. It is responsible for all planning and scheduling activities taking particular care to have at the end of the month equal or almost equal number of kilometer and on similar types of road network for all buses of the co-operative.

Maintenance of the buses is done by their owners on their own expense and initiative. The facilities used for the maintenance are also the choice of the bus owners and are usually private garages.

The co-operatives are the sole provider of interurban and/or urban transport in the areas of their responsibility, and, with the exception of very few special cases, one co-operative may not serve passengers in the territory of another one. Direction and management is provided by elected officials who form the board of direction or Council. This Council consists of a chairman and 2 members for co-operatives with less than 50 buses and a chairman and 4 members for larger co-operatives. A Secretariat, formed usually by a secretary, a clerk, and an accountant, provides administrative support to the Council. The schedules are formed by the so called "movement section" which usually consists of one or two experienced persons who often are ex-drivers or bus owners. Scheduling takes a special experience and is strongly influenced by the need to equate the mileage so that, at the end, each bus owner gets the same or similar share of the profits and the wear and the tare of the buses is again similar for all of them. This set up may, in fact, be seen as a major draw back for the co-operatives. The supervision of the co-operatives is done on first level by the prefecture services and ultimately by the Ministry of Transport. The network of lines and the schedules have to be approved by the prefecture, while changes in fares have to be approved by the Ministry. Apart from these major elements there is virtually no di-

46

rect control and interference by the supervising authorities.

Financing of Services

For the greater part of their lives, until very recently the bus co-operatives have been financially self supporting. Many of them still are. However, an increasing number of them is becoming uneconomic i.e. their operating
costs are larger than their revenues. This has to a great extent been the result of the central government's policy concerning fares and fare concessions. Fares have not been allowed to increase according to the average cost of living while at the same time a large number of concessions were given to various categories of passengers for reasons of social policy. Compensations for these concessions are not given by the government. For the co-operatives with a deficit the government provides loans with favourable terms which, nevertheless, have to be repaid and serviced by the co-operative. For the larger urban areas this policy of loans (instead of compensations or subsidies) has already a very heavy financial burden which is threatening the whole existence of these co-operatives.

Some Concluding Remarks on the Greek Experience

The experience from the bus co-operatives in Greece is basically a positive one. This form of organization of bus transport, while retaining the basic advantages of a privately owned agency, does not allow for open and unchecked competition which might result in abandonment of (non-profitable) parts of the service and so on.
For urban areas, as well as their surroundings, where there is relatively little demand for services and with great temporal variations as in most of these areas the co-operatives have performed remarkably well with great flexibility for many years. Their unit operating costs are the lowest of any other bus transport agency in Greece, including the privately owned Bus Transport Company of Thessaloniki. If the supervising authorities could reduce their interference as regards fares, or (perhaps better) if they would provide subsidies in compensation for their "social policy imposed" fare reductions, there would be no serious financial problems in the co-operatives' operation.

47

The Greek experience shows also that there are a number of disadvantages or drawbacks associated with this type of bus organization. These are mainly related to the planning and operation of the service which is not based on a systematic and scientific approach but rather on intuition and past experience. Also there is no preventive maintenance of the buses and no real incentive for investment on supporting infrastructure such as bus shelters, information boards etc.

Provided that these drawbacks are remedied and mainly if there is assured compensation for any social policy imposed constraints, the co-operatives have succeeded in providing an acceptable standard of service at minimum cost.

3 The service and operation planning process

DEFINITIONS AND CONTENTS OF THE PROCESS

DEFINITIONS AND CONTENTS OF THE PROCESS

Long-term versus Short-term Planning

"Planning" has primarily been defined as an activity that formulates the appropriate actions and measures to be taken in order to transform a present system to a future form that meets the foreseen demand according to certain goals and objectives. This, by its very definition, is a medium to long-term procedure. Short-term planning has the meaning of formulation of immediate action plans to meet the needs in the short term. It is for this reason a less vague and more "practical" process which, nevertheless, employs the same techniques and methods as long-term planning, though to a less sophisticated extent.

For a bus transportation agency, planning will involve four basic steps that are invariably found (with different names perhaps) in all planning processes:

    a.   analysis of current situation with a view to identifying problems and discovering their causes and underlying influencing factors,

b.　forecasts of future conditions including
　　　　　the level of future demand for bus (or any
　　　　　mode) transportation,
　　　c.　formulation and analysis of alternative
　　　　　plans and actions and
　　　d.　evaluation and final selection/formulation
　　　　　of the preferred (long-term) plan.

Typically, long-term planning in the bus transportation sector deals with issues such as:
　　　-　acquisition of new rolling stock (of vari-
　　　　ous types)
　　　-　construction of new maintenance and ter-
　　　　minal facilities (or extension of existing
　　　　ones)
　　　-　major reorganization of the network and
　　　　services, especially in relation to the
　　　　other modes of transport operating in the
　　　　same area
　　　-　long-term financial planning
As the emphasis has been shifting in most countries from major capital investments to managing existing facilities in the best possible way a new form
of planning became necessary, namely the kind of
planning that focuses on the short-term operations
and the productivity of existing infrastructure, processes and services. As with the traditional long-
term planning process, short-term planning is again
structured around the following four sequential activities:
　　　a.　problem identification through collection
　　　　　of the appropriate data,
　　　b.　design of alternative actions,
　　　c.　analysis and evaluation of the effects and
　　　　　other aspects (e.g. costs) of each alterna-
　　　　　tive and
　　　d.　final formulation of the preferred alterna-
　　　　　tive.
The only notable difference is the absence of a
forecasting stage which is obviously unnecessary
since the object of the process is to formulate plans
and strategies in the short term. In fact, short-term
planning in the above sense has been defined (Wilson
et al, 1984) as "the process of monitoring the operation of a transit system and planning modifications
that can be implemented during one of the next schedule changes, generally within a period of one year".
An implication of the above definition of short-
term transit planning is that the type of actions or
measures suitable to be the object of such planning,

are small scale changes to the network (i.e. new routes, extensions or changes to existing ones, changes in scheduling times and frequencies and so on).

The contrast between the complicated, computer based models used for long-term planning (especially when it is done within the urban transportation planning process) and the ad hoc, judgmental, and experience based planning process, typically used within the context of short term planning, is quite striking. Yet, it is the second type of processes that are the most widely used today, especially in the context of small to medium urban areas and bus undertakings. In the following, the process for short-term planning is analysed and presented in greater detail.

The Contents of Planning in the Short-term

The definition of short-term planning has the objective of determining the modification to be made to the system in the short-run, i.e. within the next one to three years. This time scale helps to identify the types of changes and actions that are the result of such planning. These can be grouped under two headings as follows:

A.   Changes concerning routes
  1.   New routes.
  2.   Alterations to the existing routes.
  3.   Route realignment.
  4.   Route abandonment.
  5.   Rearrangement of route structures (express routes, feeder services etc).

B.   Changes concerning operation
  1.   New schedule frequencies.
  2.   New hours of operation.
  3.   New types of scheduling (e.g. dead-heading).
  4.   Changes in layover times, or travel times (if traffic conditions change).
  5.   Fare changes (as regards the preferred structures and levels, as well as estimating their impacts).

All of the above actions are an almost daily occupation of the personnel of bus transport undertakings who strive to satisfy the demand of the public and the authorities for new or improved services, on the one hand, and the changing needs and objectives of the agency itself on the other. A properly organized and executed planning process would give the agency the means of determining which of these actions, if any, should be taken in the short-term in order to make the system most effective. It would furthermore provide the agency with the means to "defend" its actions against outside (and mainly political) pressure to act otherwise.

The short-term planning activities, like all planning activities, are basically a permanent and on-going process that has to be established within the agency's structure. Data are collected continuously, problem areas are identified and alternative actions are formulated and evaluated on an almost continuing basis.

A necessary prerequisite, is the existence of clear objectives and a policy of operation which will have to be formulated within the agency but taking into account the public preferences and requirements as well as the demands of the supervising authorities.

An example of a recommended framework for a comprehensive short-term planning process is diagrammatically shown in Figure 3.1. The major elements of this process, i.e data collection, plan formulation, implementation etc, are discussed in greater detail in the following sections.

DATA COLLECTION

"Data collection" includes the whole process of collecting the necessary information, not only in order to monitor the system's performance and actual potential problems, but also in order to find the preferences and needs of the travelling public as well as of those who work in the system. This definition makes it necessary to include in the "data collection" phase the following:

- general ridership and cost of operation data (including maintenance)
- travel times and delays
- travel needs and public attitudes information
- bus drivers' suggestions and participation.

The information that is collected is analysed by the planners within the short-term planning process and relevant statistics or proposed actions are sent regularly to the board of direction and/or the supervising agencies for the necessary decisions and actions.

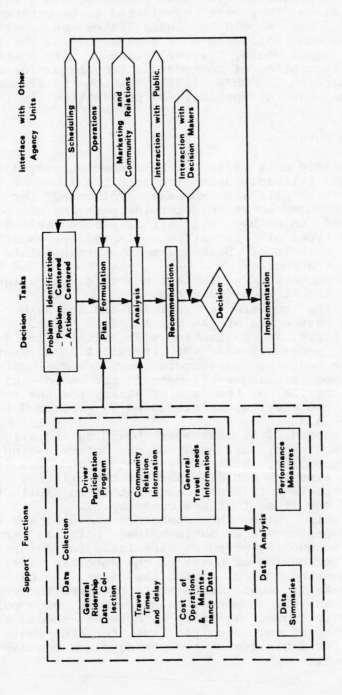

Figure 3.1: A recommended framework for a short-term bus transport Planning process (adapted from Wilson et al, 1984).

The principal contents and methods for data collection are presented in the following in greater detail, since they are considered to be extremely important, and should be established as routine procedures and collected on a regular basis. The interested reader would, however, find a very comprehensive description of methods and techniques for bus data collection in UMTA (1987), which is strongly recommended as a specialized publication in this field.

Ridership Data

Ridership data refer to the number of passengers and other relevant data for specific lines of the network. These data are normally collected for all times of the day so as to determine peak and off-peak periods and to gather statistically acceptable samples. The types of information collected are usually:
  a.   numbers of passengers at various points of the route,
  b.   numbers of passengers boarding and alighting at specific stops,
  c.   the number of vehicles and the number of passengers at the maximum load point.
The first, in conjunction with travel time data etc, are necessary for the determination of useful statistics such as passengers per vehicle-hour of service, or passenger-kilometres per vehicle-kilometre of service, or the data necessary for the evaluation of the service, as discussed in greater detail in chapter 4.
The second, i.e. passengers boarding and alighting at each stop, are used for the determination of bus stop capacity, bus stop design, and bus line capacity. Also for deciding whether the existing number of stops is sufficient, and whether to split the number of bus lines that use one stop.
The third, i.e. the number of vehicles and the number of passengers at maximum load point, is essential for scheduling purposes especially for determining the frequencies of buses on the specific line.
The method for collecting the first two categories of data is usually with staff on-board the vehicle who count the number of passengers at each point on a special form. Normally an observer should ride all vehicles of the specific line for the whole of the day for a minimum of two weekdays and one day of the weekend.

When total counting is not possible due to the great number of buses on a particular line, a certain sample of the buses can be taken. However, at the same time the total number of buses and their passengers passing a certain centrally located point (usually the maximum load point) along the line should be counted by an observer standing at the curbside[a]. This count of the standing observer is then used to expand the samples of the on-board observers.

A useful example of a counting form for the on-board ridership surveys is shown in Figure 3.2. In this form there is also provision for recording the time spent at some (or all) stops. This information can be used later to make estimates of the delay relative to the number of passengers boarding and alighting and to take measures to reduce excessive delays at critical stops (e.g. increase frequencies).

Direction	Route No.	Count No.	
			Date:
Vehicle No	Start Time	End Time	Name:
			Sheet no.: ...... of .....

Stop no.	No. of Passengers			Time at stop (mins)
	ONS	OFFS	LEFT*	

* i.e. not able to board the bus

Figure 3.2: Example of a counting form for on-board ridership surveys.

The examples of forms for the various counts that are given here, are only indicative. Each agency, according to its own needs, operation practices, and method of data manipulation and analysis, will

---

[a]. Details of this type of count are given in the following paragraphs as "stationary counts".

have to eventually produce its own particular forms for its surveys. For smaller agencies and urban areas, the task of organizing the counting programs and preparing the necessary forms can be done by joining forces between several agencies on a regional or even national basis. This will reduce costs and will ensure uniformity of approach and compatibility of the data.

The third type of riding counts mentioned above, i.e. that of the number of vehicles and their passengers at the maximum load point (e.g. the busiest stop), is made with the so called **stationary counts.**

These are made by an observer standing at the curbside. The data from these counts are mainly used to determine adjustments to the frequency of scheduled service and sometimes for scaling up the samples taken from on-board surveys, as already mentioned. They are therefore taken more frequently (e.g. once a month).

The stationary counts are normally taken over a 17-hour period from 6.30 to 23.30 in two 8.5 hour shifts. However, in some cases fewer periods of time or even only the morning and evening peak hours are checked. An example of the type of forms that can be used in "stationary counts" is shown in Figure 3.3.

Location: Date:
Weather: Sheet no. . . . . . . of . . . . . .
Direction:

TIME IN	LINE No.	ARR.	ON	OFF	TIME OUT	LEFT

Notes:

TIME IN = The time of arrival of the vehicle
LINE No.= The number of the bus line (in cases where more than one bus lines pass from the count point).
ARR = The number of passengers on-board the bus when it arrives
ON = The number of passengers boarded at the bus stop
OFF : The number of passengers disembarked at the bus stop
TIME OUT : The time of departure from the bus stop.
LEFT : The number of passengers left waiting at the stop because of a full bus, etc.

Figure 3.3: Example of a form for a "stationary" riding count.

The form in Figure 3.3, also indicates the types of data recorded in stationary counts. In general it can be said that these counts are easier to make and do not require large numbers of personnel. The information they give, however, is limited to one point in space and should better be used in conjunction with the on-board counts mentioned earlier.

In all the above counts the number of passengers on- board the bus is not (and cannot be) counted precisely. What is usually done instead, is to supply the counting personnel with information about the passenger carrying capacity of all the types of buses used in the system.

A typical bus carrying capacity information of this type would be for example:

> number of seated   : 40
> practical capacity: 80
> crush capacity   :100.

The counting personnel should then be instructed to estimate the number of passengers as follows:

a. For a fully loaded vehicle, use the capacity measure or a figure close to it.

b. For partially full vehicles, count/estimate the number of passengers standing and then add this figure to the seating capacity of the vehicle. However, note if possible any empty seats when counting and subtract these from the total.

c. For vehicles which are quite empty, an actual count may be made of the number of on-board.

d. Care must be taken with vehicles entering bus stops, since seated passengers often stand near doorways making vehicles seem somewhat more crowded than they actually are.

e. Figures should be rounded off to the nearest five, when vehicle loads are quite large, e.g. "103" becomes "105". (This is recommended, simply because there is usually no confidence and no use in any estimate with precision to the actual figure).

Travel Time and Delays

In the previous counts some information on travel time and delays at stops is also recorded, as can be seen in the examples of the counting forms in

Figures 3.2 and 3.3. If more detailed information is needed, special travel time surveys will have to be undertaken. These are made on-board the vehicles by observers with stop watches, who record the travel time between stops, the time spent at each stop, and, in some cases, the delays (i.e. time stopped) due to other reasons. This information is normally used for the bus scheduling process, where precise travel time data for each period of the day are necessary.

An example of the type of counting form that can be used for the travel time and delay counts is given in Figure 3.4. The headings of the columns in the form of Figure 3.4 indicate the type of information that is collected with this type of count.

Route :   Direction :

Time period :   Weather :

Total time (Origin to Destination):							
Total time at Stops:				(% to total time:			)
Average speed (total distance / total time):						km / hr	
Stop N°	Distance between (m)	Traffic Conditions ♦	Travel Time (mins)	Time at stop (min)	Average Travel (♦♦) speed	Total Average speed incl. stops	
Origin							
1							
2							
3							
4							

♦   The observer notes here the traffic conditions between stops, e.g.
    E= free flow, M= semi-congested, F= Forced Flow etc.

♦♦ Without the time at stops

Figure 3.4:   Example of a form for travel time and delay counts by using on-board personnel.

Origin - Destination Patterns

These types of data are collected once every two to four years. They are necessary in order to assess the adequacy of the existing network of bus lines, or to plan new lines and services and to coordinate the bus network with other modes of public transport that may exist in the same area. There are two basic possibilities as regards the Origin - Destination surveys (O - D surveys):

a. When only the O-D patterns of the bus passengers are to be measured. In this case the survey is done on-board the buses with a fairly large sample (10-20% or more) and is relatively easy and more straightforward as a procedure. It may also be combined with a "passenger attitude and preference" survey. In this case, together with the information on the origin and the destination of his trip, each passenger is asked more questions concerning his preferences and attitudes as to his public transport or other trip making choices. These O-D surveys are normally (and strongly recommended to be) made by personnel specifically trained for this type of operation. An example of the form used for an on-board O-D survey in Ottawa, Canada is given in Figure 3.5.

b. When the O-D patterns of the population at large are measured, i.e of the users as well as of the non-users of public transport. In this case a full household interview survey (or telephone survey, in cases where this is feasible and reliable) must be used with relatively small samples, due to the magnitude and cost of the whole operation.

Both types of O-D surveys require a complicated and specialized preparation and execution process which is outside the scope of this book to describe in length. The interested reader can find detailed information in specialized publications such as Ampt et al (1983), CUTA (1985), ITE (1976) and, probably the most comprehensive of all, UMTA (1987).

Cost of Operation and Revenue Data

These are probably the most widely collected data, since all bus transport agencies must produce

OC TRANSPO SURVEY

Your assistance in completing this form will help us to plan a better service for you. Please complete and deposit this card in one of the return boxes located at the front and rear doors of this bus. Should you find it more convenient, you may return this card to ANY OC Transpo driver. You may be given several cards during the next few weeks. Please complete accurately and return to us each card that you receive.

OFFICE USE ONLY

1) On which route (number) did you receive this card?_____

2) What time did you board this bus?
_____ A.M. _____ P.M.

3) Did you transfer from a previous bus on to this bus?

Yes ○   No ○

If yes,   If no,

a) from which route number?_____

which fare did you pay on boarding this bus?

b) was this an Outaouais route?

Yes ○   No ○

Adult Cash ○

Reduced Fare Cash ○

Adult Ticket ○

c) did you use a pass to board this bus?

Reduced Fare Ticket ○

Yes ○   No ○

OC Transpass ○

OC Unipass ○

If yes, which type?

Student Pass ○

OC Transpass ○

Senior Citizen Pass ○

OC Unipass ○

Outaouais Pass ○

Student Pass ○

Senior Citizen Pass ○

Outaouais Pass ○

4) What is your home address?_____

5) For your ride on this particular bus, please give the address, nearest street intersection or building name for:

a) Where you boarded this bus _____

b) Where you will leave this bus_____

6) For your total continuous trip, which includes your walk to and from the bus stop and travel on any other buses, please give the address, nearest street intersection or building name for

a) The START of your trip_____

b) The FINAL DESTINATION of your trip_____

Thank you for your co-operation.

№ 101341   (Français au verso)

Figure 3.5: Example of the questionnaire used for an on-board O-D survey in Ottawa, Canada (CUTA,1985).

evidence (at some stage) as to their cost-coverage rates, in order to get approval for higher fares and/or financing purposes. They also have to compile their yearly statement of accounts and the budget for next year, both of which are based, among others, on cost of operation data.

Typical items included in the cost and operation type of data, are:

A. Personnel Costs :
    a. Salaries for personnel in:
       - movement of buses
       - maintenance
       - administration
    b. Payments for personnel insurance, taxes etc.
    c. Other personnel payments (productivity bonuses, retirement bonuses etc)

B. Operating Costs :
    a. Diesel
    b. Lubrication
    c. Tyres
    d. Maintenance (excluding salaries)

C. Insurance fees :
    a. Buses
    b. Other property

D. Other costs :
    a. Rents
    b. Furniture
    c. Electricity
    d. Office supplies
       etc.

E. Receipts :
    a. From fares (by type of fare)
    b. From other sources.

The above types of data are collected on an annual basis for the whole of the bus operation, and besides their use for the preparation of the budget and for accounting purposes, they can be employed in economic analysis of the whole system or of specific lines. This can be done in connection with other operational data such as:

- Number of service vehicle-kilometers
- Number of service vehicle-hours
- Percentage of daily bus failures (or number of veh-hours outside service).

From these, one can calculate the unit cost data that are employed to construct cost allocation functions for the bus operation (see for example US DOT (1981)). These functions can then be used for the economic evaluation of the system or of individual lines.

Travel Needs and Attitudes Information

This information can come from two sources: From interviews at the households (either by sending interviewers for a face-to-face interview, or by telephone) and from a questionnaire survey of the passengers on-board the vehicles.

The first are, of course, more comprehensive and can be done in connection with longer-term planning surveys. They give the opportunity to see the needs and the attitudes of the public at large and not only those of the people already using public transport. They are usually done in connection with the O -D surveys mentioned earlier.

The second, i.e on-board the buses, are easier and cheaper. They can provide useful information and are recommended especially if the wider O-D surveys of the previous type are not made.

The major purposes for public needs and attitudes surveys are the following: First, to determine the attitudes of the public towards public transport and their assessment of the level of service offered. Such information can help guide the design of an advertising campaign intended to "correct" any misconceptions that the public might have concerning the transit service, as well as indicate potential areas for system improvements. Secondly, such surveys can be used to predict potential ridership, either in areas not currently served by transit, or when major fare, route or service changes are contemplated for an existing service.

The design of an attitude survey questionnaire is a highly skilled task, and a detailed discussion of questionnaire design is beyond the scope of this book. (For detailed presentations see for example Babbie (1975), Parten (1986)). However, as a simple example of such questions, we give in Figure 3.6 the basic questions regarding "attitudes" that were asked in the household interview survey in Athens in 1983 by the Public Transport Planning Organization (OAS, 1984). The presentation in Figure 3.6 is in summary form (to avoid lengthy texts) and is meant to indicate the types of questions asked. It will be noted that some of the questions are repeated under slightly different wordings. This was done on purpose so as to be able to cross-check the answers and assess their honesty.

A. General Information
     1. Age   2. Sex   3. Profession
B. Trip Making Attitudes Information
     4. Do you USUALLY take Public Transport for :
     Work .... Shopping ..... Entertainment ......
     5. (If yes in previous question no. 4)
     What are the basic reasons for using public transport in each of
     the 3 trip purposes :
                                        Work   Shopping   Entert.
          - No private car
          - Non availability of car
          - Not easy to park
          - Traffic congestion
          - Petrol too expensive
          - Parking too expensive
          - Not easy to find taxi
          - Taxis too expensive
          - Public Transport service acceptable
          - Public Transport safer
          - Other
     6. (If No in question 4.) what are the reasons
                                        Work   Shopping   Entert.
          - Public transport not available
          - Long waiting at bus stops
          - Long distance to bus stop
          - Long travel times
          - PT not reliable
          - Need to transfer
          - Private car necessary for work
          - Not clean PT vehicles
          - I like using private car
          - Need to carry shopping
          - Don't know bus network
          - Use car pooling
          - Other
     7. Do you find the system of flat fares :
          Right ... Wrong .... No Opinion ....
     8. Do you use the monthly card ?   Yes... No...
        If No what is the reason :
          - Not using Public Transport
          - Make few trips
          - Not convenient
          - Other
     9. What does it bother you most with public transport
             (name three reasons)
          - low speeds   - stops too distant   - many transfers
          - long waiting at stops   - no seats available
          - don't like crowds - not reliable - expensive fares
          - not clean   - bad behaviour of staff
          - no information on services   - other
     10. If you are now using private car or taxi, would you use pub-
     lic transport if:
          - the travel time was shortened substantially
          - it was free   - it was more reliable
          - there were no transfers   - there was no congestion
          - less waiting at stops - less walking to stops
          - cleaner and more comfortable vehicles.
          - do not use public transport under any circumstances
     11. If you live in a rented apartment, state three of the main
     reasons that made you chose this area:
     - cheap rent   - good public transport to my work - nice area
     - relatives live nearby - many services nearby - easy parking

Figure 3.6.: Short presentation of the question asked
in the attitudes household survey in Athens 1983.
The questionnaires were returned by post.

Bus drivers' Suggestions

Bus drivers, with their every day on-the-job experience, may have valuable information to give as regards the operation of the service, passenger's attitudes and complaints etc.

The ways of obtaining bus drivers' suggestions vary according to the size of the agency (i.e. the number of drivers), their educational level etc. The easiest way is to distribute a simple questionnaire to each driver once every month (or in longer intervals e.g. every six months) and collect it after a few days. A typical such questionnaire is shown in Figure 3.7. If the number of drivers having difficulties to write is relatively large, a periodic oral interview can be organized, or the previous questionnaire can be completed by an interviewer with a face-to-face interview with the driver during (or outside) service.

Name of Driver :   **Years in Service :**

Date :

Interviewer :

A. Scheduling:

B. Routeing:

C. Passenger Complaints:

D. Other Suggestions:

Figure 3.7: Example of a questionnaire form for drivers' suggestions and remarks.

64

A note on planning and statistical design of bus surveys and counts

Perhaps the principal factor of success is the proper design of the survey. Numerous texts deal with survey design, execution and analysis. Here a brief but concise summary will be given of the main points to be taken into account. The reader is again referred to the recent US, UMTA publication (UMTA, 1987).

The first question to be asked is what information is required in order to analyse the problem and/or to answer the questions posed by the study objectives. Of particular concern is how one actually defines and measures the variables of interest. In the case of a simple count these variables are easy to define and the main question centers on the sampling size and method of collection. If one is interested in a survey of "attitudes" for example, it will often be the case that no one question will precisely capture a particular attitude or concept, or that no one variable will perfectly measure the quantity or quality of interest. In such situations one usually defines several variables and uses several questions to "get at" the effect being measured. The example from the attitude questions in Athens in Fig. 3.6 is indicative of this technique. In any case, the "operationalizing" of one's data requirements in terms of variable definition and measurement is an important task in survey design.

The second important point of survey design is the question what is the size of the population and what method will be used for sampling. The population is the total, "100 percent", from which the sample is to be drawn. Implicit in the definition of the population is the definition of the elements or sampling units which comprise the population. Examples of populations include all bus riders on a given route, all travellers crossing a screenline and all households located in a given section of the city. The sampling units associated with each of these populations are, respectively, individual households.

The definition of the "population" and its associated sampling unit is obviously highly dependent upon the purpose of the survey that is being designed. Many procedures exist for choosing the sample. Generally, a random selection procedure should be used to reduce potential sampling biasses (see later paragraphs). Random sampling techniques include:
a.   Simple random sampling. In this type of sampling the elements are chosen from the entire frame

(see later paragraphs) at random. This is the simplest approach, but it assumes that the sampling frame is explicitly and exhaustively known prior to sampling, something that is seldom the case in the kinds of counts or surveys discussed here.

b. Sequential sampling. In this type, every n^{th} element in the frame is chosen, the assumption being that the elements have been listed in random order in the sampling frame. An example would be sampling every tenth passenger boarding a bus, in which case the assumption is that the bus boarding is a random process. Similarly for stationary counts one can include every second or third bus and so on. Note that a telephone directory or a directory of street addresses are not appropriate sampling frames for sequential sampling since their elements are clearly not listed in a random fashion.

c. Stratified random sampling. In this, the elements are first grouped according to some criteria and then each group is randomly sampled. Stratified samples are an efficient approach when one is interested in particular groups within the population, especially when these groups are small in size relative to the whole. As an example, one might be particularly interested in the transit needs of the elderly. Thus an on- board survey might be stratified according to age, with every tenth boarding passenger under 65 and every fifth passenger over 65 being sampled. In this way, a greater number of elderly people will be surveyed, a more accurate response from this group will be received and yet the overall survey will remain unbiased since it is possible to correct for the differential sampling rates used for the two groups when calculating, for instance, average responses for the entire sample.

d. Cluster sampling. In type of sampling, the sampling frame is first divided into "clusters", a certain number of clusters are randomly chosen and individual elements within each of these clusters are then sampled. Cluster sampling is generally not as efficient as, say, stratified sampling, but it is often a very convenient technique to use when the sampling frame is not explicitly known a priori. As an example, all households in the urban area might represent the sampling frame for a home interview survey, but

66

there may not exist any reliable lists of all households in the area. In such a case, one might define the area's census tracts as clusters, randomly select n of these, enumerate all households within each of these n tracts and then randomly interview m households within each tract. Thus, with suitable corrections for variations in tract sizes, one can sample in an unbiased way from a sampling frame that has been only "implicitly" defined. This was in fact the technique used in very many household interview surveys including the very recent one in Thessaloniki, Greece in 1988.

The previous discussion points to the need to determine an appropriate "sampling frame" and this is the third major question to be answered.

The sampling frame is the implicit or explicit "list" which is actually used to define the population and from which the sample is actually drawn. If the sample population consists of all bus riders on a given route, then the sampling frame would probably be all people actually observed to board buses on that route during a given time period. If the population consists of all households located in a given zone, then the sampling frame might be constructed from census data, assessment rolls, utility customer lists, telephone directories, aerial photographs of the neighbourhood, field enumeration etc. Some of these sampling frames may contain hidden biases. For example, not all households possess telephones. Thus, the telephone directory will provide a biased sample, at least in terms of its income distribution.

In general, bias can enter a sample in a number of ways including: ambiguous or misleading survey questions; poor sample selection techniques; incomplete responses or outright refusals by sample members etc. On the contrary sampling errors are inherent in the task; Mathematically, error refers to the sample variance while bias refers to the sample mean: an unbiassed sample is one in which the sample mean approaches the population mean as the sample size grows large.

The final important question in survey design is that of determining the sample size. This task presupposes that the desired sample precision and the sampling technique have been chosen. For instance, if a precision of d% in the estimation of the proportion of a given group within the population is desired for

67

a simple random sample, then it can be shown that the required sample size, N, to achieve this level of precision with 100(1-a)% confidence is (see also CUTA, 1985):

$$N = \left[\frac{Z_{1-1/2a} \, \sigma}{d/100} \right]^2 \tag{3.1}$$

where : $Z_{1-1/2a}$ = the (1-1/2a) percentile normal deviate,

σ = the group standard deviation.

Since σ is rarely known, equation (3.1) can be replaced, for large samples, with:

$$N = \left[\frac{(Z_{1-1/2a}) \, \sqrt{p(1-p)}}{d/100} \right]^2 \tag{3.2}$$

where p is the group proportion within the population[a]. As an example, assume that an error range (d) of 0.05 is desired at a confidence level of 95% (a=0.5). Assume p = 0.5 so that p (1-p) equals 0.25. From statistical tables it is found that:

$$Z_{0.975} = 1.96$$

Substitution into equation (3.2) yields:

$$N = \left[(1.96)(0.5) \, / \, (0.05) \right]^2 = 384$$

Thus, 384 observations must be made in order to achieve the specified level of precision.

---

[a]. Since p is what one is typically trying to ascertain through the survey, this may not appear to be very useful. A reasonable guess at the value of p, however, is usually sufficient. Also note that p(1-p) can never exceed 0.25 in value. Thus substitution of 0.25 for p (1-p) in equation (3.2) will always yield an upper bound on the sample size, given one's choice of d and a.

PROBLEM IDENTIFICATION

This stage in the overall short-term planning process typically looks for deteriorating levels of service, such as crush level ridership, or reliability problems, or inefficient services indicated by low ridership levels, as a way to identify problems requiring attention.

One way that is used to identify problems is through the use of service standards (see also next chapter and Annex 2). Service measures and service standards are used today by well organized public transport agencies around the world, either as the basis for decisions or as indicators of problems. The discussion in the next chapter illustrates the difference between a service standard and a performance indicator and shows the way that can be used to evaluate service and identify problems.

Suggestions are another method that is used to identify problems, particularly as regards those aspects of the operation with which the public is more aware. Suggestions are usually made by passengers, drivers or other personnel, community groups, and, on occasion, by business groups. Frequently, planners will have a portfolio of such suggested changes which they would like to see implemented or at least analysed more fully under suitable circumstances.

Of the two methods, the second is undoubtedly the most usually applied in practice, since it is the easiest and most straightforward. However, it is the first that is recommended here, since it is the most objective and reliable one and can be incorporated in an overall service evaluation and planning process. It also offers the best possible "protection" to the agency against undue political or other outside pressures for changes or new services that may not always be "technically" justifiable. The overall process of formulating, analysing, approving and finally implementing a (short-term) change in the network or service, is described in some considerable detail in the following.

PLAN FORMULATION AND PUBLIC PARTICIPATION

Having identified the problems, the next steps in the suggested planning process shown in Figure 3.1, concern the formulation of the appropriate short-term plans for action, their analysis which should normally include some sort of public participation and the implementation.

Plans are formulated in one of two ways. The first, which is standard in many agencies, is to have one experienced planner or technical staff to take responsibility for developing one or more actions to solve the existing problems. For scheduling changes there is generally only one solution, but for route path changes there may be several alternatives from which to choose. Each alternative must be feasible and susceptible to cost estimation, ridership, and revenue impacts, which will come in the analysis phase.

The second method is to have round table discussions with the appropriate staff members, planners, engineers, schedulers etc who will do the same analysis as the single planner in the process described above. This group method is often used when resources are tight, when a proposed plan may be controversial, or when a number of plans are being considered together.

During the process of trying to find feasible solutions to a problem, additional data may be required. It is not uncommon to collect additional data, either when the original data were collected through the regular and more general data collection phase, or when the problem has brought to light the need for new data.

There are a number of factors which help to choose from alternative plans. For example, if a change will result to increased deficits, the financial resources available will be the deciding factor. Also if extra vehicles are required, the deciding factor will be the number of spare vehicles available. Other factors which often constrain the range of solutions are general policy standards such as headways (e.g. off-peak headways should be less than 60 minutes) geographic accessibility guidelines (e.g. 95 percent of the area's residents should be within, say, 400 m of a bus stop).

The final test for any proposed plan will come when it is subjected to the reactions of the public and the view of the decision makers who are particularly aware of the political consequences.

As regards the participation of the public, action plans may be divided into two groups:
   a. Minor changes, such as changing the running time, or adding buses to a route or removing something from it. These changes typically require only internal approval from the head of scheduling or planning and can be implemented at

the next driver pick as long as no financial or
other constraints intervene. It also follows
that they do not necessitate public participation, in any institutionalized form (e.g the
well known Public Inquiry Process in Great Britain or the "scoping" in the Environmental Assessment Process in the Netherlands, etc).
b. Major ones, e.g. network changes. These
should normally be made with public participation at some stage of the process, so that they
have the widest possible acceptance of the travelling public. The process that will be followed in order to make the public aware and able
to express an opinion, may vary according to the
specific socio-political circumstances that
exist in the area. In some countries public participation may not be feasible or practical, if
the public is not familiar with such procedures
and there are no legal procedures established.
In other countries there are statutory procedures established which have to be followed.

Alternative ways for making the public aware of
the proposed changes, even in the absence of a well
established practice or statutory regulations, are
the following:
a. Open Board meetings which the public can
    attend and express its views. These must be
    appropriately publicized and prepared in
    advance, so that the participating public
    is aware of the proposed actions preferably
    before the discussion.
b. Application of the proposed measures on an
    experimental basis, say for 6 months, so
    that the public gets an opportunity to ex-
    perience them and express its views or ob-
    jections. The danger here is that an "ex-
    perimental" implementation may not always
    be feasible (at least without increased
    cost).
c. Gradual application of the change, so as to
    make intermediate improvements, if neces-
    sary, and generally to take the views of
    the public into account. This is perhaps
    the most popular way with the politicians
    because it gives them flexibility to change
    a mistaken decision without undue political
    cost while at the same time showing in
    practice their active concern for change.

Implementation of any decided action should always be done in the shortest possible time, but again adequate warning and information must be given to the public. A lot may depend also on the timing of the implementation action. The preferred time is usually a relatively calm and not too busy period preferably on a "low season" of the year.

4 Performance evaluation and service standards

DEFINITIONS

The efficient operation of an urban bus system, like all other modes of public transport, requires the existence of a framework within which this operation is continuously monitored, evaluated and adjusted. Such a "framework" consists of standards and indicators of performance which permit an objective evaluation of existing or proposed new services. The difference between a "standard" and a performance indicator has already been mentioned, but can usefully be repeated here.

A Performance Indicator (PI) is a concept designed to express, in an objective and quantitative way, a certain aspect (economic, technical or operational) of the system's performance. It is a quantifiable measure which can be reported as a single data value or as a ratio of two or more data values. The purpose of utilizing performance indicators is threefold:

a.   to provide an early detection system to signal undesirable trends;

b.   to provide data to aid in decision making;

c.   to help towards the achievement of a certain desirable performance.

In other words performance indicators provide a
mechanism to evaluate the performance of the system
and of individual routes. They also provide a guideline for adjusting bus service to meet given budget
constraints and a framework to measure the impact of
such adjustments.

A **service** **standard,** on the other hand, is a
fixed minimum or maximum value of a specific performance or other indicator, that should not be exceeded. It is a limiting value or a specific objective to achieve, which may or may not correspond to a
performance indicator. For example a standard concerning bus stop spacing will refer to the minimum
and/or maximum permissible distance between bus
stops. For such a standard there is usually no corresponding performance indicator. However, for the
performance indicator, concerning e.g. passenger
safety (no. of accidents per 100,000 vehicle-kilometers) there is usually a corresponding standard
that sets the maximum value of this indicator.

Both indicators of performance and service
standards are being used as a mechanism to provide an
evaluation of the performance of the (public transport) system as a whole and/or this of individual
routes.

Relative to the standards and performance indicators, the following cases may exist[a]:

a.   **Formal** **Service** **Standards.** These are official
policy objectives, which are used to evaluate a
particular performance indicator by establishing
specific limits that identify acceptable and
unacceptable performance levels. The formality
of the standard is a reflection of its status
within an agency as official policy and the existence of a formalized performance evaluation
and review process for the corresponding indicators. Due to the standard's official status, a
major effort is normally made to adhere to its
requirements under most situations and conditions.

b.   **Informal** **Service** **Standards.** In this case the
standard has no official or policy status within
an agency and is used as an internal guideline
only. The standard's informal nature may result

---

[a]. These categories follow the broad distinction
made in US, DOT (1984).

74

in less than universal application under various situations or conditions at the discretion of the department or manager responsible for the evaluation activity.

c. **Proposed Service Standards.** This is the situation, in which a transit system is either in the process of developing a service standard to evaluate a performance indicator, or it is currently involved in securing approval for recently developed standards or the implementation of standards that have recently been approved. Most of the agencies with "proposed" standards envision that the standards will receive formal status in the near future.

d. **Performance indicator monitoring.** This is the situation, in which a transit system does not possess (or is in the process of developing) a service standard to evaluate a performance indicator. However, despite the lack of a standard, the agency does track or monitor the performance indicator by collecting/analysing pertinent data and by calculating various indicators and statistics on a more or less regular basis. Transit systems that monitor performance indicators frequently use such general terms as "minimize" or "maximize", which indicate a desire to improve some aspect of performance, but fail to set acceptable performance levels that are quantifiable or measurable.

e. **No standards or indicators.** A final case is a situation, in which no standards or performance indicators are used by the agency.

Many agencies today, are reluctant to set and use Performance Indicators or Standards. However, as pressure increases from the supervising agencies and the passengers, to extend or change service to suit specific demands, which may not always be economically viable, the agencies are becoming more and more in favour of setting standards as a way to "protect" themselves.

THE SERVICE EVALUATION AND STANDARDS PROCESS (SESP)

General contents and objectives

Relative to the application and use of performance indicators and service standards, is the whole process of performance evaluation and service standards setting, which will be referred to in the following in short as the **"Service Evaluation and Standards Process"** - SESP.

This process is typically composed of the following:

    a.   Ongoing monitoring and service adjustments for all existing routes.

    b.   Continuous detailed review of the structure and level of service on all existing routes (Route Efficiency).

    c.   An annual performance review of all existing routes based on economic and ridership criteria and a concurrent comprehensive evaluation of proposals for new and modified services.

    d.   An evaluation of new and modified services which had been previously implemented.

The basic objective of the SESP is to enable the agency to apply the service standards and performance indicators in a systematic way, so as to continuously evaluate and adjust its service to the changing needs of the public.

The following sections show, in a summary form, the contents of a SESP, as currently applied by the Toronto Transit Commission (TTC) in Toronto, Canada (TTC 1985a).

Monitoring and Service Adjustment

Ridership on all regular routes is monitored through regular and frequent counts as part of the Ridership Monitoring and Service Adjustment Program. Additional information and statistics are compiled from customer communications, regarding daily riding experiences, from staff observation of ridership and route operations and from operations reports on passenger loadings and recurring problems, which may affect service to the customer.

This information is used to determine the average number of passengers on the vehicles at the location of highest demand on each route. The vehicle loading standards are then applied to determine if service is adequate. If maximum-hour peak-point average vehicle loads begin to approach the applicable vehicle loading standard, then provision of additional service is considered, subject to certain other crowding indicators being triggered and to the availability of vehicles. If actual average vehicle loads are beginning to drop significantly below the applicable loading standard, then a decrease in service levels may be considered.

In Toronto the Ridership Monitoring and Service Adjustment process is carried out roughly once a month, although the lead time between identifying a required service adjustment and actually implementing it is a least 4-6 months. During this time, extra vehicles may be operated on the appropriate routes on an ad-hoc basis, until the new schedules are available.

Route Efficiency Review

All routes in the system are reviewed in detail to identify more specific problems related to the route structure than would be highlighted in the Ridership Monitoring and Service Adjustment Program. The review is carried out on each route, as new riding count information becomes available, usually once a year. The analysis deals with recent route operating experience, comparison of observed ridership and service levels on each branch of the route and the level of service provided within each time period. Minor service changes to improve a route's efficiency are recommended for implementation. Major service changes are deferred for analysis in Comparative Evaluation within the Annual Service Standards Application (see below).

Annual Performance Review of Existing Routes

Each year, all existing routes in the system are ranked in descending order, on the basis of their rona: subsidy per boarding, which indicates the amount of money the agency receives in subsidy for each person boarding a transit vehicle on a specific route. This ranking is then compared to an Economic Performance Target, which is the amount of subsidy the agency receives per boarding on a system-wide basis. Routes which have subsidies greater than the Economic Performance Target are considered to be "poor-performers" because they utilize more than their share of resources and put upward pressure on fares.

Poor-performing routes are examined in detail to identify measures which could be taken to improve their efficiency and effectiveness. Minor service changes, such as decreasing the hours of service, adding a new short-turn branch, or amalgamating the service with another existing route, are recommended

for implementation. Major service changes are referred to Comparative Evaluation (see below). If there
are no feasible service changes, which can be made to
improve a route's performance, then the entire route
must undergo Comparative Evaluation.

Evaluation of Service Requests

The Annual Service Standards Application Process
(as done by the Toronto Transit Commission) also presents the major opportunity for consideration and
possible implementation of new transit services
and/or significant modifications to existing ones.
Schedule-related service changes, which do not involve significant increases in operated mileage or
capital cost, can be considered and implemented, if
warranted, on an ongoing basis as part of the Ridership Monitoring and Service Adjustment Program, as
well as
through the Annual Service Standards Application process. However, proposals which involve significant
mileage costs (e.g. additional periods of operation)
and/or vehicle costs (e.g. new routes) must undergo
more detailed analysis within the Annual Service
Standards Application. This ensures that any additional resources expended by the agency are being
used to their fullest benefit, with full approval of
the Commission and in consultation with the affected
municipalities.

As part of this process, the local municipalities within the Metropolitan Toronto region are in-
vited to submit council-endorsed proposals for new
services. The requirement for council endorsement of
all such proposals ensures that they have broad community support and provides the TTC with a mandate to
evaluate them together with any staff-generated proposals. Any recommended service change is subsequent-
ly reviewed by the appropriate municipal council before it is actually implemented.

Service requests are categorized as follows:
- Proposals for New Services.
- Proposals for Additional Periods of Opera-
  tion on Existing Routes.
- Proposals for Changes to Service Start and
  Finish Times.
- Miscellaneous Proposals.

"New services" refer to the creation of a new
and separate transit route, to the extension or modification of an existing route or to the creation of a
new branch of an existing route. Additional periods

of operation are considered, as a route's service area develops and its ridership grows. Any of these proposals, which do not conform to the System Design Guidelines, are dropped from further consideration.

As the next step, all remaining proposals are assessed in terms of their economic performance, utilizing the route subsidy per boarding measure and the Economic Performance Target in the Annual Performance Review of Existing Routes. Service proposals, which require less subsidy than the system-wide Target, are recommended for implementation. An additional economic standard is then applied to service requests at this point in the process: The Maximum Permissible Subsidy defined as the upper limit of a route's subsidy requirement, beyond which the Commission cannot afford to operate the service. Therefore, any service proposals, which have a subsidy per boarding greater than the Maximum Permissible Subsidy, are not considered further, unless a separate "social" subsidy is made available for their operation. All remaining proposals with a route subsidy per boarding which falls between the two standards are within "Comparative Evaluation".

Comparative Evaluation

Comparative Evaluation is the point in the Annual Review, where the remaining services (i.e. the poorest-performing existing routes identified in the Annual Performance Review and the Route Efficiency Review Program or the most costly proposed new routes and/or additional periods of operation) are brought together for evaluation against each other to aid in determining which of this final group of services should be given priority for implementation. The Comparative Evaluation focuses on the achievement of mobility and community objectives rather than on economic performance.

Each route in this phase is rated according to three separate measures of passenger service effectiveness, which take into account factors such as the net gain or loss of ridership, expected to result from the proposed service change, transit access time for residents and transit dependency. These three separate ratings are combined into one overall "Performance Point Total" for each route. Each total score is then divided by the dollar cost of saving associated with each service change and the routes are ranked on the basis of this score per dollar cost. This final ranking indicates which routes, com-

pared to each other, would provide the most effective
service for every dollar spent.

Available vehicles and budget mileage are then
allocated to each route, starting with the number
one-ranked service, until the resources are used up.
If there are not enough resources to recommend all
routes in the final ranking for implementation, then
the "left-over" (i.e. lowest-ranking) proposed new
routes are dropped from further consideration. In
addition, it is possible that a very low-ranking existing route could be recommended for discontinuation
and its resources re-allocated to a higher ranking
proposed new service.

The Service Standards recommendations, once approved by the agency, are then sent to the municipalities for review and comment.

The above description of a specific SESP applied
in the area of Toronto, Canada, shows the complexity
but also the usefulness of the process in providing
objective and well documented service planning to the
people of the area.

PERFORMANCE EVALUATION INDICATORS

Definitions and Basic Concepts

The performance evaluation indicators of public
transport usually embrace two concepts - **efficiency**
and **effectiveness**. Since there are no universally
accepted definitions for public transport performance
efficiency and effectiveness, some of the definitions
that have appeared in the literature are as follows:
Efficiency and effectiveness are concerned with produced and consumed output respectively (McCrosson,
1978). Efficiency is concerned with how well a transit firm utilizes its available labour and capital
resources; effectiveness is concerned with how well a
transit firm meets the goals which have been set for
it (U.S.Department of Transportation, 1978). Efficiency measures reflect resource usage; effectiveness measures rate the degree to which the transit
service achieves the rider's and the community's
needs (Fielding et al., 1977).

The well known "triangle" connecting these concepts is shown in Figure 4.1. Between the three concepts of **"service inputs"**, **"service outputs"** and
"consumption", the notions of cost efficiency, cost
effectiveness and service efficiency materialize. If
one adds the Community served by the system to be

evaluated and its constraints and demands, the complete picture of the various interactions and interrelations is obtained. The corresponding indicators fall in one of the categories shown in Figure 4.1.

Two alternative methodologies have appeared in the literature for selecting efficiency and effectiveness indicators for evaluating the performance of public transit firms. One methodology (which appears to be more widely used than the other) specifies the criteria that selected performance indicators must satisfy (Fielding and Gauthier, 1976). The alternative methodology requires the specification of transit operating objectives for the purpose of the selecting performance indicators (Talley and Anderson, 1981).

These two methodologies are compared in a recent paper (Talley, 1986) which concludes that the operating objective specification methodology for selecting performance indicators has several advantages over the criteria specification method. Details of the "operating objectives" method can be found in Anderson et al (1981), while for the "criteria selection" method a number of publications can be found, as it is the most widespread method used (see for example Fielding et al, 1977, OECD, 1980, and Fielding, 1987). Although we cannot go into any great detail within the scope of this book into the two selection methodologies, some general points can be given, so that the indicators described in this book can be better understood and evaluated.

As regards the criteria selection method, a number of selection criteria have appeared in the literature for selecting transit performance indicators and are as follows:
1. consistency with goals and objectives
2. conciseness
3. data availability
4. expense and time commitment to collecting indicator data
5. measurability
6. minimization of uncontrollable factors
7. robustness.

The selection criterion number 1 above, "consistency with goals and objectives", refers to selecting performance indicators that measure the extent to which the operations of the public transit firm are impacting upon some specified goals and objectives related to transit service.

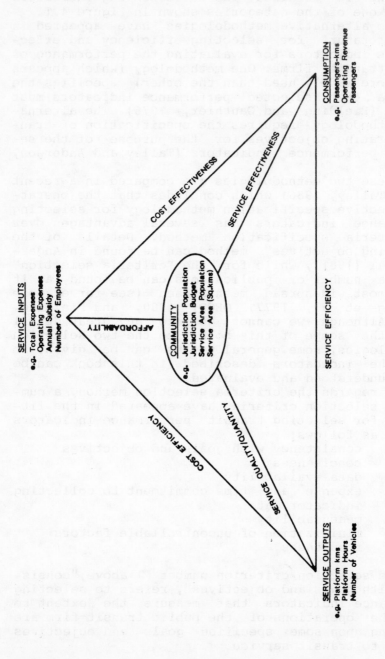

Figure 4.1: Basic concepts and interrelationships for the definition of performance evaluation criteria for a public transportation agency.

Examples of Community goals with respect to transit service are:

a. to reduce air pollution,
b. to reduce highway congestion
c. to provide public transportation to those without other means of travel.

Examples of objectives with respect to the above criteria (which differ from the goals in that they are more specific and they often specify a time period) are:

a. to increase ridership by 100 percent within a certain time period
b. to maintain farebox revenue at a minimum of 50 percent of operating cost for the foreseeable future.

These same goals and objectives can also be found in strategic planning models (or systems).

The selection criterion number 2, "conciseness", refers to selecting performance indicators that minimize the redundance and overlap among selected indicators. Not only should data be available for measurement of the indicator, but the cost and time commitment in collecting the data should also be considered in the selection of performance indicators. The criterion "measurability" simply refers to the fact that the indicator should be measurable.

The criterion, "minimization of uncontrollable factors" refers to selecting performance indicators that minimize the influence of uncontrollable factors that affect transit operations (i.e. factors beyond the control of transit management). Example of such factors are traffic congestion and highway system design.

The criterion "robustness" refers to selecting performance indicators that can be used for evaluating various transit service scenarios.

An alternative methodology to that of the criteria, is to specify the operating objectives of the transit firm, from which transit performance indicators are obtained. Those variables that appear in the efficiency operating objective and whose values (at least to some extent) are under the control of the transit agency would be the agency's effectiveness performance indicators. The methodology of selecting transit performance indicators that considers explicitly transit operating objectives is found in the work of Talley and Anderson (1979) and Anderson et al (1981). Although this second methodology appears to be theoretically more sound, it is the first that has up to now been more widely used and understood.

Selecting an Appropriate Package of Performance Indicators

The interested reader can find in the references mentioned in the previous section a whole spectrum of theoretical means and justifications for the selection of the most appropriate indicators by using either of the two methodologies. However, there are a number of practical considerations which will finally determine the actual indicators to use. Most of them have already been mentioned in the previous section when describing the "criteria selection" method. Here these "practical" criteria will be discussed further, with a view to suggesting a series of possible indicators for final selection according to the specific case in mind.

The first point to bear in mind is that performance indicators and allied information are likely to be of interest to several different groups of people and institutions; from those responsible for the day-to-day operation of public transport services, to those who must take a much broader view of transport policy, at local, regional and national levels. From this wide spectrum, the different user groups will wish to consult different subsets of the indicators. Also the way, in which these packages can be most usefully put together, naturally depends on the purposes which they will serve.

The great majority of indicators are calculated by public transport management for its own use, but some of them will be used in discussion and negotiation with various levels of government, including comparisons with other agencies. Even within a single transport system, the information has different uses. Some of it may be required in the planning of new service changes. Other indicators may be used primarily to show how successfully the operation is performing in its many different aspects and whether the performance is improving or deteriorating over time, while other indicators may still be used to compare performance in different areas or divisions of the undertaking. Many of the indicators may be applied to all three of these purposes and there will be a similar overlap between indicators used internally and those used in dialogue between operator and local authority, or those used in decision-making at the different levels of government.

In deciding which of them to include in a package designed for a particular operation, two issues should be borne in mind. Firstly, the collection of the necessary data and the calculation of the indicators is costly in staff, time and resources, even if all the data handling is computerized. Secondly, really important aspects of the operation can become submerged under huge quantities of statistical information, if the user is not sufficiently selective in deciding where to concentrate attention.

The second major consideration concerns the data requirements. Since indicators are only as valid as the data and information used to develop them, the approach to designing data elements and collection systems is critical to any performance evaluation system. Also since the development of data bases is costly and time-consuming, the subject deserves serious attention and must be seen in connection with the overall data requirements of the agency, according to what has already been mentioned in the previous chapter.

Indicators are typically ratios, composed of figures obtained from some kind of information system and data base, either financial (e.g. costs, revenues) or operational (e.g. trips, travel time). In addition, and if the agency has sufficient size and resources, data may be collected for special purposes through surveys of special studies as a supplement to the basic data system. The financial and operating data help to compose indicators concerning efficiency; market statistics provide data that are primarily related to effectiveness.

Thirdly, a very important consideration is the purpose for which the specific indicators are to be used. In relation to this point a comprehensive report prepared by a working group of the OECD's Road Research Committee (OECD, 1980) classified the possible indicators in three groups:

A. Indicators for Service Planning. These are meant to help in assessing the operating consequences of changes to existing services or routes or these of expansion of the network to new areas. They are both efficiency and effectiveness indicators. The first, because the agency will want to know the cost saving or additional cost involved and the demand on its resources and the second, because it will want to make some prediction of the likely effects on patronage.

Therefore this group of indicators may be sub-classified into those concerning:
a. costs,
b. revenues,
c. vehicle requirements and fleet planning and
d. global ones, i.e. dealing with general planning issues and variables.

   B. Indicators for "Internal" Trends Assessment over time. These are intended for the operator him-self in order to assess the trends in performance over time, and in order to compare performance bet-ween the various sections of the system. The items usually of interest, are:
a. costs,
b. service production,
c. service reliability,
d. engineering aspects of the operation,
e. safety,
f. revenues and
g. patronage.
   C. Indicators for Comparisons between different operating agencies. Finally, this group of indicators is intended for use in comparing the differences be-tween different divisions of service within an oper-ator. The comparisons are not meant as a yardstick for judging inferior or superior divisions, but rather as a reason to search and identify the causes of the differences. It is obvious that this latter type of indicators is meant for the large agencies only, especially those that operate more than one modes of public transport.

   A final point is the need to have uniform and comparable indicators in a wider area, e.g. a region or the country as a whole. This requirement, although not binding for a specific operator who would like the indicators for his own use, may be very important from the supervising organizations' point of view. Compatibility and uniformity of the indicators used, can provide a useful comparison between agencies in different areas.These will be the duty of a higher level authority to study and impose.

Examples of Possible Indicators

   As already mentioned previously, it is not pos-sible to give specific recommendations for perfor-

86

mance indicators, because there is no way to account for possible differences among operators and operating environments. What will be presented in the following, are examples of performance indicators suggested in various studies and reports. These examples can provide very useful guidance for the selection of such indicators by the interested operators or other agencies.

Table 4.1 shows a set of 8 indicators from two earlier studies by Fielding and Gauthier (1976) and Drosdat (1977). These have been selected for the context of the specific studies mentioned, by use of the "criteria selection" methodology.

Table 4.1

Efficiency and effectiveness performance indicators from two earlier studies in the U.S. (Fielding and Gauthier, 1976, and Drosdat, 1977),

Efficiency measures	Effectiveness measures
1. Cost per vehicle-hour (a cost indicator)	1. Percent population served (an accessibility indicator)
2. Energy per passenger (a cost indicator)	2. Passengers per service area of population (a service utilization indicator).
3. Annual vehicle-hours per employee (a labour productivity indicator)	3. Passengers per vehicle- (a service utilization indicator)
4. Annual vehicle-hours per vehicle (a vehicle utilization indicator)	4. Revenue per unit cost

Another example of a wider range of performance indicators, suggested in the study of the OECD Road Research Group (OECD, 1980), is given in Tables 4.2 to 4.4. These three tables give the suggested indicators as they correspond to the three categories A, B and C, mentioned in the previous subsection. The contents of the three Tables 4.2 to 4.4 have been slightly modified by the author so as to be simpler and easier to understand.

Table 4.2

Indicators recommended for service planning
(OECD, 1980)

Aspect of interest	Indicator	Application
Cost	- (*)Aver.cost per veh-hr or veh-km: Cost categorization in unit costs: variable,semi-variable,fixed - Maintenance (cost/vehicle or per veh-hr or km) - Running cost (fuel,oil, tyres)/veh-hr or km categorized by veh.type and age	for cost prediction of service changes for fleet renewal
Service production	- (*)Revenue veh-km/revenue veh-hrs - (*) Vehicles in service in peak/veh.between peaks - (*)Spare veh. required - Revenue veh-hrs/total veh-hrs	speed,(schedule planning fleet size planning
Patronage	- (*)Passengers/veh-hr (or veh-km) - Passenger-kms./veh-hr (or veh-km) - (*) Revenue per pass. or fare index	for estimating likely demand and revenue
Engineering	- (*)Categorization of by type, capacity, age - (*)Aver. out-of-service time per bus and/or categorization of faults by vehicle type	for fleet size planning and fleet renewal
Global	- No. of transit trips per inhabitant/veh-kms per inhabitant - Proportion of population within 1/2 km of route	for estimating likely demand for estimating "needs"

Note : Those marked with (*) are considered, by the OECD group, to be a basic minimum.

Table 4.3

Indicators recommended for "internal" assessment
(OECD,1980)

Aspect of interest	Indicator	Application (1)
Cost	**Indicators of efficiency**	
	- (*)Average cost per veh-hr or km	Xfsp
	- (*)Comparison of operating cost, & capital investment with budget	X fb
	- Cost categorization into unit costs (per veh-hr, veh-km, or vehicle): variable,semi-variable fixed.	Xysbp
	- Cost per employee	X f
	- Payroll cost as a proportion of total cost	X f
	- Engineering cost as proportion of total cost	X f
	- Administration cost as a proportion of total cost	X f
	- Cost per passenger-km or per passenger	y s
Service productivity	- (*) Vehicle-hrs or km	Xfsb
	- (*)Veh-hrs/veh or veh-km/veh	Xfsp
	- Veh-hrs (km)/ veh crew or veh-hrs (km)/ employee	Xfsp
	- (*)Revenue veh-hrs/total veh-hrs	X yp
	- Revenue veh-kms/revenue veh-hrs	X yp
	- (*)Crew-hrs paid/revenue veh-hrs	X yp
	- (*)Vehicles in service in peak/ vehicles between peaks	X y
	- Mean number of transfers per passenger	y
Service reliability	- (*)Lost vehicle - kms	X fsp
	- % of vehicles beginning duty more than x minutes late	X f
	- Measure of deviation from schedule or measure of average passenger waiting time	X fp
	- Measure of veh.load : % of vehicles full, or pass.-kms / seat-kms	ysp
	- Letters of complaint	X fs

(1) See end of Table 4.3 at page 90.

Table 4.3 (Continued)

Engi- neering	- (*)Categorization of fleet by vehicle type, capacity, age	X y
	- (*)Number of breakdowns in ser- vice per X,000 veh-kms	X f
	- Lost vehicle-kms due to unser- viceable vehicles	X f
	- Failure to provide vehicle for service	X f
	- Mean out-of-service time per veh.	X f
	- Spare veh./fleet size required for service	X y
	- Categorization of veh.faults by fault type,vehicle type and age	y
	- (*)Maintenance workers per veh.	X f
	- Cost of materials/engineering employee	X f X f
	- Number of veh.serviced per en- gineering employee by type of work	Xfb
	- Number of vehicles cleaned per cleaner	Xfb
Accident reporting	- (*)Accidents per 100,000 veh-kms, categorized by accident type	Xfs
	Indicators of effectiveness	
Revenue	- (*) Revenue/cost ratio	X fsb
	- Revenue per veh-hr or km	X fsp
	- Fare index or revenue/passenger relative to prices	y
	- Per cent of tickets inspected, per cent of evasion of fraud	X f
	- (*) Revenue per pass.-km	Xfs
Patronage	- Passenger-kms/veh-hr or km (or Passengers/veh-hr,km)	X fsp
	- Passenger-kms/employee (or Pas- sengers/employee)	ysp

(1) Notes on application:

X   indicates that the measure is useful in comparison between different operating divisions

f   indicates slow overall variation and ex-amination at yearly intervals

s   indicates that seasonal variation is likely

b   indicates that comparison with a budget, schedule or standard may be necessary

p   indicates that peak/off-peak variation may be of interest.

y   indicates slow overall variation and ex-amination at yearly intervals.

Table 4.4

Indicators for Comparison of Different Operations and for a more "Global" Assessment (OECD, 1980)

Aspect of interest	Indicator
	Indicators of efficiency
Cost	- Cost per veh-hr (preferably or per veh-km in relevant operating district - Cost per passenger-km (preferably) or passenger journey - Cost breakdown in unit costs (per vehicle-hr, veh-km, veh).
Service Production	- Vehicle-hrs or vehicle-kms:compare with budget - Lost vehicle-kms and proportion caused by traffic congestion - Measure of average passenger waiting time (high frequency services) and/or deviations from schedule.
Accidents	- Accidents per 100,000 vehicle-kms
Revenue	**Indicators of effectiveness** - Revenue/cost ratio (for special services where appropriate) - Fare trend relative to prices
Patronage	- Passenger-kms and passenger journeys - Passenger-kms/veh-hr or km or passenger/veh-hr or km
Global	- Number of trips per inhabitant per area - Vehicle-kms per inhabitant per area - Car ownership, income, elderly persons/school-children per area - Proportion of population within 1/2 km of service - Accessibility factors - Congestion, parking difficulty, modal split - Energy use by mode

Finally, a more recent example of performance indicators and their values is given in Table 4.5. This comes from a study in Greece (Giannopoulos, 1986), which prepared guidelines and recommendations for the operation of Urban Bus Transport in the country. The indicators proposed there took account of the data that are collected on a regular basis in

Greece, and since these data are generally limited, the suggested indicators could form a useful example for other agencies with similar problems. Table 4.5 also shows the values of these indicators for three characteristic Greek cities of small to medium size.

The reader is also referred to Annex 2 for more examples of indicators derived by the author in a worldwide survey of Public Transport agencies.

Table 4.5

Indicators of Performance suggested for the Urban
Bus operations in Greece (1985 data).

| Name of Indicator | Value for the city of: | | | |
	Patras (155000)	Heraklion (110000)	Rhodes (80000)	Larissa (102000)
1.Total Functional Cost per veh-km (in drcs)	142.02	147.68	142.95	114.64
2.Total Number of veh-kms per per year per veh.	65740	60440	56310	83950
3.Total Number of veh-kms per year per employee	13380	10410	13250	14780
4.Total veh-kms per year per cost of maintenance	0.073	0.095	0.038	0.111
5.Total veh-kms per year per cost of fuel	0.076	0.073	0.088	0.067
6.Total receipts from tickets to total cost	0.598	0.572	0.739	0.702
7.Total receipts from tickets to total veh-kms	84.93	84.48	105.67	80.53
8.Total veh-kms to total subsidies and loans	0.017	0.037	0.021	0.053
9.Total service veh-kms to total veh-kms	N/A	N/A	N/A	N/A
10.Number of passengers per unit cost	0.029	0.034	0.023	0.046

Table 4.5 (Continued)

11.Number of passengers per service veh-kms	N/A	N/A	N/A	N/A

Notes:

a. Size of agencies (number of buses): Patras 91, Heraklion 45, Rhodes 36, Larissa 28.

b. All cost units in Greek Drachmas approx. 130 Drcs per 1 US $ in 1988).

c. If available, the number of veh-hours would be preferable in the above indicators instead of the number of veh-kms.

d. N/A = Data currently Not Available in Greece.

e. The numbers in parenthesis indicate the 1981 population of the corresponding urban area.

APPLICABILITY AND WORLD-WIDE USE OF STANDARDS, PIs AND THE SESP

The definition and use of performance indicators and service standards,for the evaluation and monitoring of the performance of a public transport agency, seems a theoretically justified and reasonable way to proceed. In practice however, there is not sufficient or widespread acceptance and use of these tools, as one might expect. In general, the larger and better organized the agency, the more likely it is to adopt and use a SESP. In this author's knowledge the process established by the Toronto Transport Commission and described briefly above, is one of the most comprehensive and well organized that can be found in the industry world-wide.

In smaller agencies, the management can usually gain a quite detailed knowledge of the performance of the system from its day-to-day contact with the operations. For example, such agencies usually rely heavily on supervisor and driver input for both finding problems and identifying solutions. Not surprisingly, the problems that are most often brought up by drivers are those relating to crush loading and insufficient running time rather than empty buses and slack running time. This situation, even though subjective to a large extent, may be adequate for small

93

agencies. However, in general, although the drivers' knowledge of the route can be invaluable when route changes are being considered, it cannot replace the information gathered through a comprehensive and more objective approach, as provided by the performance indicators and service standards.

As already said before, during the preparation of this book, a world-wide survey was carried out with the help of a questionnaire sent to all Public Transport agencies registered in the UITP's Handbook of Public Transport (UITP, 1985). The purpose of the survey was to investigate the application of service standards and/or a service evaluation process. Of the total 200 agencies asked, some 55 answered and the results are shown in detail in Annex 2. However, some overall conclusions can be mentioned here.

The percentage of agencies using actual (legislated) service standards is very small. Of the total number of answers to the questionnaire, only 10% had proper standards, 40 % said that they are using some type of informal standards, while of the remaining 50% that use no standards the great majority (90%) used some forms of simple performance indicators, and only 5 agencies reported that they do not use anything.

In another question, the majority (nearly 80%) indicated that they think the existence of a standard, is a positive and helpful thing. Only 10% indicated no use and/or no desire to use, for the time being, of service standards.

Of the agencies that use standards there is a wide diversity in the number and type of standards used. This is partly explained by the differences is local conditions and operating environments, but also due to lack of knowledge and staffing problems. Although just a few agencies define more than 10 performance indicators and service standards the great majority uses 3 or 4 key standards while some indicators are mentioned simply as indicative measures of performance.

A similar situation was reported by Wilson et al (1984) in a survey of a small number of firms in the U.S. In this survey, the reasons for the low use of standards and to a certain degree performance indicators, are stated to be the following:

1.   Public transport agencies are only interested in a few problems, such as overcrowding and underutilization, and a few indicators and standards can identify these problems.

94

2. The planning staff does not have time to deal with more than a few indicators and standards.
3. The data are limited or suspect and can only be meaningfully used to compute a few indicators.

The performance indicators or the standards used, depend upon the type of data collected and the key planning issues. Since the key concerns are with ridership (or revenue) the majority of such standards are ridership oriented, e.g. passenger/hours, passenger/miles, passenger/bus trips, and peak load factors (i.e. the percentage ratio of passengers on board at the maximum load point on the route, divided by the seated capacity of the vehicle). If the data collection emphasis is on revenue rather than ridership, the first three measures are often used with revenue substituted for ridership. Other service measures that are frequently used are subsidy per passenger, revenue/cost ratio, and the percent of buses on time. There is no uniformity in the exact definition of these service measures; some transit authorities define them by time period, others by bus trip or driver run, etc. Annex 2 gives the results of the survey in more detail.

Another recent survey among 300 North American transit agencies (US,DOT 1984), has given somewhat more encouraging results. The distribution of the use of standards or performance indicators (among the 109 agencies that answered the survey) by size of agency, is shown in Table 4.6. There is an average of approximately 4 Formal Standards per agency and nearly 5 Performance Indicators while also a considerable number of Informal Standards or Proposed Standards were reported. In general, comparing the results of our survey with that in the North American agencies, it can be seen that in the latter the use of standards and performance indicators is much more widespread than in the rest of the world including Europe.

Suggestions for specific Standards can only be made after careful consideration of the local conditions and constraints. There can be no standards of "universal" application because the requirements and conditions of service differ widely from place to place. However, the material contained in this and in the following chapters of this book about the network, the rolling stock, the operation of the system, etc., can form the basis for a "standards formulation process". Such a process will stand the best chance

95

to take account of the local conditions and produce
the necessary standards or indicators of performance
that will best represent the conditions in the network.

Table 4.6

Use of service standards and performance indicators
in N.America according to US,DOT (1984).

Type of System	No.of replies	No.& types of Standard or Performance Indicator used					
		F	I	PS	PI	Total Stands.	Total (PIs)
Large	19	89	37	24	91	150	91
Medium	28	135	38	19	116	192	116
Small	62	188	122	32	265	342	265
Total	109	412	197	75	472	684	472

Note:
F = Formal Standard
I = Informal Standard
PS= Proposed Standard
PI= Performance Indicator

5 Guidelines for the network

GENERAL

A bus "network", in the sense used in this chapter, is the system of bus lines, stops, terminals and the rest of the necessary infrastructure for the safe and efficient movement of buses and passengers. Contrary to the networks of other mass transit modes, a bus network has the great advantage that it is flexible and it does not require substantial permanent infrastructure for the movement of its vehicles (provided of course that the existing street network has adequate standards to accommodate buses). It is rather a designation of routes for the buses to follow and some necessary installations along them for the use of the passengers (bus stops, signs etc). The principal characteristics, as well as some guidelines for the planning of these "installations", are given in this chapter.

BASIC FORMS OF BUS NETWORKS

As "form" or "type" of a bus network is meant its shape in terms of the arrangement of the bus routes (or lines) in space. The form influences the service provided to the public as well as the proper operation of the system. Among others it influences:

- the "coverage" of the area, i.e. the percentage of the area within a certain acceptable distance from the bus lines
- the number of transfers required for the passengers between bus lines for the passengers to reach their final destinations
- the timetables and bus frequencies, and consequently the mean waiting time at bus stops
- the location and operation of the terminals.

The form of the street network of the urban area, where the bus system operates, does not necessarily predetermine the form of the bus network.

The principal forms of bus network are discussed in the following.

A. Radial

In this type of bus network all or almost all major lines "radiate" from a central point, which invariably is the central area of the city or some suburban center (see Fig.5.1a). The objective is to serve the major corridors of movement to and from a certain focal point. The bus lines in this type of network usually have one terminal point in the central area and one in the periphery, but this creates congestion in the center and the need to find expensive space for bus terminals. Alternatively the bus lines may pass through the center and terminate again at the periphery, but in this case the lines are longer and their operation more unstable.

The advantages of a radial type of network are the minimization of the transfers, since the majority of passengers are going towards the "focal" point, the exploitation of corridors of dense movement and the strengthening of the functions of the focal point.

The disadvantages include contribution to greater congestion in the focal point area, especially when the terminals of the lines are there, non-existent or very poor service to peripheral movements and uneven coverage of the area (the central areas being covered by many "overlapping" lines, while the suburbs may not be covered at all).

It is recommended that a radial type of bus network is used in smaller urban areas (say below

100,000 population), where there is relatively little chance of congestion in the center and the needs for peripheral movements are relatively less. For greater urban areas a "mixed" type of network is recommended.

B. Orthogonal or Grid

This type of bus network is characterized by lines set along an orthogonal grid as shown in Fig. 5.1b. Some of the lines go through the center but many do not and the main objective is to offer a uniform "coverage" in the area.

Some of the main advantages of this type of network is the fact, that the system of lines and routes is more easily understood by the public and that the area is more uniformly covered by the bus system.

Of the disadvantages, perhaps the major one is that this type of network induces more transfers for somebody to reach his final destination and, as a consequence of that, the fact that the frequencies (and thus the required number of buses) have to be increased to compensate for the loss of time in the transfers.

This type of network is recommended for bigger urban areas where the densities of development can sustain greater bus frequencies, as well as for the so called peripheral movements. It follows that, if the road network of the area is of the same type, i.e. orthogonal, this is an additional reason to adapt the bus network to this type of road network.

C. Mixed

This is a mixture of types containing both the orthogonal and the radial form in various parts of the area. Figures 5.1c and 5.1d show examples of this mixed type of network. The first figure shows what is known as a set of trunk and feeder lines, in which there are a number of main (trunk) lines going through the area and a number of feeder radial lines serving the suburbs. Figure 5.1c refers to urban areas, while Figure 5.1d is a situation that can be seen when the bus network serves a central urban area as well as its adjacent satellite towns or villages.

The mixed type of bus network is probably the more widely used type of bus network, simply because no urban area can be ideally suited for either of the previous types.

99

In the literature (e.g.CUTA, 1985) one can find definitions of several other types of networks, e.g. **Linear, Modified Radial, Territorial** etc. While one could of course distinguish, from a theoretical point of view, many different types this is not considered necessary here, as all these types can be thought of as parts or special cases of the three basic ones mentioned above. For example, the modified radial network is a radial with some circumferential routes, while the territorial is a mixed type of network that serves the surrounding towns and suburbs like the one depicted in Figure 5.1d and usually combined with "Time Transfer Points", i.e. transfer points where the bus schedules have been coordinated to minimize waiting times to transferring passengers (CUTA,1985).

TYPES OF BUS ROUTES (AS REGARDS SERVICE CHARACTERISTICS)

General Description

Just as one can distinguish different types of bus networks, the bus routes or lines that form them can be classified into different types, as regards their service characteristics. It is useful to make these distinction here.

As regards the time periods of operation, a bus line can be either of:

i. **Continuous operation**, i.e. operating continuously throughout the day and night (or most of the night), or

ii. **Part time operation**, i.e. operating for part of the normal hours of operation.

As regards the type of routing of the buses, one can distinguish the following 4 types of operation:

a. **Fixed Routing.** In this type of operation the route and the bus stops are fixed and the drivers are obliged to follow it under all circumstances. Of course this type of operation does not preclude the changes planned in routes and stops, which can be effected due to major road works or emergencies, or normal network modifications.

b. **Fixed Routing, but with some stops compulsory and some on request.** In this type, the driver follows a fixed route but does not stop at all stops. There are a number of stops where he has to stop and others where he stops only if there are passengers to be picked up or get off the bus.

100

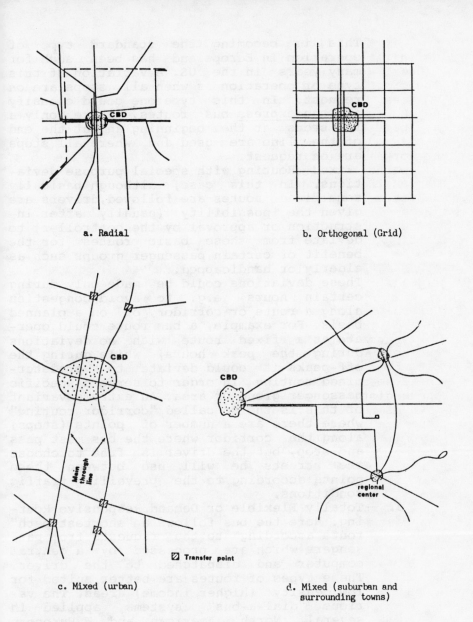

a. Radial

b. Orthogonal (Grid)

CBD

CBD

CBD

Main through line

regional center

☒ Transfer point

c. Mixed (urban)

d. Mixed (suburban and surrounding towns)

Figure 5.1 : Sketches of alternative forms of bus networks.

This is becoming the standard type of operation in Europe and has been such for many years in the US. A variation of this type of operation is when all stops are on request. In this type one could classify all the _express_ bus routes, where only a few stops at the beginning and at the end of the line are used and where all stops are on request.

c.   **Fixed Routing with special purpose deviations.** In this case, although basically some fixed routes are followed, drivers are given the possibility (usually after instruction or approval by the controller) to deviate from these basic routes for the benefit of certain passenger groups such as elderly or handicapped.

These deviations could be made only during certain hours, e.g. to avoid congestion along a route or corridor, or on a planned basis. For example, a bus route could operate as a fixed route with no deviations during the peak hours, while during the off-peaks it could deviate to a predetermined routing in order to serve a specific passenger group or area. An extreme variant of this is the so called "corridor routing" where there are a number of points (stops) along the corridor where the bus must pass and stop, but the driver is free to choose the streets he will use between these points according to the prevailing traffic conditions.

d.   **Totally Flexible or Demand Responsive Routing.** Here the bus follows a "shortest path" route according to the requests from passengers which are processed by a central computer and dispatched to the driver. These types of routes are better suited for low density (higher income) areas. The various "dial-a-bus" systems, applied in several North American and W.European countries, are examples of this type of operation.

Comments and Suggestions on the Types of Bus Routes

Some comments on the above types of routing, based on the experience from their application so

102

far, are necessary in order to help bus management in their choice.

Undoubtedly the first two types of routing, described in (a) and (b) above, are the most commonly found types with a number of advantages, especially for the high density -areas in many cities of the developing world. They are basically variations of the same type (i.e. of the first) trying to improve on some of its drawbacks. On the contrary, the demand responsive routing, described in (c) and (d) above, requires a rather sophisticated organization of the whole operation, and is supposed to serve well only under certain circumstances. More specifically, the following comments can be made.

The first type of routing, is the standard type of bus line routing found in all urban areas. It has the advantage that the line is well defined and its use by the public is well understood and simple. Also, from the operator's point of view, it is the easiest to plan for and supervise. However, and especially under circumstances of heavy traffic congestion along the designated route, there are a number of drawbacks associated with Fixed Routing. Probably the major of these drawbacks are the delays due to the compulsory stop of the buses in all stops and due to the traffic congestion along the route, which cannot be avoided if the route is compulsory. Also, in the hours of heavy demand, it is very often the case that the buses "fill up" with passengers in the early stops of the route and subsequent stops remain "unserved" for longer periods of time. At the same time the filled-up buses cannot deviate from their predetermined route in order to reach their destination stops earlier and the situation is difficult to remedy unless of course one is prepared to use extra buses.

The second type of bus line operation, described in (b) above, tries to ameliorate some of the drawbacks of the previous type. By designating some stops as "stops by request", the buses may not stop there if there are no passengers, thus saving some delays along the trip. The variation of this type, known as "express" route, tries to maximize the savings from not stopping at all stops. In this case the bus usually stops only at some first few and some last few stops of the line to pick up and let passengers, while for the rest of its trip it operates practically like a private bus (with or without deviations from the main route).

The so called "express" lines, should have the

following characteristics in order to be successful:
-   They should ideally connect two centers (usually a suburban to an urban or even regional one) or, more generally, two areas of high demand, with areas of low demand in between.
-   The stops at which the bus will stop must be clearly marked on the vehicle, preferably at a place easily visible to the passengers before they alight the vehicle.
-   The drivers should have the possibility to divert to a less congested route during the part of the trip with no stops, preferably after consulting by wireless a central controller.
-   The lines should use, wherever possible, special bus lanes, preferably at contra-flow with the rest of the traffic.

The third type of bus line operation allows deviations from the main designated route, for certain purposes, mainly to serve special groups of passengers. In this last case, and although a higher level of service is provided to these special groups of passengers, there may be complaints from the regular passengers, if these deviations delay their journey unduly. The operation must therefore be very well planned, with certain limits and **very clear instructions to the drivers,** so as to avoid excess deviations from the main route. If the authority to deviate concerns only the by-passing of congestion spots, then this type of operation may in fact shorten travel times, a fact usually mentioned as one of its major advantages. In general, this type of operation incurs extra costs to the operator, especially if the requests for deviations come in via the phone and are then dispatched to the vehicles. One other drawback is the fact, that the vehicles used in this type of service must be capable of going through all types of streets. This means they must be smaller in size and perhaps with special mechanical characteristics which is a factor that imposes even greater costs in the operation.

As a conclusion, it can be said that fixed routing with special purpose deviations is difficult to plan and operate and has to be evaluated carefully. The evaluation will be based on CUTA (1985):
-   The amount of capacity of the whole system that can be allocated to the deviations.

- The additional delay acceptable to the other passengers.
- The Level of Service to be offered.
- The extra costs.
- The type and amount of equipment (buses, radios).
- The possible subsidization of the service by other authorities or the community.

The last type of bus line operation mentioned in (d) of the previous section, i.e. the demand-responsive operation, requires a high degree of organization and sophistication which many operators, especially the small ones, do not possess. In general, the higher the flexibility the higher the costs of operation but also the higher the level of service offered. Experience so far shows that the successful stories in this type of operation (mainly in the economic sense) are few and all of them in the developed countries, where most of the applications still in operation are known.

DETERMINATION OF BUS LANE ROUTING

The General Philosophy

The general "philosophy" in determining the routing of a new line or the extension to an existing one can be expressed by the following (efficiency related) motto:

" provide the maximum of service
(i.e. coverage, frequencies etc)
to the areas served, with the
minimum possible final cost to
the operation" .

An alternative approach, perhaps more realistic in many cases, is the following (effectiveness related) motto:

"provide the maximum of service
to the areas served within the
resources (including subsidies)
available".

The term "final" cost denotes the difference between the overall cost of operation for the line and its expected receipts.

105

The important point in the above "philosophy" is
the recognition, that one should take into account
the efficiency and/or effectiveness of the operation
along with the provision of good service to the public. This is a point often forgotten, especially when
the system works under strong control and interference from a central authority, usually the elected
local government.

A major help towards translating the above principle in practice can be the adoption of a number of
specific criteria or standards for both the planning
of the route, including the determination of its
course, and its operation afterwards. As regards the
latter, the relevant guidelines are given in chapter
7. For the former, the following sections contain
some of these criteria.

Suggested Criteria

A. Existence of a Minimum of Passenger Demand

A new line has to have some justification in
terms of revenues, so a major consideration has to be
the amount of passenger demand that is likely to be
generated. Logically speaking, it would not be un-
reasonable to expect that the revenues of the new
line should at least cover the costs of its operation. So the basic rule would be that the minimum of
passenger demand that could justify the specific new
route would be the one that generates enough revenue
to cover the cost of its operation.

Exceptions to the above basic rule can of course
be made in order to achieve specific social or planning objectives, but these exceptions should be as
restrained as possible.

The application of the criterion of "minimum
passenger demand" calls in practice for a simple and
reliable way to estimate the expected passenger demand, as well as the cost of the operation.

As regards the "demand", use of data from previous similar cases can be made, or a calculation
based on the estimation of the number of people that
will be within reach of the new line. Through a simple trip rate applied to this population the estimation of the total daily number of trips can be made
and then the estimation of the modal split of these
trips to determine the number of trips by bus. An
alternative way would be to calculate only the so

called "direct" or "diverted" passenger demand. This will be based on existing passenger flows in existing bus lines which will be diverted to the new one (if such lines exist). To this the "generated" demand will have to be added. The "generated" demand will materialize at a later stage and cannot be properly estimated. However, in some cases (e.g. extensions of lines to previously unserved areas) generated demand may be the one that justifies the line. It is therefore recommended to allow for a modest amount of generated demand which can be empirically estimated from previous experience if possible.

The estimation of the cost of operating the new route can be done with a simple cost allocation model based on data from other lines. The necessity to repeat the process for alternative route configurations before choosing the preferred one, makes the establishment and use of simple models quite useful. Several operators have established simple rules that are applied routinely when evaluating a new line (see for example TTC, 1980-84).

In general, and as a rough rule of thumb, it can be said that, if the total daily (direct or diverted) passenger demand for a new bus route does not exceed 1,800-2,000 passengers in both directions, this new route cannot be justified at least as a full time, whole day operation.

As a second alternative, one can examine the operation of the line as a part time operation, e.g. during the peak hours only. If the peak hour demand is also too small, say below 150-200 passengers per hour, then the line should be dropped altogether. The above figures are meant as indications of order of magnitudes only and are given as help for quick and inexpensive checks of the feasibility of a new route. Final selections and decisions <u>must</u> be based on a proper cost-revenue analysis, as indicated above. A final point to be made concerns cases where more than one alternative routes attract acceptable numbers of passengers. In this case the obvious way is to select the routing which maximizes the passenger flows.

B. Creation of "Straight" Lines

A bus line should ideally be as close to a straight line as possible, i.e. with no deviations. A "deviation" is a major change of direction in the form of a loop or circle or G etc. This gives passengers the impression that they are wasting time in unnecessary routing or that they do not follow a more or less direct route to their destination. So perhaps the major guideline here should be that there are no deviations allowed in a bus route.

However, in certain cases they are inevitable in order to serve, with one line, a wider area than usual and avoid introducing a second line. In these cases certain rules are suggested to alleviate the negative impacts of deviations on passengers. These "rules" are the following:

a. The maximum bus travel time, while in a deviation, should not exceed 10 minutes including the time spent at stops.

b. The length of the deviation should not make the total length of the line greater than 20% (preferably) or 30% (maximum) of the length of the same trip by car.

c. The average travel time per passenger in the specific bus line should not increase more than 25%, as compared to the same travel time if the deviation was not made.

d. In each line, the maximum number of deviations is preferably one and absolute maximum two.

e. A deviation should be preferably placed at either end of the route and not in the middle.

The above points (a) to (d), are not alternatives to each other but are meant to be examined together. In other words if one of these points is not satisfied, the deviation should not be made or should be adjusted accordingly.

C. Avoidance of "Overlapping" between Bus Lines

When relatively large parts of an area can be served by more than one bus lines, for the same destinations, then the lines are "overlapping". This is something that should obviously be avoided, as it results in wasted resources which could be used more productively elsewhere. Overlapping can be considered to occur, when more than two lines overlap in the above sense in central areas, and more than one for suburbs or non-central areas.

As a general rule, overlapping of bus lines should be avoided, especially in non-central areas. However, this is not always possible, especially in the dense street network of central urban areas in most cities. For this reason certain guidelines are here necessary, not in order to avoid this problem but in order to create some decision rules, as to when this problem should be "acceptable" and when not, in which case action should be taken to ease it.

Bus line overlapping can only be acceptable in the central or densely populated areas but even then under the following circumstances:

a. The combined scheduled headway of the overlapping lines (i.e. the headway of the arriving buses irrespective of the line they belong) is greater than 3 minutes in the peak, and 6-8 minutes in the off-peak hours. When headways fall below these figures, action must be taken to reduce the number of lines that overlap and divert them to serve other areas less served by the existing network or charge the schedules (e.g. by "deadheading" some trips).

b. The average bus occupancy rates in the overlapping section is greater than 60% of the maximum occupancy for the type of buses used.

c. The length of the section, over which overlapping occurs, should not be greater than 50% of the total length of each of the overlapping lines.

The above points are particularly applicable in the case when the overlapping lines use the same stops. When this occurs, special problems arise and the above points are meant to help avoid serious congestion and delays. The usual practice to regroup bus stops so as to avoid queueing congestion of buses does not solve the problem but may only alleviate it, especially when the number of lines is high (there are for example extreme cases with one bus stop serving more than 30 bus lines).

In relation to the above points concerning overlapping, one should also consider the discussion in the next section about density of lines.

D. Other Criteria

There are finally a number of other criteria or guidelines, that must be taken into account. These are:

a.   Obviously the roads that are going to be used for the bus lines should be adequately surfaced and their geometric characteristics should allow a comfortable movement for buses, including the possibility of overtaking stopped vehicles etc. The width of the lanes used by the buses must be at least 3 meters. Other considerations concerning the roads to be used by buses, include the existence of sidewalks with adequate width (at least 2 meters) to support the bus stops, the existence of wide turns, especially if longer buses (or articulated ones) are foreseen for operation, the existence of overhead structures etc.

b.   The total length of a bus line should not exceed a certain limit. This is set by mainly functional criteria, as well as for reasons of preferences of the travelling public. A lengthy line is more likely to experience delays and unreliability of travel times than a shorter one, while too long travel times do not attract passengers anyway. A reasonable limit, often quoted in the literature, is that total travel time (in both directions) should not exceed 2 hours (preferably), or 2.5 hours (maximum) for purely urban lines. This limit is increased for lines which connect the urban area with suburbs or peripheral townships etc.

c.   For reasons of easier use and memorization of the network by the travelling public, it is recommended that, wherever possible, both directions of travel for the same route should be on the same roads. If this is not possible (e.g. use of one-way streets etc), it is recommended that the two directions of travel for the same route are not further than 300-400 meters from each other.

d.   Finally, and not disregarding the provisions in (b) above about the length of lines, it is recommended that the routing of the bus lines goes through the urban center instead of terminating there. The existence of bus terminals at the city centres causes congestion and harms the environment, without improving substantially the service provided to the public.

DENSITY OF A BUS NETWORK

The term "density" provides an overall measure of the length of a network its coverage of the area, and generally its geographical distribution in space. The density of a bus network, is a function of the density of development in the area, the form and density of the principal roads (i.e. the appropriateness to accept buses), the frequencies of service along the bus routes, the acceptable walking distances etc. The main aim here is to provide at least one bus line at an adequate walking distance from all parts of the urban area.

As the density of the bus network is the end result of a complex process of route planning and design that is influenced by many factors, most of which are area-specific, it is not desirable to give specific and inelastic standards for the density. What is to be attempted here is to give some examples of densities that have been observed in existing urban areas, as well as some general figures that seem to be fairly common in the majority of the urban bus networks.

For urban areas with high densities of development the maximum distance between "parallel" bus routes should not exceed 800 meters, so as to have maximum walking distances for the population served by them of 400 meters (or walking time approximately 5 minutes). For central areas, these distances are of course much smaller, especially when the form of the bus network is radial. For urban areas with low densities or in the suburbs, where the acceptable walking distances are usually greater, the maximum distance between routes with bus lines can reach 1600 meters or more.

The above distances are purely indicative, as they obviously depend on the local conditions and especially those that affect the acceptable walking distances. For example, if the topography has high gradients, the walking distances are smaller and thus the maximum acceptable distance between lines is also smaller. The same applies for the existing "walking environment" in terms of safety for the pedestrians, visual intrusion, or even the prevailing weather conditions. The less favourable for walking these factors are, the smaller the distances between "parallel" bus routes should be.

Another factor, that will ultimately affect the maximum distance between the lines of a bus network, is the frequency of the bus service in these lines.

111

In general, it can be said that, in order to serve a given level of passenger demand, it is preferable to have a smaller number of lines with higher frequencies than more lines with low frequencies of service.

The distance between bus routes is not a unique measure of density. On one hand, it is the walking distances to the stops that count and, on the other, in many cases, the notion of a distance between lines is not clear because of the radial alignment of many road networks.

The previous points concerning densities can be adjusted to take into account distances from bus stops. In this case it can be said that a "reasonable" density of the bus network is the one, in which 70-75% of the population of a densely populated urban area is within 400 meters walking distance from a bus stop. For less densely populated areas, or the suburbs, a percentage of 50-60% of the population should be within 800 meters from a bus stop.

Finally, another way to express the "density" of a bus network is by ratio of length of bus network per square km of area served. This is a standard expression of density and can be used as an aggregate measure of "coverage" of the area from the bus network. Table 5.1, gives some indicative values of this ratio according to the average density of the population. In this table, as length of the network is meant the total length of streets, over which bus lines run. The figures given in Table 5.1, are indicative of the order of magnitude and should be used only for comparative purposes in a general sense.

Table 5.1

Indicative densities of urban bus networks.

Population Density (*) (persons / sq.km)	Density of bus network (network kms(**)/sq.km)
>4600	2.50
3900 - 4600	2.00
3000 - 3900	1.65
2300 - 3000	1.25
1500 - 2300	1.00
750 - 1500	0.60
<750	0.30

(*) Total population over total area of urban area.
(**) Total length of roads over which buses run (not total length of bus lines).

BUS STOP LOCATION

Spacing of Bus Stops

The spacing of bus stops along the lines of a
bus network refers to the number of stops per km of
line or the average distance between stops. This is a
very important element of the bus network affecting
the average walking distances of passengers in order
to reach the lines but also the operation of the line
as it influences travel times, delays etc.

As the distance between stops increases, the
walking time to and from the stops increases, but so
do the travel times as buses have to stop at fewer
stops. So the total travel times, including walking
times, may increase. Conversely if the distance between stops decreases, so does the walking time but
buses have to stop at more stops and thus their travel time decreases. This trade-off between spacing of
stops and total travel time is diagrammatically depicted in Figure 5.2A. Clearly the aim should be to
set the spacing of bus stops, along a certain bus
line of the network, in a way that total travel time
(for the door-to-door trip) is around the minimum
shown in Figure 5.2A. For central areas a maximum
walking distance of 400 m from the bus stop is considered as acceptable. This is higher for suburban
areas.

In connection to the walking distance consideration for bus stop spacing, is the total "coverage" of
the area, i.e the amount of urban space within acceptable walking distance of the bus stops. This
"coverage" or "area of influence" for each bus stop
is denoted by a contour around it, which defines a
walking distance of, say, 400 meters <u>on the existing
street network</u>. All these contours form the total
"coverage" area of the bus network as shown in the
sketch in Figure 5.2B. These contours can be approxi-
mated by circles of an appropriate radius depending
on the density and form of the road network.

The criteria determining the general position of
a bus stop and therefore their spacing, relate mainly
to the type and density of land uses along the line,
the location of points of high concentration of demand, of course, the potential traffic effects from
the operation of the stop. Some general guidelines
for the general position of bus stops could be mentioned here:

a. The initial selection of a position for a
bus stop would be near a major concentra-

tion of passenger movements, such as shopping centers, hospitals, schools etc. Also near points, where two or more lines of public transport intersect or near big parking lots (to encourage park-n-ride).

b.   As a second consideration, the traffic effects of the proposed stop must be examined, especially if it is in the congested urban center. A detailed discussion about the traffic effects and considerations when placing a bus stop is given in the next section.

c.   If both the previous considerations have been satisfied, one must then consider the walking distances that result to this particular bus stop in relation to the other stops and the overall travel times of the line (see also Fig. 5.2).

Concerning walking distances and with all due regard to the previous point (b), it might be preferable to choose a point near an intersection, so as to minimize walking for passengers who want to access the crossing street.

d.   When the basic bus stop points have been determined according to the above, it may be possible to reduce their spacing further by putting stops on request in between, i.e. stops where the bus driver stops only if there are passengers wishing to use the stop. This point is of course valid only in cases, where Fixed Routing with some stops on request is a permitted type of operation.

Although specific bus stop spacing figures cannot be definitive and inflexible, some general indications about "reasonable" average distances between bus stops can be given.

These suggested average distances, based on existing experience, are the following:

i.   150 - 250 m. for the urban center or areas with high densities of population (i.e. demand for public transport).

ii.   200 - 350 m. for areas of medium density of population (e.g. around 2000 persons per km^2), and

iii. 250 - 500 m. in suburban and low density areas.

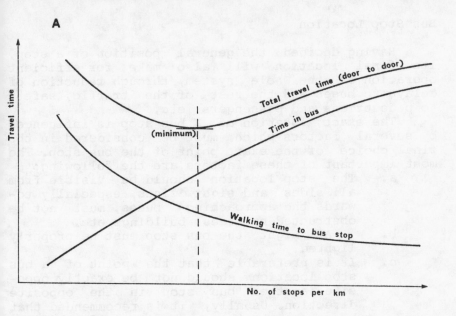

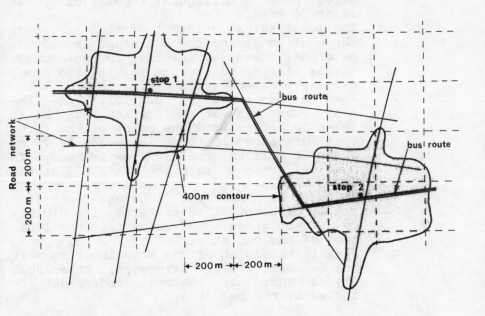

Figure 5.2: (A): Diagrammatic representation of the relation between density of bus stops and total travel time for the door-to-door trip. (B): Sketch diagramme of the "coverage areas" of bus stops.

Bus Stop Location

Having decided the general position of a stop, its final location will also make for efficient operation of the whole system, through reduction of delays to buses and the rest of the traffic, safety to pedestrians and passengers, etc.

The exact location of a bus stop is influenced by several factors which must be considered in the final choice of the exact point of the bus stop. The most important of these factors are the following:

a. The stop location should be visible from all sides and sight lines, especially towards the approaching buses, must not be obstructed by trees, buildings etc.

b. At night the bus stop must be properly lighted.

c. It is preferable that the point of a bus stop location should not be exactly opposite another bus stop in the opposite direction. Usually, it is recommended that bus stops at the two sides of the same street have a horizontal separation of at least 20 meters.

d. The longitudinal gradient of the street at the section around the bus stop, should not be greater than 4%, in order to avoid undue stress of the buses when leaving the stop, excessive noise levels etc.

e. When the buses have to turn left after the stop, the bus stop location must be at least 50 meters from the point of the turn. This distance must be increased to 75 or even 100 m if the traffic flow is heavy. In case of a right turn the minimum distance is 35 meters.

f. If there is a specific land use such as a school or hospital in the area, its vicinity must be given preference for the location of the bus stop.

g. Finally the point of bus stop location must not be near trees, driveways, other such object that may obstruct and/or get affected by the bus stop.

Of particular importance is the location of the stop with regard to the intersections. Three possible cases in this respect can be mentioned:

a. Stops at "near-side", i.e. before the intersection.

b. Stops at "far-side", i.e. after the intersection.
c. Stops at "mid-block",i.e. at the middle of
a building block.

There are relative advantages and disadvantages
associated with these three cases of bus stops and
these are presented in the following. (Considerable
parts of the description of these advantages and disadvantages come from CUTA, 1985).

Near-side Bus Stops are located at the intersections where transit flows are heavy but traffic and
parking conditions are not critical. From the driver's point of view they are preferable because they
make it easier to rejoin the traffic stream, particularly where curb parking is permitted in peak
periods. They are generally applicable where signalized intersections are frequent and where curb parking is permitted throughout the day. Buses stopping
on approaches to intersections can use the distance
of the intersection to re-enter the main traffic
flow. Near-side bus stops can be provided where buses
turn right and where right-turning traffic is not
appreciable.

Advantages of near-side bus stops include the
following:
a. They create a minimum of interference at
locations where traffic is heavier on the
far-side than on the approach side of the
intersection.
b. Passengers generally board buses close to a
crosswalk.
c. Buses are usually required to come to a
full stop at intersections. In starting,
they proceed across the intersection slowly. They are therefore under better control
and less likely to be involved in collision
or conflict with pedestrians, than if they
proceed through the intersection to stop at
the far side.
d. Street lighting is generally better near
the crosswalk, where passengers board and
alight at a nearside stop, than a bus
length or more beyond an intersection. This
factor is more significant on collectors
and local streets than on CBD or arterial
streets.
e. Passengers usually complain, when a bus
driver, stopped for a traffic signal or
stop sign, refuses to open doors because

117

the designated stop is far-side. Boarding or alighting of passengers at other than marked stops leads to excessive stops and slow operation and creates claims liability, if a passenger slips or falls.

f.   A bus driver has a better view of approaching passengers at a near-side stop, where he can see directly ahead, to the left and to the right. (At far-side stops he can see to the front only, except indirectly by mirrors). When the driver has the passengers in view, they are less likely to be left out and they are not encouraged to take chances with the traffic to catch the bus.

Disadvantages of near-side stops include the following:

a.   Heavy vehicular right turns can cause conflicts, especially where a vehicle makes a right turn from the left of a stopped bus.

b.   Buses often obscure STOP signs, traffic signals or other control devices, as well as pedestrians crossing in front of the bus.

c.   A bus standing at a near-side stop obscures the sight distance of a driver entering the bus street from the right.

d.   Where the bus stop is too short for occasional heavy demand, the overflow will obstruct the traffic lane.

Far-side Bus Stops are preferable where sight distance or signal capacity problems exist and where right or left turns by general traffic are heavy. They are also preferable wherever buses turn left, because they allow sufficient maneuvering distance from curb to left lanes and allow buses to stop after clearing the intersection.

Advantages of far-side bus stops include the following:

a.   They reduce conflicts between right-turning vehicles and stopped buses.

b.   They provide additional intersection capacity by making the curb lane before the stop line available for traffic.

c.   They eliminate sight distance deficiencies on approaches to intersections, especially for the pedestrian crossing the road.

d. They encourage pedestrian crossing at the rear of the bus.
e. They require shorter maneuvering distances for the buses to enter and leave moving traffic.
f. At signalized intersections buses can find gaps for re-entry into the traffic stream at the times when traffic lights are red.

Disadvantages of far-side stops include the following:
a. Stops on a narrow street or within a moving lane may block traffic on both the bus route and the cross street.
b. A bus standing at a far-side stop obscures sightdistance to the right of a driver entering the bus street from the right.
c. Where the bus stop is too short for occasional heavy demands, the overflow will obstruct the cross street.

<u>Mid-block Stops</u> are generally applicable in downtown areas, where multiple routes require long loading areas that might extend an entire block. They can also be used where traffic, physical or environmental conditions prohibit near or far-side stops and where large factories, commercial establishments or other major bus passenger generators exist:

Advantages of mid-block bus stops include the following:
a. Buses create a minimum of interference with sightdistance of both vehicles and pedestrians.
b. Waiting passengers assemble at less crowded sections of the sidewalk.

Disadvantages include the following:
a. The removal of considerable curb parking may be required and the parking restriction not strongly enforced.
b. Patrons from cross street will have to walk further to board the bus.
c. Pedestrian jay-walking is more prevalent, thereby increasing vehicular friction, congestion and accident potentials.

As a conclusion, the following guidelines for bus stop location can be given.

1. <u>Through-bus Movements</u>
Normal traffic flow or a light right turning movement with no special turn indication:

1. Locate bus stop at far-side of inter-section.
2. If physical curb treatment renders a far-side impractical, move across intersection to nearside.
3. If near-side is impractical, move to mid-block.

2. **Turning Bus Movements**

   a. **If Bus Turns Right**
      1. Establish near-side stop prior to turn. If total traffic right turns are appreciable, locate bus stop some distance prior to intersection.
      2. If right turns are very heavy, the bus stop may have to be located far-side after turn or mid-block.
   b. **If Bus Turns Left**
      1. Establish far-side stop after turn.
      2. If impossible, establish mid-block stop after turn. A mid-block stop prior to turn may be feasible, if traffic is sufficiently light and the building block long enough to allow the bus to move from stop to left turn position without traffic conflict.

3. **Stops at Transfer Points**

   a. **For Through-bus Movements**

      1. If there is heavy transfer between North and West movements, establish far-side stop for North movement, near-side for West movement.
      2. If heavy transfer exists between North and East movements, establish far-side for East movement, near-side for North movement.
      3. If heavy transfer exists between South and West movements, establish far-side for West movement, near-side for South movement.
      4. If heavy transfer exists between South and East movements, establish far-side for South movement, near-side for East movement.
      5. Combinations of 1 through 4 above as the transfer movements dictate.

120

b. For Turning Bus Movements

    1. If heavy transfer exists between a straight through-bus movement and a right turn, both of which operate on the same street in the block preceding the turning movement, establish the stop in the mid-block before the turning movement. If one of the movements involves a left turn, interchange points should be located at least one block prior to left turn, unless traffic is sufficiently light and the block long enough to allow bus to move from stop to left turn position without traffic conflict.

    2. If heavy transfer exists after a turning movement, establish stop according to 2 (a) and (b) above.

DESIGN GUIDELINES FOR BUS STOPS

Design Methodology

The design of a bus stop entails the determination of three main design elements :

    a. the geometric characteristics ,

    b. its placement with regard to the rest of the traffic flow on the street and

    c. the traffic arrangements (including road signs and markings) in its vicinity.

The aim of the design in all three of these elements is the fast and safe service of buses and passengers with the minimum of obstruction to the rest of the traffic. Furthermore, the aim is to avoid harmful effects on the visual quality of the surrounding environment and, wherever possible, to even enhance this environment through proper architectural design of the bus stop and its furniture (i.e shelters, signs, telephones etc).

The geometry of a bus stop will ideally result from the capacity requirements in terms of the maximum number of buses that will stop there. The 1985 U.S. Highway Capacity Manual (TRB, 1985) includes for the first time a special chapter on the capacity calculations of transit lines. It is stressed there that the capacity and design of the bus stops usually

121

determines the capacity of the whole line. The calculations for bus stop capacity given there, also determine the necessary geometric characteristics of the stops through determination of the numbers of stopping spaces for the buses. The application of the calculations suggested in the 1985 Highway Capacity Manual, requires specialized knowledge which is usually not available, while it is strongly doubted that they can be applicable to cases in small to medium-sized urban areas in countries outside the U.S. For this reason the geometric characteristics of bus stops are given in the following sections based on experience (as well as on some of the recommendations of the U.S. Highway Capacity Manual) in the form of ready to use tables.

The steps suggested for determining the three previously mentioned elements of bus stop design are the following:

a. Identify the areas along the bus route, that appear to be likely concentration points for the potential passengers.

b. Identify the potential bus stop locations along the route, by applying the general criteria for bus stop location mentioned previously.

c. Determine the exact position of the bus stop in these locations, by applying the detailed criteria mentioned in the preceding sections, (for near-side, far-side, or mid-block stops), and by careful consideration of the potential transfer requirements with the other lines of the bus network.

d. Determine the type (curbside or lay-by) of each stop and the geometric characteristics of its horizontal and vertical alignment.

e. Determine the road signs and markings to be applied.

f. Choose the types of bus stop furniture, i.e. whether to use a bus shelter and of what type, information displays, maps etc (see also chapter 9).

g. Perform cost calculations and prepare tender documents (usually for more than one stop) or construction specifications, in case of own construction.

Types of Stops

There are three types of stops according to the position of the stop in relation to the rest of the traffic:

a. At curb-side, i.e. at the side of the street without any change in the existing road or pedestrian walk.

b. At a lay-by, i.e. at a recess from the street

c. At a bus bay, i.e. in a separate stopping area adjacent to the main traffic stream.

The first possibility has the advantage that it is easy to set up with no major construction other than the necessary road signs and markings. It has, however, the major drawbacks associated with the obstruction to the other traffic and danger to pedestrians and passengers.

The second possibility, by using the lay-by, reduces the obstruction to the other traffic and makes the movement of passengers, to and from the bus, safer. It requires, however, more space from the sidewalks and in effect from the roadway as a whole and some new construction which may sometimes be quite costly (especially if there are public utility networks at a shallow depth under the pavement). A major problem with lay-bys is that quite often they are not used by bus drivers for the simple reason that, with the driving habits in many urban areas, the bus is not given priority by the rest of the traffic and, as a result, there are delays in re-entering the traffic stream. This problem is unfortunately not always solved by giving priority to the exiting bus. In fact this is already a standard provision in the "Codes of the Road" in almost all countries. Observance of this provision is usually poor, unless there is strong and consistent enforcement. It is therefore often the case that buses stop at the near-side traffic lane and disregard the lay-by.

The third and final type of bus stop, i.e. the bus bay, is of course the best in terms of safety and delays to other traffic. It requires however, sufficient space and good geometric characteristics for entering and leaving. It is usually recommended for cases where there are great numbers of passengers (e.g. near a major shopping center or hospital etc) or at transfer points (e.g. between buses and LRT or Metro or between two or more bus lines).

In the following we discuss the suggested geometric characteristics as well as the road signs and
markings of the bus stops in each of the above three
types.

Stops at the Curbside

For stops at the curbside, the geometric characteristics to be decided are in effect the dimensions
of the space to be left free from parked cars and the
position of the shelter, if one is to be used. Existing regulations in most countries (usually the Codes
of the Road) provide that parking is prohibited at a
certain distance from the bus stop. This distance is
usually 5 - 15 meters from either end. This provision
is meant to facilitate the "entry" and "exit" of
buses to the bus stop and does not include the space
required for the buses to stop. The length of this
space depends on the average number of buses that
will be using the stop, the size of the buses and the
specific position of the bus stop with regard to the
intersections and the rest of the traffic stream.
Table 5.2, shows the recommended stopping length
for the buses using the bus stop. The provision in
this table is for one or two buses to stop at the
same time, which covers the majority of cases of bus
stop capacity requirements. Further requirements of
space for more buses will have to be determined by
using the detailed capacity calculations shown, for
example, in the U.S. Highway Capacity Manual (TRB,
1985).
Figure 5.3 shows the minimum recommended sizes
of curbside bus stops for <u>one bus</u>. It is particularly
pointed out that, as shown in Figure 5.3A, for the
stops after the intersection, parking must be prohibited over a length of 20m also at the side of the
street exactly opposite the bus stop. This is necessary in order to facilitate the functioning of the
intersection at the critical area of the stop line.
This requirement is not necessary, if the street is
wide enough (e.g. more than 2 lanes in each direction). In the case of a bus stop <u>before</u> the intersection the "No Parking zone in the opposite curbside
can be reduced to the normally allowed one for any
corner, i.e. 5 metres.

The above, are also applicable in the case where
there is no on-street parking near the bus stop. In
this case the above lengths are useful for the posi-

124

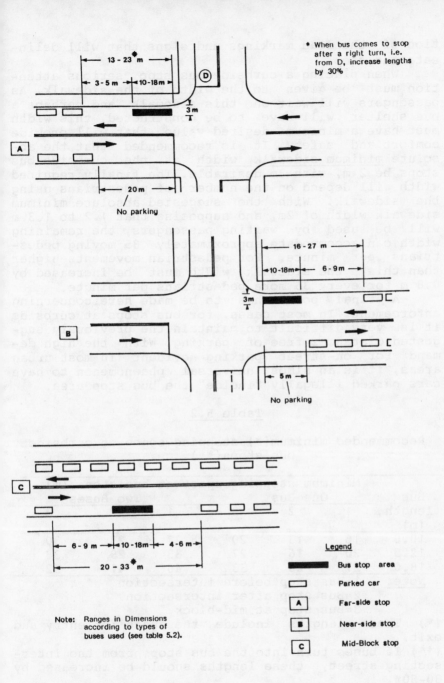

* When bus comes to stop
after a right turn, i.e.
from D, increase lengths
by 30%

No parking

No parking

Legend

▬▬ Bus stop area

▢ Parked car

[A] Far-side stop

[B] Near-side stop

[C] Mid-Block stop

Note: Ranges in Dimensions
according to types of
buses used (see table 5.2).

Figure 5.3: Minimum recommended lengths of curbside
bus stops for one bus.(For two buses see table 5.2.)

tion of the road markings and signs that will delineate the stop.

When placing a curbside bus stop, serious attention must be given to the width of the sidewalk. As passengers will wait on this sidewalk and perhaps a bus shelter will have to be constructed, this width must have a minimum desired value that will provide comfort and safety. It is recommended that the absolute <u>minimum sidewalk width</u> at the curbside bus stops be 2 m, with 3m desirable. The finally required width will depend on the number of pedestrians using the sidewalk. With the suggested absolute minimum sidewalk width of 2m, and supposing that 1.2 to 1.3 m will be used by waiting passengers, the remaining width can accommodate approximately 35 moving pedestrians per minute. For pedestrian movements higher than this, the sidewalk width must be increased by 0.8 m for every 35 more pedestrians per minute.

A final point has to be made here concerning enforcement. In most cases, for bus stops at curbside it is very difficult to maintain the previously suggested distances free of parking. With the high demand for on-street parking evident in most urban areas, it is an almost universal phaenomenon to have cars parked illegally "inside" the bus stop area.

Table 5.2

Recommended minimum(*) stopping space at curbside bus stops(**).

Bus length (m)	Minimum stopping space at bus stop (m)					
	One Bus			Two Buses		
	1	2	3	1	2	3
10.0	16	13	20	27	23	30
12.5	20	16	27	33	29	38
18.0	27	23	33	46	41	52

Note: 1=Bus stop before intersection
2=Bus stop after intersection
3=Bus stop at mid-block

(*) These lengths include the space for entry and exit.
(**) If buses turn into the bus stop from the intersecting street, these lengths should be increased by 30-50%.

It is recommended to apply proper signing and road markings of the whole bus stop area and, where possible, even <u>physical restrictions</u> of access. Figure 5.4 shows a suggestion how this can be done for all three types of stops. There is a detail at Figure 5.4 concerning the approach triangle to the stop. There, apart from the road markings shown, it is suggested to put two small posts 0.50m high to physically restrict the entry to the bus stopping area. Figure 5.5 shows in a sketch how the bus stopping area at a mid-block stop will look like with proper road markings and signs.

Stops at Lay-bys[a]

This type of bus stop is safer and less obstructive for the rest of the traffic. However, as already said, it is at a disadvantage, when the rest of the traffic does not give way to the outgoing bus and then bus drivers do not observe them or when cars are illegally parked inside them. These difficulties, coupled with the increased space requirements, make this type of bus stop not very common in the dense urban areas, especially in developing countries.

Therefore, the conditions under which a lay-by can be considered, are the following:

a. High traffic volumes and travel speeds on the main road, that make the stopping of buses at the curbside dangerous and causing delays to the rest of the traffic.

b. High numbers of passengers waiting at the bus stop, making the necessary bus dwell times at the stop quite long, say more than 25-30 seconds per stop.

c. Relatively low numbers of buses that will be using the lay-by. An indicative figure is no more than 10-15 buses per hour in the peak hour.

d. Existence of adequate width at the road side for the lay-by and the sidewalk next to it (see figure 5.7).

e. Prohibition of parking at the curbside where the lay-by will be constructed.

Should the above considerations apply, the construction of the lay-by should be examined further and detailed designs could be made. The necessary geometric characteristics for this design are given in Figure 5.6 while the general arrangements and road markings in Figure 5.7A.

_____

[a]. Instead of the term "Lay-by", the terms "recessed bus bay" or "turnout" are occasionally used.

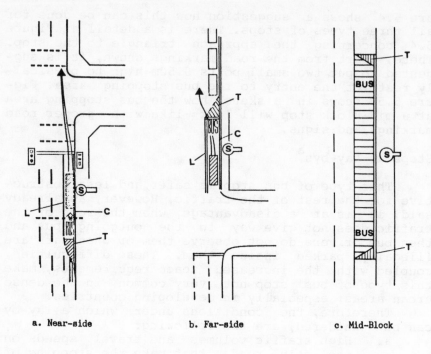

a. Near-side **b. Far-side** **c. Mid-Block**

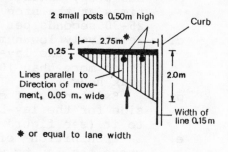

Legend

(S) : Bus stop sign

(C) : Yellow line 0.15m wide, parallel to the curb at 0.10m.

(L) : Continuous yellow or white line 0.25 wide

(T) : Triangle marked on the pavement with parallel lines and 3 posts for physical restriction of access. Dimensions and layout of this triangle are as as follows:

The word "BUS" is written with lines o.10m wide, 5.0m high, and width of each letter 0.50m.

2 small posts 0.50m high

Curb

0.25

2.75m*

Lines parallel to Direction of movement, 0.05 m. wide

2.0m

Width of line 0.15m

* or equal to lane width

Figure 5.4: Suggested road markings and physical restrictions of access at or near curbside bus stops.

Figure 5.5: Perspective view of possible curbside bus stop markings and signs. (Source: Boston Redevelopment Authority, 1973, also published in CUTA, 1985).

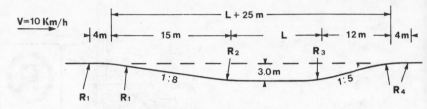

(A): Entrance with low speed, 10kms/hr. Radius of curb curves, R_1=20m, R_2=10m, R_3=10m, R_4=15m.

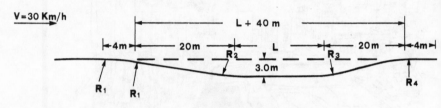

(B): Entrance at 30kms/hr. Radii of curb curves, R_1=40m, R_2=20m, R_3=20m, R_4=40m.

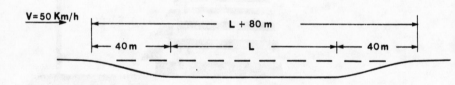

(C): Entrance at 50 kms/hr.
Radii of curb curves as in (B).

Figure 5.6: Geometric characteristics of bus lay-bys.

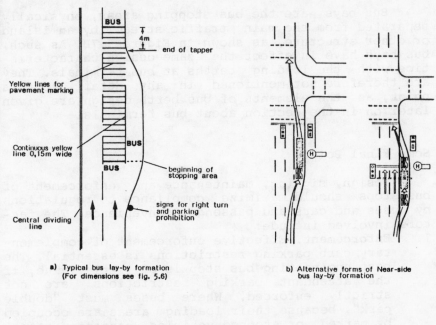

a) Typical bus lay-by formation
(For dimensions see fig. 5.6)

b) Alternative forms of Near-side
bus lay-by formation

Labels in figure a):
- Yellow lines for pavement marking
- Continuous yellow line 0,15m wide
- Central dividing line
- BUS
- 4m
- end of tapper
- beginning of stopping area
- signs for right turn and parking prohibition

A. LAY-BYS

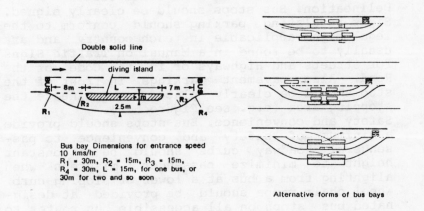

Labels in figure:
- Double solid line
- diving island
- 8m   L   7m
- 2 5m
- R₁   R₂   R₃   R₄

Bus bay Dimensions for entrance speed
10 kms/hr
R₁ = 30m, R₂ = 15m, R₃ = 15m,
R₄ = 30m, L = 15m, for one bus, or
30m for two and so soon

Alternative forms of bus bays

B. BUS BAYS

Figure 5.7: Possible horizontal arrangements of bus lay-bys (A) and bus bays (B) and the corresponding road markings and signs.

131

Bus bays

Bus bays are the bus stopping areas, physically separated from the main traffic stream by an island or other structure, as shown in Figure 5.7B. As such, bus bays have in effect the same design characteristics with the loading berths at bus terminals. They are therefore not mentioned in any detail at this point, as the elements of bus berth design are given later on in the section about bus terminals.

Some Final Points

Design, signing, maintenance and enforcement of bus stops should maximize compliance to regulations by buses and cars and passenger convenience. The factors involved include:

1. **Enforcement.** Effective enforcement of complementary curb parking restrictions is essential. The best engineering bus stop is of little value, if the attendant parking restrictions are not strictly enforced. Where buses must "double park", because their loading areas are occupied by parked or stopped vehicles, passenger safety is reduced and traffic flow is impeded.

2. **Delineation.** Bus stops should be clearly signed. Signs regulating parking should conform to the legal signs applicable in each country and are usually to be found in a Manual on Traffic Signs for Streets and Highways or in the Code of the Road. Also pavement markings in front of the stop should be clearly placed to delineate the stopping area (e.g. see Figure 5.5).

3. **Safety and convenience.** Bus stops should provide a minimum of safety and convenience to passengers. Roadway curbs should be of constant height to minimize passenger missteps when alighting from a bus at a lower or sloping curb. Wheel chair ramps should be provided at designated bus stops on all accessible bus routes to provide for street crossing by handicapped people.

BUS STOP SHELTERS

General Considerations and Criteria of Installation

Bus stop shelters are used for the protection of the waiting passengers from bad weather conditions, provision of some seats for the elderly, information material and, generally, convenience for the travelling public. Furthermore, bus shelters are increasingly seen in many cities as an important element of civic design and one source of income for the agency that owns and maintains them through the advertisements that are usually placed on them. Indeed, the provision of modern and well maintained bus shelters is an element that can greatly enhance the environment of a city and enrich its character and beauty. Since bus shelters are relatively expensive, as compared to a simple bus stop sign, and since they also require important maintenance finance, they are not installed in every stop. The suggested criteria for installing a bus shelter are the following :

a. The average minimum number of passengers using the stop must not be lower than a predetermined level appropriate for each urban area. A suggested figure for that minimum level could be 150 passengers per day (24 hours) or 800 per week for large to medium size cities and 100 per day or 600 per week for small cities and towns. Below these levels, bus shelters could of course be installed but at a lower priority as compared to other bus related infrastructure.

b. At bus terminals there should always be shelters installed.

c. When the bus stop is "substantially" used by elderly or handicapped people there should also be shelters installed. The limit to determine if such use is "substantial" is the percentage of the elderly and handicapped using the stop to the total daily passenger movement in the same stop. A figure of 15% has been used by some agencies, mainly in the US for that percentage (e.g. MBTA, 1977).

d. Bus shelters should be placed at places that are particularly exposed to adverse weather conditions, e.g. winds.

e. Finally, perhaps the most important criterion is that there should be enough space

133

available for the installation of the shelter, according to what will be said in the following about their dimensions and space requirements. This is probably the biggest restriction in the provision of bus shelters in the usually congested urban areas. As it will be seen, walkways with widths less than 2.0 metres cannot accommodate a bus shelter.

The question of bus shelter design and installation is of primary importance not only to the bus transport agencies, who are primarily concerned with the comfort of their passengers and the attractiveness of the system to them, but also by the local authorities. The latter are concerned in addition to passenger comfort, with the creation of an aesthetically acceptable and enhanced environment in the urban area.

In increasing numbers, urban areas assign the task of constructing <u>and</u> maintaining bus shelters to private companies, free of charge, who, in turn, are given rights to exploit the shelters as advertising space. The system has been applied in France, Belgium, W.Germany and other European countries with great success so far (see Figures 5.10 & 5.11).

Design Characteristics of Bus Shelters

To design a bus shelter is not a very simple task. It requires a combination of architectural structural, and traffic engineering skills as well as a substantial design study. This can be justified by the fact that a uniform bus shelter design will be applied to all installations throughout the urban area and therefore the design must comply with aesthetic as well as technical and economic considerations.

Figures 5.8 and 5.9 show some typical dimensions of bus shelters and their location with respect to the rest of the walkway. The size is determined by the acceptable size of the queue of the waiting passengers, calculated at a density of 0.3 - 0.5 sq.m per waiting passenger, and the total cost. An important point is the position of the shelter in the walkway. It has to be placed at the back or the front of the walkway, so that it leaves adequate space for the movement of pedestrians in front or behind it. The width that is left for the movement of pedestrians on the sidewalk must not be less than 0.8m (see Fig.5.8) so as to allow a minimum pedestrian flow of

134

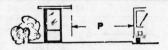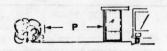

A. Two alternative positions of the bus stop on the sidewalk
   p ⩾ 0.8 m

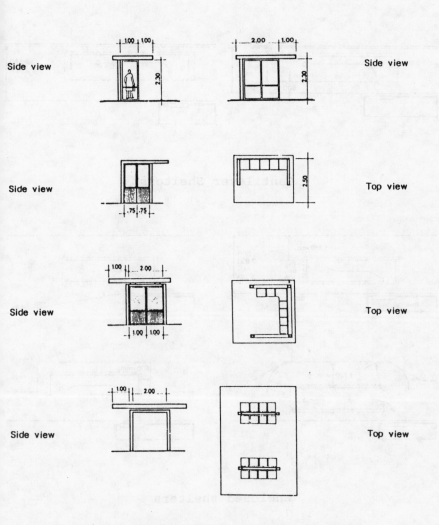

Side view

Side view

Side view

Side view

Side view

Side view

Top view

Top view

Top view

B. Alternative dimensions and lay-outs of simple bus shelters

Figure 5.8: Alternative dimensions and position of bus shelters on the walkway (dimensions in m).

135

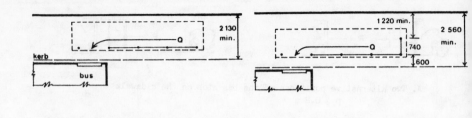

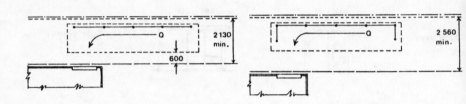

Cantilever Shelters

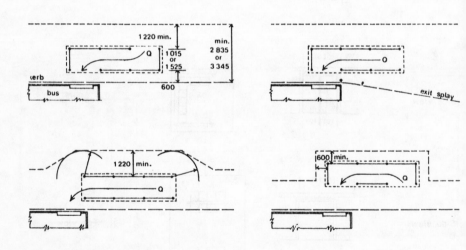

Enclosed shelters

Figure 5.9: Typical arrangements for cantilever (i.e. open at the sites) and enclosed shelters (source: CPT,1981). All dimensions in millimetres.

136

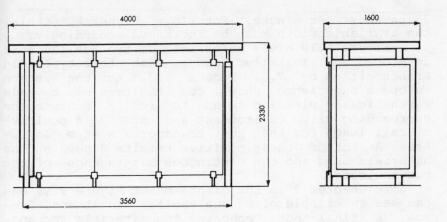

STANDARD TYPE SHELTER 4000 × 1600 mm

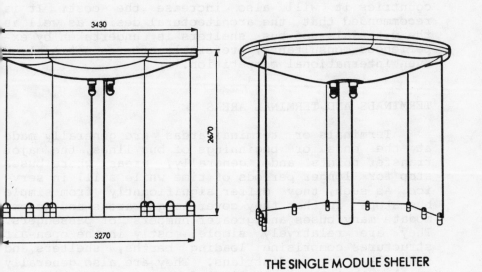

THE SINGLE MODULE SHELTER

Figure 5.10: Overview and dimensions of types of bus shelters used in France (courtesy J.C. Decaux Ltd).

137

35 persons per minute. For flows higher than this, the available width must be increased accordingly.

Figure 5.10 gives an example of two bus shelters developed and installed (along with other types) in French cities by J.C. Decaux Ltd. As the Western European experience shows, bus shelters can be made aesthetically pleasing so as to really enhance the surrounding city environment and provide a positive overall image for the bus transport system in the area. A lot of these positive results depend on the materials used and the continuous maintenance of the bus shelters.

In Chapter 9 in the diagramme of Figure 9.6, one can see an example of a bus shelter in Athens, Greece. A final note concerns the materials for constructing bus shelters. The choice of the materials depends on their availability in the local or national market, their cost and the particular design chosen. Usually, a steel skeleton structure is used with surfaces made of glass and a roof made of plexiglass or hard plastic material. Use of an aluminium skeleton structure instead of steel is aesthetically better, and lighter as a structure, but in most countries it will also increase the cost. It is recommended that the architectural design as well as the materials of bus shelters is undertaken by experienced consultants, preferably after a national or even international competition.

TERMINALS AND TERMINAL AREAS

Terminals or terminal areas are generally made at the ends or beginnings of bus lines, the major transfer points and, generally, areas where buses stop for longer periods of time while still in service. As such, they differ significantly from simple bus stops in that they cover larger areas and accommodate many buses and greater numbers of passengers. They are relatively simple, mostly in the open-air structures comprising loading berths, shelters and sidewalks for pedestrians. They are also generally smaller than the sophisticated bus stations which are usually covered within buildings including shops, restaurants and other amenities. Although the scope of this book precludes any lengthy discussion of bus stations (these are after all mostly for intercity buses), most of the design elements that will be given here for bus terminals are the same for bus stations.

The layout and size of a bus terminal, depends on the number of bus movements that it will accommodate, the number of passengers, the availability of space, the general effects on the surroundings etc.

The critical elements in the design of a bus terminal are therefore:

- The determination of capacity and the number of loading berths.
- The geometric characteristics and horizontal layout of these berths.
- The determination of capacity and the geometric characteristics of the walkways for the movement of pedestrians.

These are discussed in the following.

Number and Capacity of Loading Berths

The passenger loading capacity of a single berth depends on the boarding and alighting time per passenger and their number. The relation is a straightforward one and is as follows:

$$L = \frac{3600\ B}{Aa + Bb + C} \qquad (5.1)$$

where:

L = The number of passengers loaded per hour through the berth.

B = The number of passengers boarding per departure.

b = Boarding time per passenger (secs).

A = The number of alighting passengers per arrival.

a = Alighting time per passenger (secs).

C = Clearance time between successive buses (secs).

The denominator in relation (5.1) expresses the total dwell time per bus in the berth. Certain authors such as in De Leuw Cather (1983) include in the total dwell time also the times of early and late arrivals of buses.

From the above expression giving the number of passengers loaded per hour through the berth, the total number of berths that are necessary to accommodate a given number of passengers can be easily calculated. Levinson, (1975)[a] gives the following expression for the calculation of the required number

---

[a]. Also found in Taylor (1977) and CUTA (1985).

139

of berths at maximum load point conditions:

$$N = \frac{P(bpS + C)}{3600\ S} \qquad (5.2)$$

where:

N = The number of berths.
P = The capacity of the line at the maximum load point i.e. the maximum number of passengers per hour.
b = The boarding time per passenger (secs).
p = The percentage of passengers boarding at the heaviest stop, to the number of maximum load point passengers.
S = Bus Capacity (no. of passengers).
C = Clearance time between buses at the stop (secs).

For both the above relationships one must know the average boarding and alighting times per passenger. These should normally be determined by observations on the particular bus network under study, as they differ according to the type of buses used, the system of fare collection etc. The change in these times according to the type of fare collection and the total number of boarding[a] passengers is shown in Figure 5.11. Typical values range from 2.0 to 4.0 secs per boarding passenger.

The following example illustrates the use of both the above relationships (5.1) and (5.2). Suppose we want to calculate the required number of berths at a busy stop serving a transfer point on the network. The number of passengers that have been estimated to board the buses per hour at this point is 900, with an average number boarding per departure equal to 20 and alighting 10. Assuming a clearance time of 30 secs (i.e. from closing the doors of one bus to opening the doors of the next one) and boarding and alighting times per passenger of 3.0 and 2.0 secs respectively, the following results are obtained.

From relationship (5.1) the total number of passengers that can be loaded per hour per berth is calculated to be L = 800. Therefore the required number of berths is : 900 / 800 = 1.12 which is normally rounded to 2. If the relationship (5.2) was to be used, and assuming the line haul capacity at maximum load point to be 2,800 passengers per hour and that

_____

a. Since boarding times are generally greater than alighting ones, it is the boarding passengers that are taken into account.

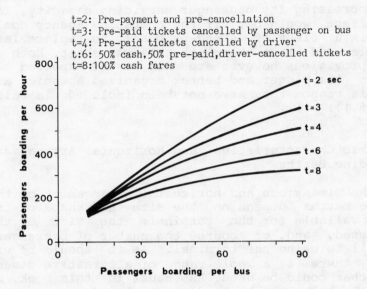

t=2: Pre-payment and pre-cancellation
t=3: Pre-paid tickets cancelled by passenger on bus
t=4: Pre-paid tickets cancelled by driver
t:6: 50% cash,50% pre-paid,driver-cancelled tickets
t=8:100% cash fares

Figure 5.11: Effect of the type of fare collection and the number of boarding passengers on boarding time (t) per passenger. (Source: De Leuw Cather (1983) modified with some data from Greece).

the percentage of passengers, boarding at this stop to the maximum load passengers is 30%, the number of required berths is calculated from relationship (5.2) to be (with bus capacity = 70) :

$$N = (2800(3x0.3x70 + 30)) / (3600x70) = 1.03 \text{ or } \text{approx. } 2.00$$

It is recommended that the elements of the above relations (5.1) and (5.2) be defined for each specific case through measurements and data collected for the bus operation concerned. The above values can only be indicative for the sake of illustration.

A final note must be made here about the other factors that may affect the capacity of a bus berth.

These are mainly connected with the operating practice of the bus agency. For example if a holding area is provided for buses that arrive early, so that they do not block the loading aisles before they depart, the total dwell time in the berth would be shorter, thus increasing its passenger servicing capacity. The same effect would be, if the operating agency could maintain a fleet of stand-by buses to replace late arrivals and thus keep the headway short. Both of these provisions however are not to be expected but only in the bigger and better organized agencies and for this reason they have not been included in relation (5.1).

Geometric Characteristics and Horizontal Arrangement of Loading Berths

The dimensions and horizontal arrangement of the loading berths depend on the size and shape of the space available for the terminal, the size of the buses used, and, of course the number of passengers who will be using the terminal. As it should be expected, there is a whole range of alternative dimensions that could be used. As usual in this book, we will give below the berth dimensions and arrangements for the most usual types of buses. These are:

1. The standard 12.0 metre bus with 2.5 m width, 2.5 m and 3.5 m front and rear overhangs respectively and a minimum turning radius of the outer front corner 12.9 m at crawl speed.
2. The articulated bus of 18.0 m length, 2.5m width and a turning radius of the outer front corner of 13.0 m.

Small deviations from these measurements do not change the berth design appreciably.

There are two commonly used horizontal arrangements of bus berths. The **Parallel** and the **Shallow (or deep) Sawtooth.** Figures 5.12 and 5.13 show respectively these two types of berth arrangements as well as their suggested dimensions.

More specifically, in Figure 5.12 two alternative "parallel" arrangements are shown. The parallel arrangement has as its main advantage the ease of implementation, since it uses existing curbs and has minimum costs. It also offers flexibility for re-arrangement to accommodate different types of buses and/or new requirements for space and expansion. Its main disadvantages are the relative difficulty with which buses park in their spaces and the inability to restrict buses to their own designated parking positions, coupled with the ease with which other vehicles or pedestrians can interfere with buses. It is usually quite likely, in the parallel arrangement to have disorderly parking of buses, which results in not very productive use of the available space and rather long queues at peak times of demand.

For the parallel berth arrangements shown in Figure 5.12, it has to be noted that the dimensions given are for **free and unrestricted entry and exit** of the buses. The "traditional" parallel arrangements, where each bus parks almost directly behind the other, require difficult maneuvering and cannot be recommended for a bus terminal.

The sawtooth arrangement (Figure 5.13) has as its main advantage the ease of manoeuvering of buses into their designated positions which in this case cannot be "violated" as in the parallel arrangement. A possible disadvantage is that the sawtooth may require overall more width of roadway than the parallel arrangement.

Overall the sawtooth arrangement provides a saving of about 2.0 m in length over a parallel one with the same level of service (De Leuw Cather, 1983). Because of its general superiority of function and design, it can be said that the sawtooth type is gaining in popularity and is the preferred type of arrangement.

Capacity of Walkways

The final basic element of a bus terminal area concerns walkways for pedestrians who walk around in order to board the buses. Certain elements of the capacity of a walkway in terms of the number of passengers who can pass through a certain width of walkway (i.e. 35 persons per minute for a width of 0.8m) have already been given in the section about "Design Guidelines for the Bus Stops - at the curbside". These elements were principally concerned with the actual capacity (i.e. the ability to move), per unit width of the sidewalk and, as such, they can also be used in the context of the design of walkways for terminals.

However, when large volumes of pedestrians are involved on a regular basis, comfort and safety should also be considered besides capacity. We are then also concerned with the "level of service" in

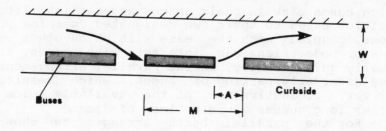

Standard Bus 12.0 m				Articulated Bus 18.0 m			
M	A	W		M	A	W	
		min.	rec.			min.	rec.
23	11	6.50	7.00	29	11	6.50	7.00
22	10	6.75	7.25	28	10	6.75	7.25
21	9	6.75	7.25	27	9	6.75	7.25
20	8	7.00	7.50	26	8	7.00	7.50
19	7	7.00	7.50	25	7	7.00	7.50
18	6	7.25	7.75	24	6	7.25	7.75
17	5	7.25	7.75	23	5	7.25	7.75
16	4	7.50	8.00	22	4	7.50	8.00
15	3	7.75	8.50	–	–	–	–

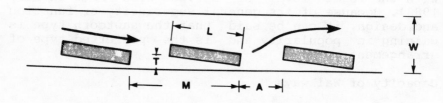

Standard Bus L=12.0 m				Articulated Bus L=18.0m			
M	A	W		M	A	W	
		min.	rec.			min.	rec.
19	8	7.00	8.00	27	10	8.00	9.00
18	7	7.50	8.25	26	9	8.50	9.25
17	6	7.50	8.50	25	8	8.50	9.50
16	5	8.00	9.00	24	7	8.75	9.50
15	4	8.50	9.00	23	6	9.00	9.75
14	3	9.00	9.50	22	5	9.00	10.00

Figure 5.12: Two alternative designs of "parallel" bus berths and dimensions for free, <u>unrestricted</u> entry and exit.
Note: If maneuvering is permitted, the values of (A) can be reduced by 70%.

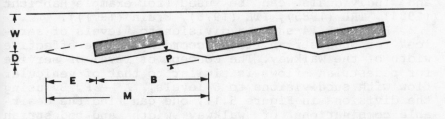

M	E	D	P	W		W + D	
				min.	rec.	min.	rec.
A. Standard Bus L = 12.0 m							
20	7	1.00	1.53	7.25	7.50	8.25	8.50
20	7	1.25	1.91	7.25	7.50	8.50	8.75
20	7	1.50	2.29	7.25	7.50	8.75	9.00
20	7	1.75	2.67	7.25	7.50	9.00	9.25
20	7	2.00	3.04	7.25	7.50	9.25	9.50
19	6	1.00	1.46	7.25	7.50	8.25	8.50
19	6	1.25	1.81	7.25	7.50	8.50	8.75
19	6	1.50	2.18	7.25	7.50	8.75	9.00
19	6	1.75	2.53	7.25	7.50	9.00	9.25
19	6	2.00	2.89	7.25	7.50	9.25	9.50
18	6	1.00	1.38	7.50	7.75	8.50	8.75
18	6	1.25	1.72	7.50	7.75	8.75	9.00
18	6	1.50	2.06	7.50	7.75	9.00	9.25
18	6	1.75	2.40	7.50	7.75	9.25	9.50
18	6	2.00	2.74	7.50	7.75	9.50	9.75
B. Articulated Bus L = 18.0 m							
25	7.5	1.00	1.53	7.50	7.75	8.50	8.75
25	7.5	1.25	1.95	7.50	7.75	8.75	9.00
25	7.5	1.50	2.30	7.50	7.75	9.00	9.25
24	6.5	1.00	1.46	7.75	8.00	8.75	9.00
24	6.5	1.25	1.81	7.75	8.00	9.00	9.25
24	6.5	1.50	2.20	7.75	8.00	9.25	9.50

Figure 5.13: "Sawtooth" bus berth layout and alternative dimensions
Source: for standard bus: De Leuw Cather (1983)

accommodating pedestrians of a certain facility. In this respect the work done by various organizations and individuals can be used (for example Habricht (1984), TRB (1985), ITE (1976), Fruin (1971)).

Figure 5.14 shows a division to "levels of service" for pedestrian flow according to the effective width of the walkway. The concept of level of service for pedestrian flows is similar to that of vehicular flow with subdivisions to 6 levels, A - F. By using the divisions in Figure 5.14, one can find the desirable combinations of walkway width and pedestrian flow for a given level of Service.

Generally, level of service C is recommended for the design of the facilities. Therefore, by using Figure 5.14 and starting with the estimated level of pedestrian flow on the vertical axis, the necessary walkway width can be found as the same figure indicates. The shape and magnitude of the areas indicating the various levels of service may vary in different countries as the capacity and levels of service of a walkway depend on the physical dimensions of the body, the psychological preferences regarding bodily contact with the others and other complex human characteris tics regarding balance, timing, sight etc. In this respect it should again be reminded (as in previous occasions) that the division in levels of service shown in Figure 5.14 is indicative only and it may have different configurations in different countries.

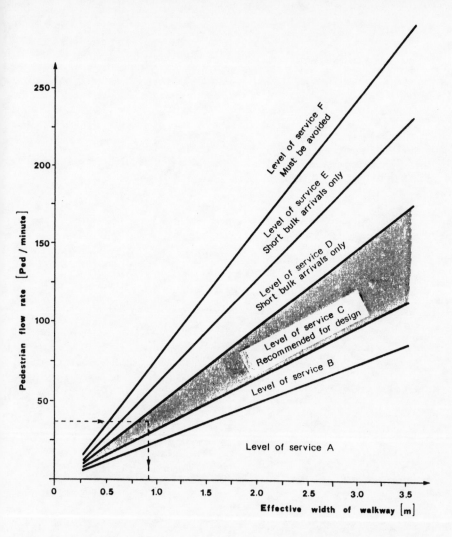

Figure 5.14: Levels of Service for pedestrian flows on walkways according to the effective width. Level C is recommended for design. Levels D and E for short bulk arrivals only. Level F must be avoided.

6 Guidelines for the rolling stock

This chapter deals with the rolling stock as an element affecting the operation and the productivity of the agency, as well as the level of service offered to the public. It is not concerned so much with the mechanical performance of the vehicles as such, but more with their functional and operational characteristics that are evident and influence the travelling public in their choice of mode.

In most countries there is a specific procedure that has to be followed before a certain type of bus can be introduced into service. There are usually administrative decrees from the central or regional governments, called type approvals, that postulate the basic characteristics of the vehicles which can "legally" be used by the operators. These "type approvals" usually take into account the types of buses currently offered by the manufacturers, especially those that are locally manufactured. They, however, define new or "desired" characteristics of the vehicles, so that they satisfy certain requirements peculiar to the specific urban areas and countries.

Another problem facing the operators is the question of choosing the appropriate type of vehicle for an urban bus operation. This usually requires definition of a whole range of detailed specifications and standards as well as specific technical information. The material in this chapter provides some of this information and generally helps towards a better understanding of the influence of the appropriate type of rolling stock on the whole operation.

There are four main aspects of the operation that relate directly to the type and condition of the rolling stock:

a. **Safety.** The mechanical parts of an urban bus and especially the body structure, the chassis, the suspension, the types of doors and their mechanisms, the control systems (brakes, steering) and other characteristics of the vehicle (e.g. the height of the steps) are elements that influence directly the safety of the operation.

b. **Comfort.** A "traditionally" negative aspect of public transport, as compared to the private car, is the lack of comfort during the trip. Although by its very definition a "mass" transit operation cannot provide the same level of comfort as that of the private car, an acceptable level must be provided so as, combined with the other advantages of public transport, to make modal choice turn in favour of the latter. Elements of the rolling stock that directly influence the comfort of the passengers are the number of doors, the number and position of the seats, the existence and position of handrails, the ventilation of the interior, the size and position of the windows etc.

c. **Efficiency of Operation.** This aspect encompasses all those elements of the operation of a bus that directly relate to the proper and efficient execution of the daily service requirements. For example, the ability to maneuver, the acceleration/deceleration rates, the horsepower of the engine, its fuel efficiency etc.

d. **Effects on the Environment.** These effects, which primarily include air pollution, noise levels, and vibrations have become very important for the congested urban areas where the buses usually operate. Elements of the rolling stock, such as levels of emissions (mainly for smoke and Nitro-

Oxides) as well as noise levels, are therefore important aspects of the whole operation to which both the travelling public and the authorities are, and are becoming more, sensitive.

The specific characteristics, that each type of vehicle offer in relation to the above aspects, have to be weighted against the total cost of purchasing and maintaining the vehicle over the whole period of its economic life. A proper cost-benefit analysis may not be sufficient to show the entire range of costs and benefits, especially in terms of the above four aspects, and therefore a more qualitative analysis may be more appropriate.

In the following sections the reader will find guidelines and suggestions regarding the most important and "passenger related" elements of an urban bus. The examination has taken into account the range of existing technology and the variety of material currently available, or reasonably within feasible technical and economic availability.

THE PASSENGERS SECTION

The part of the bus that is used by the passengers is obviously very important because it is this part that the travelling public notices most of the time. The most important elements of the passengers section are:

- the seat arrangement
- the dimensions of the seats and seat upholstery
- the dimensions and position of the windows
- the handgrips and handrails
- the lighting arrangements
- the ventilation system and heating
- the floor
- the information system for the passengers.

With the exception of the last item which will be dealt in full detail in chapter 9, all other elements of the above list are examined in the following sections.

Seating Arrangements

A. Criteria of Selection

The seating arrangement that will be selected will have to be determined by the type of service that the vehicle is to provide, the method of fare collection and the door location. Seat arrangement, door location and internal circulation are all tied together. For longer routes the design should aim to maximize the number of seats, while for shorter ones the opposite may be the aim. The most usual criteria in the analysis of seating arrangements are the following:
- ratio of standing to seating passengers
- minimum distance from doors
- existence of sufficient leg-room
- psychologically comfortable sitting
- ease of cleaning and maintenance.

The relation of seating to standing passengers is usually expressed by the ratio of total to seated passengers. This ratio has the values shown in Table 6.1 and, according to the value selected, the number of seats for a bus of a given size can be determined (as well as the corresponding space for standees). The basic decision here is whether the operator will opt for a seating arrangement that provides the minimum number of standees or the opposite (or of course something in between). Once this is decided, the specific number of seats will be determined by the value of the ratio in Table 6.1.

The criterion of minimum distance from doors refers to the seating arrangement in relation to the doors. Obviously the distance that a passenger has to walk in order to reach the nearest door must be as short as possible and the way there as easy as possible.Although the possibilities that exist in terms of this criterion are rather limited, it is worth investigating them before finalizing the preferred arrangement.

The criterion of sufficient space for leg-room is of critical importance for the comfort of the seating passengers. It affects, on the one hand, the total space required by the seats, and, on the other, the comfort of the seated passengers especially in the case of double seats where sufficient room must exist for the entrance to the inner seat (i.e. close to the window).

Psychological comfort is also very important in seat arrangement, because a passenger may be exposed to psychological stress in addition to actual physical discomfort. He/she may have a feeling of being boxed in or over-exposed or be greatly dissatisfied with his seating partner. Hence, he/she might minimize the use of the public transport system because of these psychological discomfort factors and not because of the actual quality of the seats or service. Relative to this criterion is our suggestion, presented in the following, for slightly offset seats when in double row.

Table 6.1

Values of the ratio total/seating passengers[a] for a standard 12m bus. A:Urban Operation, B:Suburban (or longer) routes.

Level	For maximum number of seats	For maximum number of standees	Comments
minimum	A= 1.25[b] B= 1.00	A= 2.50 B= 1.25	Max.ease of movement for the standing passengers
suggested	A= 1.70 B= 1.10	A= 3.00 B= 1.25	Restriction in the ease of movement and comfort of stand. pass.
maximum	A= 2.00 B= 1.25	A= 7.00 B= 1.50	Max. density of standees movement with great difficulty

Notes:
a. The suggested values of the ratio in this table are given in order to determine the number of seats and the seating arrangements. They should not be confused with the suggested occupancy rates in Table 7.1 which are suggested loading rates and concern the way the system is operated.
b. A value of 1.25 means for example that all seats are occupied and that there are standees equal to the 25% of the seated passengers.

B. Seating Formations and Angles

The above considerations have resulted in the suggested seating formations that are shown in Figures 6.1 and 6.2. More specifically, as regards the position of the seats in relation to each other, Figure 6.1 shows the suggested minimum distances between the two rows of seats. A minimum distance of 0.7 m between the front and the back seat is considered necessary for sufficient leg room and ease of passage for the passenger of the inner seat. Also when two seats are together, the outer (i.e. towards the corridor) is suggested to be placed 0.10 m "behind" the inner one (towards the window), so as to achieve maximum ease of entry for the inner seat. This is shown in Figure 6.1c.

As regards the seating angles the following three possible types can be mentioned:

a.   **Transverse** type of seating. This is the conventional arrangement used in the great majority of cases today (see sketch below). It provides a high seating capacity with little variety. Visibility is fair but poor loading characteristics may be experienced with this type of arrangement. To improve these characteristics a variation of the transverse type is the one shown in figure 6.1c, which has the outer seat a little retracted with relation to the inner one (window) as already suggested earlier.

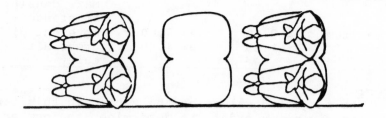

b. **Longitudinal** (see sketch below). This provides good capacity in peak hours when the maximum number of standees is needed and is very useful over the wheel covers of the bus. This type of arrangement provides poor restraint during vehicle acceleration, poor visibility, limited space per person and is very impersonal, since the passenger would have many people sitting or standing around him.

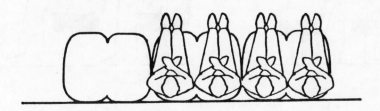

c. **Angular** (see sketch below). Angular seating has poor capacity but good visibility, comfort, privacy, sufficient room for belongings and may also be used over wheel covers.

The ideal seating formation would contain a variation of angular, longitudinal and transverse seats. A wide variety allows the passenger to sit alone or with somebody else. Using three types of seats would also make the interior interesting with a relaxed atmosphere.

The main disadvantage of a variety of seating is that it consumes more space and it is not appropriate for handicapped, especially blind persons for whom the ideal is to have the same type of seats throughout the vehicle.

Based on the above considerations, the alternative seating arrangements shown in Figure 6.2 can be suggested. These are only indicative of a wide range

155

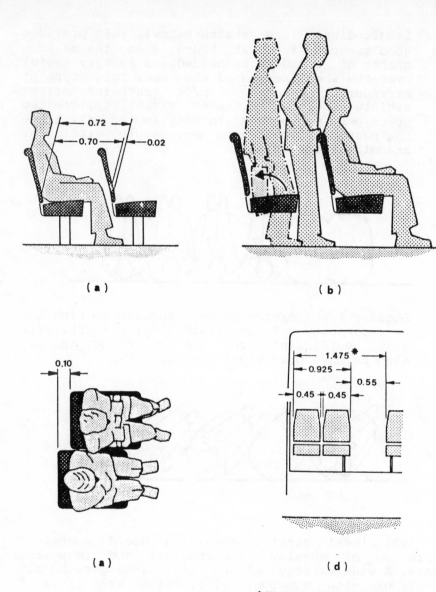

Figure 6.1: Suggested placement of bus seats in relation to each other (source: VOV/VDA, 1979).

156

MAXIMUM NO. OF SEATS
(Long distance lines or Suburban)

MAXIMUM NO. OF STANDEES
(Short length high demand lines)

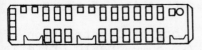

A. No. of seats: 45

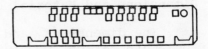

A. No. of seats: 31

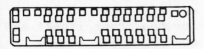

B. No. of seats: 44

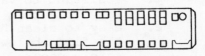

B. No. of seats: 29

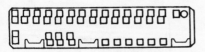

C. No. of seats: 42

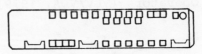

C. No. of seats: 26

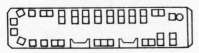

D. No. of seats: 35

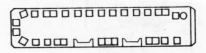

D. No. of seats: 28

Figure 6.2: Examples of seat arrangements for a 12 m standard bus with 3 doors (alternatives A,B,C) and 2 doors (alternative D).

157

of alternative arrangements, which may differ slightly with each other but with different advantages and
disadvantages, mainly as regards the space requirements and the comfort of passengers. Special mention
is made of the fact that in Figure 6.2 each alternative arrangement is related to an objective regarding
total passengers to standees ratio.

Dimensions and Material of Construction of the Seats

The dimensions and the form of construction of
the seats varies considerably. Some basic criteria
for selection are:
a.   comfort,
b.   suitable in its dimension to accommodate
      the "95 percentile" person,
c.   resistant to vandalism,
d.   easy to get in and out of,
e.   easy to clean both for the seat itself and
      the floor below it and
f.   safely secured with no protrusions.

In Figure 6.3 a suggested set of dimensions of a
typical bus seat are presented, based on recommendations of the German Federation of Public Transport
Operators (VOV/VDA, 1979).

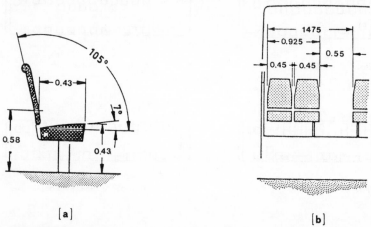

[a]   [b]

Figure 6.3: Suggested dimensions of seats (based on
VOV/VDA, 1979).

The seats are recommended to be constructed of
two sections of moulded fiberglass with foam between
the two sections (as shown in Figure 6.4). Fiberglass

158

is recommended since it is easily repaired when scratched or slightly damaged. This type of seating unit also has good energy absorption from impact, vibration, shock and sound, so it increases the over-all safety inside the bus. Furthermore, it is pleas-ant in appearance having no seams or rivets, and can be easily replaced in case of excessive damage since the whole unit is usually bolted to the floor. Alter-native types of construction include wooden, poly-ester, or even upholstered seats. As regards uphol-stery, it may be necessary to note that it is very rarely used in urban buses because of its cost and easy damage.

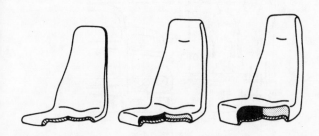

Figure 6.4: Seat construction from fiberglass with foam of varying widths between.

Dimensions and Position of the Windows

Window style and quality reflect some comfort considerations while adding to the overall quality of the interior and exterior environment. They also con-tribute greatly to the "psychological" comfort of the passengers, as discussed earlier. Furthermore, the windows must be resistant to solar radiation (this may not be so important for countries with cold and rainy climates), cracking and shattering. Typical light as well as infrared and ultraviolet transmit-tance for bus windows is 30-35%.

As regards the dimensions of the windows and their position in relation to the floor of the vehi-cle, the aim is to achieve full visibility for the seated passengers as well as for those standing. In almost all modern designs of urban buses today the width of the windows is practically the whole side of the bus. So the critical elements of the window de-sign remain the height and the distance from the floor. In Figure 6.5 two possible designs are shown. In both the height of the window is 0.95 m but the distance from the floor differs. In the case of Figure 6.5B, the floor for the standing passengers has been lowered to allow for easy viewing for them. This arrangement, however, has the disadvantage that it creates an extra step inside the vehicle, thus increasing the difficulty of access to the seat, especially for handicapped persons.

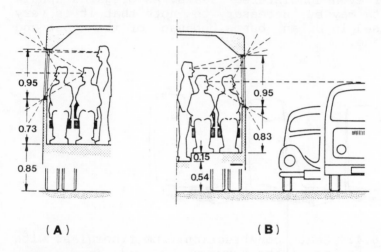

(**A**)   (**B**)

Note: Total height from floor
to roof should be 2.05-2.15m.

Figure 6.5: Suggested minimum dimensions for the windows and their distance from the floor for two cases of floor height from the ground.

Handgrips and Handrails

Handrails are the horizontal or vertical tubes that are installed in the interior of the bus for the safety of the standing passengers. The horizontal ones usually run parallel to the central corridor on both sides directly above the edge of the seats (see Fig. 6.6B). They may have hanging handgrips for greater convenience. The vertical handrails are placed at points were there are no seats and/or at the end of the horizontal ones.

Other handrails of special purpose and nature are recommended at the following places:
   a.   The middle of the steps at double doors for entry and exit (Fig. 6.6A). These cannot be

160

installed if the door is specially equipped
for the entry and exit of people in wheelchairs.

b.   The side of folding doors (obviously not
the side where the door folds), as shown
in Figure 6.6C.

c.   The edge of the seat close to the corridor
as shown in Figure 6.6B.

d.   The folding door itself, so that when it
opens it "offers" the passenger a handgrip
at the side(s) of the entrance.

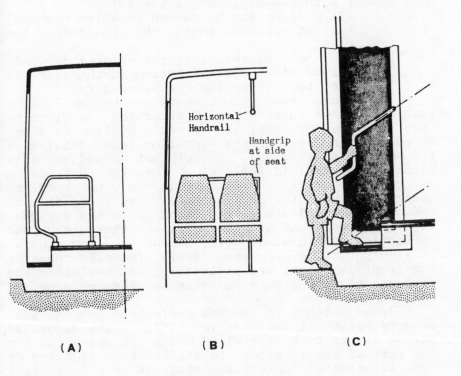

(A)   **(B)**   **(C)**

(A) In the middle of the steps (for
     double doors)

(B) On the corridor seat and hori-
     zontally above the seat

(C) At the side of single doors (for
     door opens at the other side)

Figure 6.6: Types of handrails and possible positions.

Special attention must be given to the material of construction of the handrails or, to be more precise, the material that covers the handrail. Usually, in certain climates in the winter, if the metal part of the handrail is uncovered it may be too cold to hold. For this reason handrails may be covered with a plastic cover that also helps improve its appearance.

Interior Lighting

The interior lighting of the passenger section must comply with two basic requirements:

a. It must be strong enough to allow for convenient reading inside the bus during the night.

b. It should minimize, if not eliminate, windshield glare and reflection in the dark for both the driver and the passengers.

The above two requirements may be conflicting with each other unless special attention is given to this problem. Usually, the driver's section is separated from the rest of the interior (see details in the driver's section), a fact that should normally eliminate windshield reflection for the driver. In any case the driver should have at his panel complete control of the interior lighting, so as to be able to reduce it immediately in cases where the external lighting conditions are very dark and there is strong reflection on his windshield. His control may consist of simply turning off some lights (usually those of the front section) or, preferably, of regulating the strength of the lights by dimming them when necessary.

In an effort to reduce reflection for the passengers Navin et al (Navin, 1975) have suggested strong lights to be installed under the seats and for the rest of the interior, to utilize the lighting of the illuminated advertisements. In any case spot lights should be avoided and, instead, neon tubes should be preferred both because they emit glare-free quality of light and because they have reduced thermal emission rates.

Ventilation and Heating

Ventilation and heating are essential parts of passenger comfort when travelling in a bus. The optimum would be air conditioning, i.e. full climate control inside the vehicle. This, however, is some-

162

thing that will increase the cost of the bus and is considered by the majority of operators as a "luxury". If a fully air conditioned vehicle cannot be seriously anticipated, a properly ventilated and heated vehicle is absolutely necessary. One of the reasons stated by many travellers for not choosing public transport is that vehicles are often crowded and "stuffy". So the subject of ventilation and heating is very important.

As regards **heating**, a temperature between 10 and 15 degrees Celsius for the passengers section is the optimum. Below 10 degrees, passengers will start to feel cold and above 15 (or may be 17 degrees) they will have to take off their coats, both situations causing inconvenience. For the driver's section the temperature must be slightly higher than the rest of the bus (i.e. around 18 degrees Celsius), so that he can work with normal work clothing on. The obvious source for heating is the engine coolant, the hot air being circulated through air ducts all over the vehicle. The proper difference in the temperatures between the driver's section and the rest of the vehicle is maintained by the appropriate placing of the outlets of the air ducts that bring the hot air.

A serious problem associated with the heating is the mist that stays on the windows when the outside environment is very cold. De-misting for the driver's windshield must definitely be provided by mechanical means, usually through blowing air with a fan on the windows, as in any private car. For the rest of the windows however, de-misting is a serious problem which can partly be solved by placing the ventilation and/or heating air outlets at appropriate places, so as to have the air circulating close to the windows. There are other more expensive ways, however, namely to have the window glass specially treated on the outside to increase insulation.

As regards **ventilation**, this must be working in conjunction with the hot air circulation system, and must be provided both when the vehicle is in motion and when it is standing or at crawl speed. This latter requirement is very important as most urban bus operation is at low speeds and natural ventilation, through the movement of the vehicle, cannot be sufficient. Figure 6.7 shows a possible ventilation arrangement. The air intakes are located at the top two sides of the vehicle (Fig. 6.7A) and the air comes in the interior via special air outlets that can direct it to specific areas of the interior. The outgoing air is let out from the front of the vehicle as shown in Fig. 6.7B. The whole system is working both with the help of a set of fans, when at low speeds or stationary, and through the air current when moving.

An alternative arrangement for ventilation is shown in Figure 6.8. There, the air comes in again from the top and is directed towards the windows (see cross section in Fig. 6.8). Then it goes out via outlets near the floor of the vehicle. This system of ventilation should be combined with strong mechanical support (fans) to ensure proper air circulation as well as in order to serve as a good de-misting device.

A special note must be made here about the need to fix a maximum rate of air movement inside the vehicle. This should be arranged so as to avoid creation of "drafts" or other unpleasant sets of air coming on the passengers.

Ventilation, heating and possibly full air conditioning (climate control) must be the subject of a special study by experts who will design or recommend the most appropriate system, according to the climate of the urban area concerned and the specific cost and performance requirements of the operator.

The Floor

Two principal considerations are related to the floor of the vehicle. The material of which it is constructed and its height from the ground.

The material of the floor should be:
- not slippery
- wear and tear resistant
- sound absorbent
- possibly shock absorbent
- easy to clean.

These characteristics (with the possible exception of the last one) are met, to an acceptable degree, by using rubber or synthetic covers with "dots" or "corrugations". However, alternative designs may be possible and they should be properly investigated.

The height of the floor, presents one of the most difficult problem areas in bus design. From the viewpoint of both the operator and the mechanical aspects of the vehicle, "the higher the better". However, from the viewpoint of the user, which is our primary concern, "the lower the better".

Reducing the floor height changes the basic physical configuration of a bus. The simple construction of solid axles on the large wheeled existing buses, demands that the floor be relatively high off the ground because of the vertical travel distance needed for the axles. The high floor hinders the ease of boarding and alighting for all passengers, thus increasing dwell times, and for some elderly and handicapped people limiting access to the service completely.

In weighing both possibilities carefully, the following advantages and disadvantages of a low floor can be formulated.

Advantages of a low floor:

a. Reduced first step height and fewer steps, which in turn means:
    - increased accessibility to the interior
    - reduced boarding and alighting times
    - safer boarding and alighting
    - more easily modified to accommodate persons with varying degrees of handicap.

b. Lower overall height of the vehicle, which:
    - lowers the centre of gravity for reduced vehicle sway
    - is pleasing in appearance.

Disadvantages of a low floor:

a. Increased expense on the other mechanical systems, including capital costs. An example of a mechanical configuration that would allow a low floor (approx. 0.42m from the ground) according to Navin et al (1975) is: independent suspension, engine at the rear, rear wheel drive, small wheels with duplex tyres and a tandem wheel configuration at the rear. All these increase the initial cost of the vehicle.

b. The passengers viewing may be slightly limited because they will be lower to the ground.

c. Wheel wells (or "covers") protrude more into the vehicle.

Overall, and taking the passenger's point of view, it can be said that every effort should be made to produce lower floors. However, if that requirement is perceived to increase the capital cost of the vehicles excessively, other means could be investigated, namely to increase the height of the "boarding platform" at the bus stop, or increase the number of steps etc.

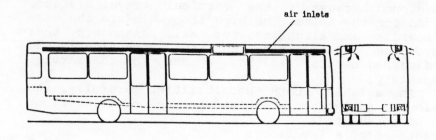

air inlets

A: Side view   Cross-section

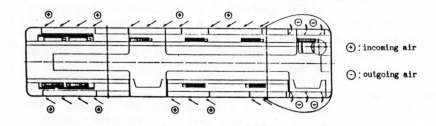

⊕ : incoming air

⊖ : outgoing air

B: Overview

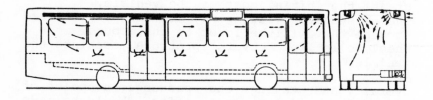

C: General air circulation

Figure 6.7: One possible bus ventilation system (adopted from VOV/VDA, 1979). Incoming air enters the vehicle through slots at the top, middle and rear sections of the bus, while the outgoing air passes through slots at the top of the vehicle in the front section.

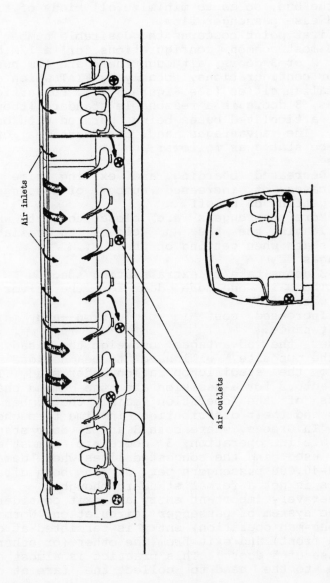

Figure 6.8: An alternative ventilation system to that of Figure 6.7. Air comes in through the top and goes out through outlets near the floor passing near the windows. This system, if combined with mechanical fans to push the air towards the windows, can provide adequate de-misting (see cross section).

Air inlets

air outlets

DOORS AND THE SYSTEM FOR ENTRY/EXIT

Entry/Exit Considerations

Entry/exit considerations should be made in relation to the size of the seats, the seating arrangement, the fare collection system and the door width. They concern the number and the best possible placement of the doors and the system of entry and exit to and from the bus, so as to minimize all kinds of time delays and ease passenger flow.

The first point concerns the desirable number of doors. The most common configurations for a 12m bus are either 2 or 3 doors, although there are 12m buses with 4-door configurations, notably by FIAT which are used in Italian cities (see Figure 6.18). For articulated buses, 3 doors is a reasonable standard (though there are articulated buses being operated with only two doors). The advantages and disadvantages of 3 doors may be stated as follows:

Advantages
- Decreased boarding and exiting time in cases of increased number of passengers getting on or off.
- More passengers are closer to exits when leaving the bus and closer to available seats when getting on the bus.

Disadvantages
- 3 doors take up extra seating space.
- There is one more door for the driver to watch.
- Increased cost in production and maintenance.

Whether the advantages outweigh the disadvantages or the opposite, will have to be decided according to the specific operation under study. The critical factors for a decision are the demand characteristics of the operation (mainly the number of passengers and their distribution in time throughout the day). In Greece, where both 3 and 2- door standard buses are in operation, 3 doors are almost exclusively used in the congested lines where demand exceeds 30-40,000 passengers per day in both directions (this is not a formal standard though).

Another very important entry and exit consideration is the system of passenger circulation. Normally, with one-man operation, entry is permitted at one point (the front) and exit from the other (or others, in the case of 3 doors). This practice is almost entirely due to the need to collect the fare at one

168

point for easy control. It results, however, in greater boarding delays. If the system of fare collection permits, it would be preferable to allocate more doors for boarding than for exiting off because the boarding times are generally greater. The decision as to which door will be used as entrance or exit will be related to the fare system in operation and the practice followed in the urban area under consideration.

Door Location

Generally speaking, the positioning of the doors should minimize the door-to-seat and seat-to-door walking distances and allow for smooth passenger flow and convenience.

For a 3-door configuration the location of the doors is more or less fixed, i.e. one at the front opposite the driver, one at the middle, roughly between the two wheel axles, and one at the rear (at approx. 1-2m from the end of the bus).

For a 2-door bus configuration there are two basic alternative positions of the front doors. The first, which can be called "conventional", has the front door almost directly opposite the driver's seat ahead of the front wheel axle. The second has the same door more towards the middle of the bus behind the front wheel axle.

The conventional door location has the following advantages and disadvantages:

Advantages

a. It allows for easier passenger/driver communication upon or before entry and is especially useful, when the system of fare collection provides some form of payment inside the vehicle, because then the presence of the driver nearby induces greater passenger compliance with the fare regulations (it is always assumed that we have one-man operation).

b. Fare collection is not restricted in any way.

c. It allows for driver supervision of the doorway without the use of mirrors.

Disadvantages

a. When the vehicle is full, standing passengers near the door obstruct the driver's view and interfere with his work.

b. The passengers entering from the front may have to walk further for available seats.

c. It increases the chances of passenger / driver interaction over and above what is necessary for safety and service requirements.

d. Dwell time is increased when a passenger communicates with the driver upon entry, thereby blocking the flow of passengers into the vehicle.

The alternative door location, i.e. behind the front wheel axle, has the following advantages and disadvantages:

Advantages:

a. It minimizes the distance between the doors and the seats.

b. It allows for speedier boarding and alighting because of available room all around the inside of the door.

c. Doors are closer together which allows double entry lines (if the system of fare collection permits).

d. It reduces unnecessary passenger/driver contact upon entry.

Disadvantages

a. No direct driver supervision of entry.

b. No communication with the driver upon entry.

In general it can be said that the conventional door location is preferable when (in connection to one-man operation) the fare collection system involves some form of payment in the vehicle upon entry (exact fare, card validation, etc). Although the driver is not usually required to really supervise the fare collection procedure, his presence has usually a positive impact on payment behaviour. For all other cases the alternative door location may be preferable.

Door Design and Operation

The various bus manufacturers today have produced a variety of door opening and operating mechanisms. With regard to the door design the following criteria and constraints apply:

Door Width: The door should be wide enough for two people simultaneously entering or exiting with parcels or articles. A door width around 1.2m is probably a good standard to follow for

170

double doors, which are the standard in modern buses.

Safety: The doors must contain a pressure release mechanism in case a boarding or alighting passenger gets caught in a closing door. Ideally the door should be designed to stop on contact with people during the opening and closing operation. Another feature may be that the doors should be operable only when the bus is standing still and vice versa, i.e. the bus cannot move unless the doors are closed. This is done with the use of "interlock" mechanisms (but the driver should be able to over-ride the interlock mechanism).

Performance: Opening and closing operations of the bus doors should be quick. A minimum time of 2 seconds has been noted as acceptable (Transbus, 1979) in order to combine good safety and efficiency. The performance of the door should be steady and reliable and the mechanism used to open and close the door should also be easy to service. The actual operation of the door is usually left to the driver.

The way in which doors open and close is also very important in terms of space requirements as well as in terms of safety and efficiency.

The following four types of door operating mechanisms are the most common (see Figure 6.9):

a. Double Folding Doors (Fig.6.9b). These doors offer the advantages of safety, proven reliability and fast opening/closing times. However, they usually tend to be complicated and heavy and they take up a relatively large amount of space in the entrance/exit area.

b. Outward Opening Glider Doors (Fig.6.9c). This type of door mechanism offers fast opening and closing times, it leaves the entrance/ exit width almost totally unrestricted and is generally reliable. The problem with this type of door operation is that it requires a considerable distance, from the side of the bus. A passenger's safety is then questioned, if he is standing close to the exterior side of the bus as the doors open or close.

c. Sliding Doors (Fig.6.9a). These doors are similar in operation to the sliding doors on small utility vans or, in a smaller

171

scale, to the doors of some Metro railways.
They offer good passenger safety because
they do not extend a large distance from
the outside of the bus and they do not reduce the entrance/ exit width. Their reliability and speed of operation, however,
have not been reported as good as with the
previous doors. They also require special
construction of the body structure of the
bus to allow the space for the entry of the
doors when open.

d. Rotating Doors (Fig.6.9d). This type of
doors open by sliding simultaneously along
two perpendicular tracks. Their operation
is quick, reliable and they only moderately
reduce the entrance/exit width. They are,
however, recommended only for relatively
narrow doors for single file operation.
Typical door widths, for which this type of
operation is quite acceptable, are up to
1.00m so that each of the two door sections is not more than 0.5m wide. If these
dimensions are exceeded, these doors tend
to be quite heavy and protrude a great distance into the interior of the bus thus
taking up a lot of space.

The steps

The steps form a critical part of the whole bus
design and are closely related to the height of the
floor. Their design, and especially their height,
affects the ability of passengers to use the bus conveniently at the boarding and alighting times. Depending on the height of the bus floor from the
ground, Figure 6.10 shows two recommended types and
dimensions of steps.

The first (Fig.6.10A) has 3 steps of 0.2m height
and 0.3m width. So, allowing for a 0.2m distance of
the first step from the boarding platform and a 0.14m
height of the platform itself, a total of 0.74m
height of the floor is allowed for.

The second (Fig.6.10B) has 2 steps allowing for
a total floor height of 0.54m from the ground. The
top step has a slight inclination of 3% to allow for
easier boarding and to effectively shorten the height
of the step from 0.2m to 0.18m.

Relative to the step design, a very important
consideration is whether special provision should be

172

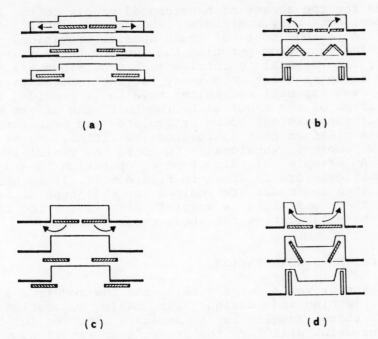

(a)   (b)

(c)   (d)

<u>Figure 6.9</u>: Alternative types of door operation.

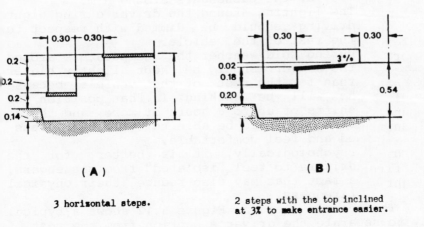

(A)   (B)

3 horizontal steps.   2 steps with the top inclined
at 3% to make entrance easier.

<u>Figure 6.10</u>: Two types and dimensions of steps.

173

taken for the access of handicapped people to the bus system. For many operators (and supervising bodies) the increased cost of such special provisions may dissuade them from pursuing the subject further. However, in several countries such provisions are not only acceptable but compulsory for the operators. In this case special mechanisms have to be provided for the steps of the front door (so that the driver has direct supervision) to be articulated and transformed into a platform that is lowered and lifted, so as to allow people in wheelchairs to board the vehicle.

An example of this type of operation in a diagrammatical form is shown in Figure 6.11. It is noted that when the buses are equiped for this type of service they must have a special sign indicating that they have facilities for wheel chair boarding.

THE DRIVER'S WORKSTATION

The driver's area within the bus requires special planning and design. Our basic suggestion is that there should be a separate section for the driver which will form the driver's workstation. This is supported by the following considerations:

- For reasons of safety the driver must be isolated as much as possible from the distractions that could result from the proximity of the passengers around him.
- The lighting around the driver during night driving should be dimmed with respect to the rest of the vehicle.
- During cold weather the temperature around the driver should be kept slightly higher than for the rest of the vehicle, because he will be working in that position for shifts of up to 8 hours or more and therefore he should be able to be lightly dressed and feel comfortable.
- Psychologically, it is better for the drivers to feel "isolated" from passengers, a fact that may also reduce their physical tiredness.

The shaded area in Figure 6.12 shows a typical way to separate the driver's section from the rest of the bus. The dimensions given in this figure are for the standard 12m long, 2.5 m wide urban bus as used in most urban buses today.

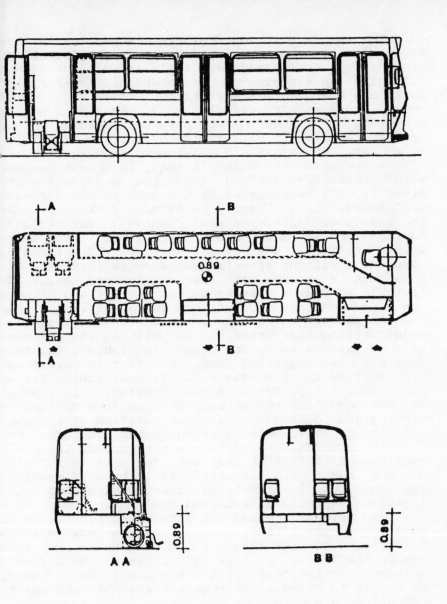

Figure 6.11: Sketches of the arrangements for loading wheelchairs on a bus. The steps of the door are mechanically extended to form a platform which is then lifted to bring the wheelchair to the level of the bus floor. The whole boarding operation is supposed to take less than one minute.

For the interior of the driver's section, driver ergonomics have been employed to study the driver and his working environment as early as in 1959. Figure 6.13 gives an example of an ergonomic analysis of parts of the driver's workstation, while Figure 6.14 shows a more recent example (VOV, 1983) in metric dimensions. The most direct physical features of bus design, relating to driver ergonomics, are the driver's seat, the windshield and the instrumentation.

As regards the **driver's seat**, this must be much more thoroughly studied than the passenger seats since it will be occupied by the same person for several hours. Also it cannot be as easily vandalized as the passenger seats. The seat cushions, seat back and surface material must be of high quality to ensure driver comfort. The seat's vertical and horizontal movement positions as well as the angle formed by the seat back with the seat cushion must be easily adjustable so that a larger percentile of the drivers can be accommodated comfortably and safely.

An example of a drivers seat with its basic dimensions (and their ranges) as well as the position of the driving wheel is shown in Figure 6.15. This seat has been suggested for the standard German bus type SLII by the W.German Federation of Public Transport (VOV, 1983). Its main characteristic is that it is designed to reduce body fatigue from continuous sitting and to induce an upright position of the spinal cord to avoid back aches and other symptoms.

As regards the **driver's windscreen,** the basic requirement is that it must not reflect the interior of the bus. This is particularly true after dark, when the bus is travelling without high beam headlights on a poorly illuminated road.

One simple method of accomplishing this is to reduce the area of the inside of the bus which a driver can see reflected on the windscreen. For this reason the dividing "shield" between the driver's section and the rest of the bus should be darkened, so as not to allow light from the rest of the bus to the driver's section.

An alternative way to reduce the reflections on the windscreen is to curve the windscreen in such a way, so as to focus the light rays onto some point with non-reflective material in the interior. This means either an elliptic or a cylindrical type of windscreen (or both), fitted in such a way that the driver's eyes are near one of the focuses, while the second focus of the ellipse is in a dark non-reflective area (see sketch in Fig. 6.16).

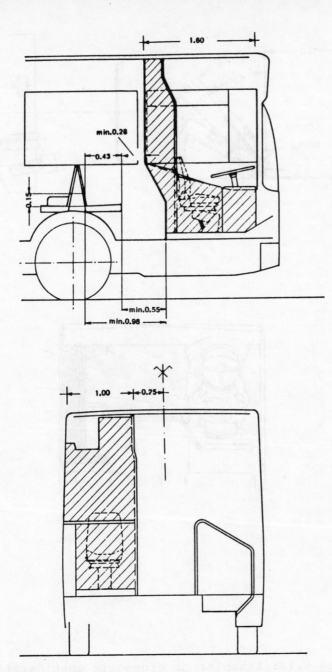

Figure 6.12: Typical lay-out and dimensions of the driver's section (VOV, 1983).

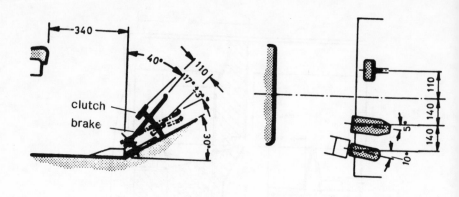

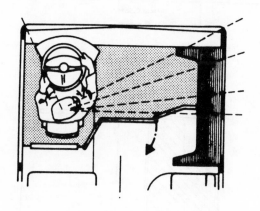

Figure 6.13: Examples of ergonomic considerations for the bus driver's foot instruments and the driver's side view which greatly influence the driving comfort in an urban bus.

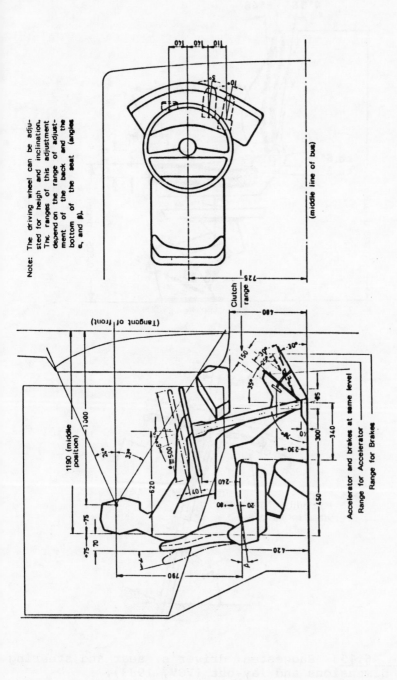

Figure 6.14: A recent ergonomic study of the driver's seat and section for the German standard SLII bus (VOV, 1983).

Note: The driving wheel can be adjusted for heigh and inclination. The ranges of this adjustment depend on the range of adjustment of the back and the bottom of the seat (angles α and β).

(middle line of bus)

Clutch range

(Tangent of front)

1190 (middle position)

Accelerator and brakes at same level
Range for Accelerator
Range for Brakes

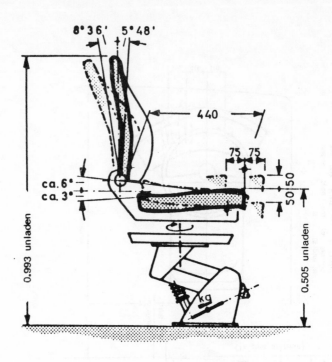

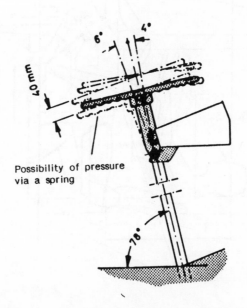

Possibility of pressure
via a spring

Figure 6.15: Suggested driver's seat and steering wheel dimensions and lay-out (VOV, 1983).

180

Finally, as regards the Instrumentation and Controls, proper relative positioning of the driver to the major vehicle dynamic and electrical controls are necessary for comfortable and safe operation of the vehicle. For the instrument panel and display the following are worth noting:

- Indicator lights should be colour-coded to distinguish between emergency or standard procedures.
- Under regular operation, the driver should not be confused by the instrument panel, i.e. only essential displays should show.
- Positioning of controls and displays should not hamper one another.

Normally all warning displays are red and regular procedure displays are either green or blue. All indicator lights are recommended to be shown with figure displays (not words) and not seen when off. Dials may be used for some indications, e.g. engine temperature, oil pressure and fuel level. Some of the desirable indicator and warning lights to be contained on the display screen include:

- speedometer
- engine temperature, oil and fuel indicators
- environmental control indicators
- various warning lights.

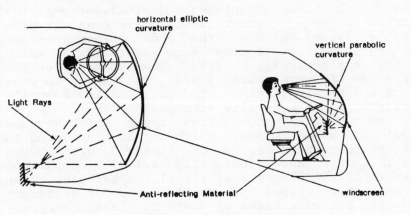

Figure 6.16: Two examples of a windscreen that reduces or eliminates reflections to the driver by focusing light rays to non-reflective dark points.

All control switches should be in one area, preferably the right side of the control panel. Internally lighted 2 or 3-way rocker switches, rotary switches, and rheostats can be used for the various electrical control functions.

THE EXTERIOR OF THE BUS

Many features of the exterior design of a bus are dominated by the decisions made concerning its interior (or passenger section). Since the doors, the system of steps, the entry/exit points and the windows have already been discussed under the general heading "the passengers section", only the exterior body shape and the lighting arrangements will be of interest here. The overall exterior dimensions of the vehicle, as well as its overall style, are also of importance.

As regards body shape, the primary requirement of the bus body design is that it suits all the needs of the interior shell. It should also have a simple and lasting style, preferably with a low profile to achieve an aesthetically pleasing appearance. Two main styles of exterior shape are the most commonly used in bus types today. The first has a "wide bottom - tapered top" shape with inwardly inclined sides. The second is the more traditional almost rectangular shape. Both have advantages and disadvantages. The positive features of the first one are that it provides a larger window area and optimum interior lighting as well as a more aerodynamic shape, which is also aesthetically pleasing. The second gives the impression of more space inside, is easier to construct and repair in cases of damage and is generally considered as structurally stronger.

Figure 6.17A shows five types (of the same shape) of urban buses, which can be considered as covering the whole range of standard urban buses today. In the same figure (Fig. 6.17B) a comparison is shown of the theoretical (line) capacity of three representative types of these buses for different headways. The advantages of scale in terms of capacity (and hence productivity of personnel) of the larger buses are evident. These advantages should of course be weighed against cost and other considerations before any meaningful selection can be made (see also section on selecting the appropriate rolling stock, below).

In Figure 6.18 drawings of standard buses used in the Federal Republic of Germany are shown. These are for urban (SLI) and interurban (Stulb) transport.

As regards the **external lights** most bus manufacturers (but also safety regulations in many individual countries) have predetermined the position and shape of the external lights. Some general comments, however, can be made and these are the following:

a. <u>Headlamps</u>. For most urban and suburban applications a pair of single lamps with a high beam and a low beam are adequate. These should preferably be of the quartz iodide low glare type to prevent discomfort to the drivers of oncoming vehicles.

b. <u>Turn Indicators</u>. Turn indicators are located on the extreme outside corners of the bus, so as to be seen clearly from the front and side or back and side. The colour is normally bright orange and the lens should have a minimum width of 10-12cm. Both the headlamps and the front turn indicators can be inset with respect to the front bumper of the bus to prevent possible damage. Additional turn indicators are suggested at the sides of the bus.

c. <u>Tail Lamps</u>. The lighting arrangement for the rear of the bus usually consists of an integrated lens design extended in the vertical or horizontal direction and located on the extreme outside corners of the back body shell. The tail lamps can also incorporate the back turn indicators. The brake lights should be of variable intensity and indicate the magnitude of the bus deceleration through the intensity of the lamp. (This feature can however be overlooked as it increases costs and can be replaced by the standard intensity red light stop lamps as in most of the bus makes today.)

Finally, as regards the **external dimensions** of the bus there is a wide variety. These depend on the carrying capacity, form of construction and maneuverability, which come with each type and make of bus. Table 6.2 shows the dimensions of three types of buses.

Medium-size Bus

Standard Bus

A

Double-decker

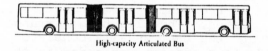

Articulated Bus

Articulated Bus

High-capacity Articulated Bus

B

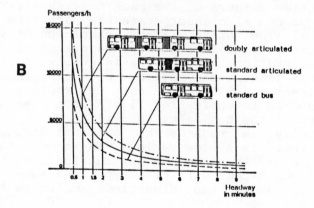

Passengers/h

doubly articulated

standard articulated

standard bus

Headway
in minutes

Figure 6.17: Five types of urban bus (A) and a comparison of 3 of them in terms of theoretical line capacity (undisturbed operation without batch operation; standing area occupied) (B).

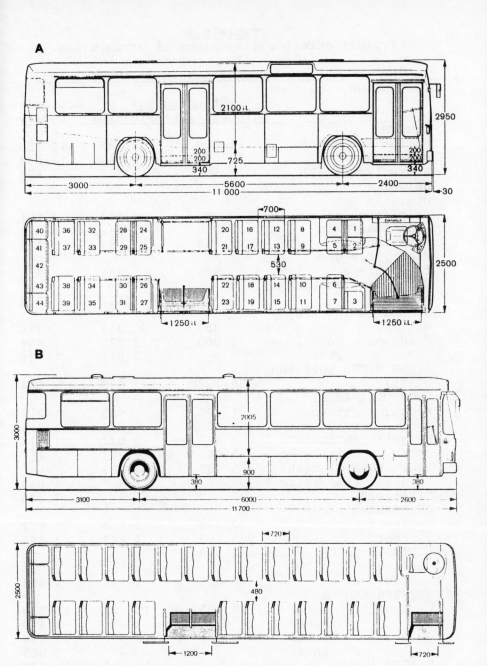

Figure 6.18: Drawings of the standard buses used in the F.R.Germany (A) the urban SLI bus, (B) the standard intercity bus (Stulb).

185

Table 6.2
Typical exterior dimensions of urban buses.

Description	Standard bus European(a)	Standard bus American(b)	Articulated(c)
LENGTH			
Bumper to bumper	11 000	12 192	18 185
Over body	10 020	12 090	18 034
WIDTH (External)	2 500	2 588	2 591
HEIGHT			
Overall:			
– at front axle	2 980	3 017	2 591
– at rear axle	3 000	3 042	3 073
– maximum	3 040	3 060	3 175
Floor from ground at front steps	920	886	955
Ground to 1st step-entrance	345	342	368
Ground to 1st step-exit	350	355	368
Headroom – normal	2 060	2 070	1 981
– rear	–	2 011	1 981
AISLE WIDTH (between seats)	950–1280	635	584
DOOR/CLEARANCE)			
Width: – entrance	1 300	965	1 214
– exit	1 300	673	1 214
Height:– entrance	2 060	2 032	1 214
– exit	2 060	1 993	2 159
WHEEL BASE (length)	5 400	7 223	–
"Tractor"(for artic.)	–	–	5 649
"Trailer"	–	–	7 300
OVERHANG			
– front	2 460	2 118	2 652
– rear	3 160	2 842	2 583
WIDTH OF TRACK	2 000		
– front	–	2 164	2 055
– rear	1 835	1 943	2 055
TURNING RADIUS			
– Wheels: – outer	10 800	11 328	11 735
: – inner	–	–	7 470
– Body : – outer	11 500	12 801	13 198
: – inner	–	–	7 803
WEIGHT (empty)in kgs	–	11 754	16 740

(a) Based on Ikarus 3-door standard model used in Athens, Greece.
(b) Based on FLYER D900 MODEL 10240 used in the US.
(c) Based on M.A.N. SG-270 Articulated model 10260.

CONSIDERATIONS REGARDING THE MECHANICAL COMPONENTS

Although the main scope of this chapter is to provide information on the parts of the rolling stock that directly affect passengers and their appraisal of a bus system, some attention should also be given to the various possibilities concerning the purely mechanical parts of a bus. This is necessary because these parts, although not affecting passengers directly, they do influence vehicle performance in terms of speed, comfort, frequency of breakdowns etc. A minimum of general knowledge about these mechanical elements of buses would be very important to planners and managers. Therefore provision of this general knowledge is attempted in the following sections.

<u>Frame and Body</u>. The frame and body include the side structures, roof, bumpers and the actual frame (if the body is not of the so called integral design).

The primary concerns in body design are safety and strength. These are of course interrelated. If sufficient structural rigidity is provided to serve under normal operation loads, in addition to withstanding rapid decelerations and inward protrusions in the event of a crash, then safety for passengers is increased. U.S. standards set by the Safety Car Program of the National Highway Safety Bureau limit inner body deformation to 7cm (3 inches) when a bus is struck by a normal vehicle at 46km/h (30 mph).

The roof of the vehicle should be able to resist collapse in the event of a roll-over.

An additional requirement for the body is that it should be constructed of durable light weight and corrosion free material that should be easy to repair in the event of damage.

The **conventional design** (known as the non-integral design) is to have a frame and independent body. The body is usually bolted to the frame. The major disadvantage of this design in bus applications is greater weight and higher ground clearance. The weight is increased mainly due to the main frame rails (chassis) underneath the vehicle and this in turn necessitates a larger engine and suspension system, while it sacrifices some of the vehicle's maneuverability. The use of such frames also means that the floor must be high enough to allow the frame adequate ground clearance and hence defeats the important objective of a lower floor, discussed earlier.

Another more modern type of construction is the so called "**integral design**" (box corner and sill

187

type). It uses no beams or major frames, but rather the shape of a lighter material to obtain the required strength. The design advantages here are that the effective "frame" is incorporated into the body of the vehicle. As a result one has a much lighter vehicle and a saving in body materials, since the metal can serve a double purpose. It is also possible to design a much lower floor, because there are no frame beams to allow for clearance.

This configuration is ideally suited to the needs of an urban bus but it must be stressed that in operations where buses are usually overloaded and the road surface is rough, the non-integral, conventional type of design should probably be preferred.

Suspension. The suspension system, in its entirety, consists of the seats themselves, the springs and dampers of the bus and the tyres. The major role is played by the so called mechanical suspension system which consists of the springs and the dampers. The two primary objectives of the suspension is to eliminate shock and to improve vehicle handling and safety characteristics. It should also be designed so as to reduce pitching and rolling motions under various acceleration conditions. In addition to supporting the vehicle under all loads, the suspension must prevent shocks from being transmitted to the body. This is necessary for a comfortable ride and for reduced vehicle component wear. Safety considerations are also important. The suspension must be designed so that the wheels maintain contact with the road surface at all times. Finally the suspension system and its related components should be as compact as possible to prevent unnecessary protrusions into the passengers compartment.

There are three major methods for providing suspension between the wheel and the body of the vehicle.

Leaf springs are the most popular and simple type of suspension. These are often used in conjunction with the solid axle design (i.e. wheel on the axle) for heavy load applications, but are poorly suited for independent suspension. The springs require a large operation area under the vehicle and this necessitates some protrusion into the passengers compartment. The leaf springs tend to lose their stiffness with time and hence require repair or replacement.

Coil springs can be used on all types of suspension systems. They are compact, relatively durable and are well suited to independent suspension systems. However, for a coil spring to be used in a vehicle with a weight such as that of a loaded bus, the spring would have to be very hard. As a result the spring would not give in for small shocks and would create a rather rough ride.

Air or hydropneumatic suspension is another technically successful possibility but not as widely used as the two previously mentioned possibilities. The reason is that this system is probably the most expensive one, but its ride characteristics are far superior. A compressible fluid such as air is kept in a bag or cylinder and this acts as the effective "spring". This method of vehicle suspension has the property of being able to absorb shocks more easily, while at the same time it supports greater loads. The rigidity of the suspension and height of the vehicle can be varied by changing the pressure of the supporting fluid. Some problems have been reported about the maintenance of the air (or other fluids) bags but these are bound to be sooner or later solved.

Steering and Maneuverability. Safety and ease of operation are the prime considerations in designing a steering system. The driver should have positive control of the vehicle under all situations and at all speeds. The vehicle must react with quick response to the driver's actions. The vehicle must also be able to rapidly maneuver in heavy traffic situations. Also components and parts related to the steering system should be designed so as to require a minimum of maintenance and have a life equal to that of the vehicle without any of the steering linkage developing "play". The main devices used to fulfil these criteria are those related to the overall design of the vehicle, such as a low centre of gravity, minimum overhangs from wheel to bumpers etc and those related to steering, mainly power steering, and a high steering lock angle.

Power Train. This term refers to all mechanical components used in accelerating or decelerating the bus. These are the engine itself, the transmission and the braking system.
a.   **The Engine.** The diesel engine is the standard in almost all types of buses today. It should have a wide power range in order to give good tractability and ease of driver control under all operating conditions and above all to have low air pollutant emissions (mainly of smoke and

189

Nitro-oxides). It should also have low noise levels and be reliable and easy to maintain. Alternatives to the diesel engine, like the kinetic energy fly wheel or electric power, are discussed in a later section when dealing with the potential future advances in bus design.

b. **The Transmission.** The power transmission system should be as efficient as possible. It should deliver the maximum amount of engine power to the rear wheels at all times. When starting to move or at low speeds the change of speeds should be made without what is known as "jerk". At high speeds the transmission should have a mechanical lock-up so that its efficiency is near 100%.

c. **Braking System.** For the braking system three simple rules apply:

1. It should provide the same maximum deceleration rate achieved by the average mid-sized car.

2. It should be such that 100% control is possible of the vehicle when it is under maximum deceleration. This means that anti-lock systems should be installed for all the brakes.

3. It should be easy to maintain and change.

SELECTING THE APPROPRIATE ROLLING STOCK

The Importance of "Appearance"

According to an earlier reference[a] on this subject (Institute for Urban Transportation, 1971) the rolling stock is the largest visible outward image of the bus agency itself. Whether or not a member of the public utilizes the bus service, he most certainly notices the bus. Regardless of the efforts on advertising, promotion and public relations, the buses themselves will most probably set the initial image of the agency in the mind of the public. Great care must therefore be exercised in selecting the rolling stock that will maintain the desired image not only when it is new, but over the years of its useful economic life.

While the outer appearance of the buses is important for initial impact and impression, the

---

[a]. This section borrows from that reference.

inner appearance is perhaps even more vital. In the passengers section, the passenger experiences the direct impact of the vehicle's qualities and this is the lasting impression, that helps to satisfy and hold customers.

As the rolling stock of a bus transport agency is going to be required to satisfy different types of customers and services, it should have the appropriate characteristics to provide a proper "mix" of services to the various segments of the market. For example, for regular route services, equipment should provide an interior lay-out that makes boarding and alighting fast and easy, provides reasonable seat comfort and sufficient room for standees to be uncrowded and so on. Since in a smaller city most passengers on regular routes will not ride for great distances, there may be no need to reach very high levels of comfort in either the seating or suspension of the vehicle. On the other hand, if streets are rough or poorly maintained, as a rule it may be wise to opt for equipment affording the smoothest ride.

For suburban services passengers often have to travel a considerable distance to reach their destination. In such cases, equipment should be carefully selected and designed to provide maximum seating capacity and comfort. It is reminded that for this reason the suggested ratios in Table 6.1 for suburban lines are distinctly smaller than those for urban lines.

Finally for special services, the particular needs of the specific service will essentially determine key features of the buses used. For instance, in gearing service to make travel easy for the handicapped, special devices may be necessary on buses. To meet the needs of those who have difficulty in moving up or down steps, the minimum number of steps of low height are needed, along with additional handrails.

Also the buses used in conjunction with demand-activated (dial-a-bus) special services should be highly maneuverable so as to be able to reach any place to which they may be called quickly and easily.

The bus should be seen as a "symbol" of public transport and can be used as a promotional device. Symbolism is very important in promotional work, a fact illustrated by the pains taken by large business firms to develop a distinctive trademark or a logo that is instantly recognizable. When the symbol is "attached" in the public's mind to a quality product, the symbol becomes a complete advertising message each time it is observed. Buses offer a unique opportunity to do so and take advantage of the symbolism a city has, or is trying to create for itself. There is a potential for tie-ins and the opportunity for public transport promotion is great. These thoughts must be taken seriously into account when buying new rolling stock and make sure from the beginning that new buses satisfy at least some of the above "appearance" considerations.

Factors Affecting the Selection of the Rolling Stock

In deciding on the equipment to be acquired, the management should start with certain broad, largely non-technical considerations based on the service functions that the given equipment is to perform. These considerations will form the basis of guidelines for developing technical specifications to be used in making valid mechanical and operating comparisons between different makes and types of equipment. Below we discuss briefly the most important of these considerations which fall under the headings:
-    demand characteristics
-    operating conditions
-    quality of the ride
-    maintenance.

Demand Characteristics. These are the first to be considered. Obviously the starting point is the calculation of the number of passengers that the vehicle may be called upon to carry at any time. However, "qualitative" aspects of the demand are also involved. For example, on a smaller transit property, where excess equipment is an expensive luxury, a vehicle needs to be versatile enough in capacity and design to be used in a variety of other services besides transit, such as school service or charters.

Equipment that meets the general demand characteristics should, of course, bear primarily some relationship to the expected volume of traffic at any one time. As a simple rule of thumb, if numerous trips per day with a large volume of customers are likely, it makes sense to have relatively large vehicles so that the customers can be handled as quickly and conveniently as possible. On the other hand, if maximum use of the vehicle in regular route service calls for the handling of relatively large numbers only once or twice a day, it would be unwise to acquire a bus with large seating capacity, only to haul around empty seats most of the time. For example if the peak hour load is 50 passengers twice a day, and if passenger loading never rises above 30 passengers at any other time, it is not worth paying a high price for the extra seats (which may mean buying a bus that costs up to twice as much) merely to meet demand ten times per week. Careful scheduling and utilization of smaller buses could alleviate the standee problem. The use of high-capacity vehicles for some other services, in addition to the regular transit service, such as lucrative weekend charters, may however make large vehicles a wise choice.

<u>Operating Conditions.</u> As regards operating conditions, these are also very important. The width and clearance of roads and streets over which service may be operated are among the first decision factors to be considered along with the sharpness of curves and corners. These conditions may severely limit the equipment that can be used.

The local topography, in terms of hills and valleys, is another important factor. Sufficient engine power must be provided to meet schedules and avoid excessive stress on engine itself. A combination of steep hills, narrow streets and tight corners calls for a bus with a high degree of maneuverability as well as power. Hilly terrain also calls for extra braking power. The combination of power and maneuverability necessary to meet operating characteristics is probably the key factor under such conditions.

Noise and air pollution are also sensitive factors. The background noise on busy streets will tend to cover the operating noise of a bus, but in quieter residential neighbourhoods, or other special land uses (e.g. churches, auditoriums etc), excessive bus noise will stand out annoyingly, as will the pounding and vibration caused by heavy buses. Transit must be a "good neighbour" in extending its reach into residential areas. It may sometimes be difficult to make very large and heavy buses acceptable by those who live along the routes.

Air pollution from buses may be a very serious problem. In the usually polluted urban areas, buses can be a formidable source of air pollution (mainly smoke and NO_x). It is sometimes to be strongly recommended to purchase buses with extra horsepower (i.e. more than would normally be needed under the foreseen operating conditions), so that the engine would work at low "non-polluting" revolutions and strain. Relative to the air pollution problem is of course also the maintenance provided.

Quality of the Ride. This concerns the comfort and quality of the ride for the passengers. The suspension of the vehicle (whether it is metal springs, tension bars or some sort of air bag system) is of primary importance in assuring overall vehicle riding comfort. Beyond that, the heating and ventilating features should be given serious thought. As a rule of thumb, all vehicles must have a good ventilating system, mechanically assisted and, in most cases, also a good heating system. In very hot or very cold climates air conditioning or heavy duty heating respectively, should also be considered.

Another important factor affecting the quality of the ride is the "feeling of spaciousness" in the vehicle. This feeling (as already said) is formed by the distances between seats, the seat arrangement, the window size and location, and even the decorations and the colours.

The level of illumination as well as a "modern" appearance of buses and (above all) their cleanliness are also very important items in passenger appeal. Exterior and interior designs should be carefully selected so that a fresh, cheerful and modern appearance can be easily maintained.

Maintenance. Finally, an important consideration in selecting a type of bus is the ease of its maintenance. Without question, the vehicle must be easy to maintain. Ease of maintenance involves not only the upkeep of the mechanical devices of the bus, but cleaning and washing as well. As many of the mechanical components of a bus as possible should be provided in a modular form so that they may be pulled out or replaced quickly and easily without putting the vehicle out of service for long periods of time. The modular approach should apply to any components likely to cause trouble. If extra initial cost is involved in purchasing buses with modular components, it must be weighed against the cost of a breakdown in service resulting from having a vehicle down as well as the cost of owning extra buses to act principally as stand-by equipment.

For purposes of the so called "housekeeping" maintenance, i.e. of the interior of the bus, this should be designed and constructed so as to avoid as many dirt-trapping surfaces or obstacles as possible. The exterior of the bus should also be so designed and constructed that it may be washed easily and quickly. The continually rising cost of labour will make it more and more expensive to provide high main-

194

tenance standards if cleaning is done by hand. Mechanical means of cleaning should be foreseen.

Small versus Large Buses

This question, which is usually asked when buying new rolling stock, is addressed here separately because of its importance. The optimum size of buses to be used depends on the operating costs in relation to the benefits that will accrue from improved frequency of service, travel times and in the end increased passenger volumes (i.e. revenues) that will be attracted to the public transport system.

Some transit managers are reluctant to buy smaller buses, pointing out that the major operating cost is the salary of the driver, which does not vary according to the size of the vehicle he operates. This is certainly a valid argument but it can be true up to a certain limit. It will be remembered that earlier on, the point was made not to have a lot of empty seats during most of the time so that we provide capacity for just a few peak hours per week. Also another thing to consider may be whether or not the vehicle itself is part of a package of service that certain parts of the public need and are willing to buy. In other words the whole service that is to be offered to the public must be examined and decided upon, before the various types of vehicles in the rolling stock is determined. For example, it may be better to own two smaller buses than one large one, if the demand is not concentrated enough. As already mentioned, unless the total demand per bus trip is high, it appears unwise to have large chunks of mostly unutilized seating capacity tied up in a given vehicle and thereby "locked" to a given route at a given time.

The trend over many years has been for operators to increase the size of the buses they use on urban services in order to provide adequate peak capacity at the lower cost per seat-kilometre which the larger buses can achieve. This trend is explicable by the fact that the operators are mainly interested in lowering their total operating costs per seat-kilometre run. However, with the many possible types of service needs in modern urban areas and the small likelihood that any one type of vehicle can satisfy all those needs, acquisition of several types of equipment may be the wisest course of action. This approach becomes very feasible and realistic as there is a large variety of different sizes, shapes and makes of buses in the market. It does however mean making sure that the equipment fits properly into the appropriate marketing mix for the area and at the same time does not render the agency's objectives and policies, with regard to cost and revenue, unobtainable.

What seems to be also important is the way in which buses of different sizes are run in the system. A recent study by TRRL (Oldfield and Bly, 1985) tried to calculate the net benefit (both economic and social) of running different sizes of buses in central London. It concluded that small buses operated in competition with existing services, and using the same routes as big buses, so that most passengers could catch either type of bus, depending on which one arrived first, would easily attract sufficient revenue to cover their costs and would provide a net social benefit. By contrast, small buses operated on services which are physically separate from those of big buses and competing with them would in most circumstances find it difficult to break even.

Some Final Remarks

Some final points of interest need to be mentioned here concerning the rolling stock of an agency.

The first point concerns the provision for the replacement of buses at a staggered pace so as to avoid serious replacement costs if all buses reach replacement age at the same time.

This is a very important consideration, especially for a transit firm starting from scratch. If at the start similar rolling stock is acquired all at one time, it will tend to wear out all at about the same time. Unless a transit enterprise foresees a steady enlargement of service over its first four or five years of operation, so that several new buses will be added each year, both new and used equipment should be included in the initial fleet. Some of the older buses should only be kept for a year or two and should then be replaced by new equipment.

Ideally, a bus agency adds some new vehicles each year. This practice will help keep the average age of the fleet low. It will also prevent the need for very large capital expenditure every ten or twelve years. The constant influx of new equipment should also help to maintain a good image for the service.

A second point relates to the need to provide proper **maintenance facilities** for the types of buses

196

used. Many bus manufacturers require the existence of proper maintenance facilities as part of the contract for selling the buses. This question of maintenance is very important and will to be considered separately below.

BASIC MAINTENANCE FACILITIES AND EQUIPMENT

The facilities described here form what can be called a typical maintenance depot for a medium-sized bus agency. Smaller agencies may have to combine some of these facilities to simplify operations, or they may even do their maintenance on a contract basis with outside garages. Larger agencies on the other hand, may require a more sophisticated type of facilities and they almost certainly need to have more than one depots (average number of buses per depot 200-300). A typical maintenance facility therefore in the above sense would include the following parts[b].

1. **Maintenance Pit or Hoist Area.** The maintenance pit provides a simple means of daily undercarriage inspection. A mechanical hoist takes a little longer per vehicle to operate; however, it is more useful for steam cleaning of bus undercarriage, engine work, tyre changes and brake work. The pit is excellent when used for preventive maintenance on brakes, since it simplifies weekly adjustments, which may take only three to five minutes. Hydraulic hoists have the disadvantage that they require maintenance and higher costs of purchase but, unlike the pit, people cannot fall into them nor can a careless driver drive a bus over the edge into it. Small-scale bus operations may not need both of them, but it appears more useful for maximum maintenance efficiency to have both. If an operation were to have just one facility, the pit would probably be the best choice. A **steam cleaner** should be located somewhere near the pit or hoist area. The steam cleaner is important in order to clean the engine and engine parts regularly to reduce the danger from fire due to accumulation of

---

[b]. This section draws from a variety of sources but mainly from the Institute for Urban Transportation (1971) and the author's own experience from the Urban Bus Corporation in Greater Athens.

grease and dirt and also to enable the maintenance inspectors to see the parts clearly. If
the parts cannot be closely observed, inspectors
may miss heat spots and friction points that
should be noted and repaired for proper preventive maintenance. The undercarriage also needs
to be steam cleaned periodically.

2. <u>Body Shop and Paint Shop</u>. Both of these areas
would be found in all but the smallest agencies,
where they may have to be combined with other
facilities. Current experience shows that, if a
company has between 40 and 100 buses, one will
be in the body shop and one in the paint shop
each day. Naturally for more than 100 buses
these facilities will be busier.

3. <u>Machine Shop</u>. This is the area where proper repair work can be carried out on the mechanical
parts of the vehicles that are on repair at the
pit or hoist area. For a small agency a complete
machine shop may not be very practical. Much of
this work may be contracted out. But, in properties with more than 60 or 70 buses, a machine
shop with a lathe, valve grinder and other small
repair tools would definitely be needed.

4. <u>The store and stock rooms</u>. The store room is
used to store large items such as rebuilt engines and transmissions. If the agency is far
from a supplier of this type of equipment, it
may be very important for interruption-free
service to keep a spare engine and transmission
on hand.
    The stock room is a basic area for spare
part storage and inventory control. All parts
are stored there, to be placed in service on the
buses at a later date. Each item is checked out
through this room. Inventory counts and records
are kept there and the stock room can also be
used for employee time cards, records, work reports etc.

5. <u>Maintenance Superintendent's Office</u>. The Maintenance Superintendent's Office is the centre of
maintenance operations. It is the origin point
for work orders and the place where information
is gathered for a study of improvements in maintenance. This office need not be large, but it
should be located close to the site of opera-

tions for purposes of close supervision and intervention in the work.

6. **Fueling and Service Area**. This is the area, used for fueling, day to day servicing (if necessary) and fueling inspections. It is necessary and recommended for even the smallest agencies, although in actual practice many small agencies have their buses fuelled and serviced at normal petrol stations, just as they do their overall maintenance and repair works on a contractual basis at outside garages. If a fueling and service area exists here checks of coolant levels, oil levels and torque fluids are done there, as well as the fueling of the buses. The fueling area need not be connected directly to the maintenance facility. Whether it is or not depends on the amount of space available and the actual "fuelling" practice of the agency.

What is definitely recommended, especially for warm climates, is to have a roof over the fuelling area. It is also necessary to have there some provision for cleaning the interior of the bus. On a very small property, the cleaning job may have to be done manually. If so, the bus should not be cleaned in the fueling area, but in a parking area adjacent to it. If the cost of a mechanical cleaner can be justified, it should be placed at the end of the fueling and service area and should be used while the bus is being serviced.

7. **Wash Area**. The wash area is a necessity, if equipment is to be kept attractive in appearance. Financial constraints will determine whether a mechanical washer can be used. Initial cost of a mechanical washing system is relatively high but, given the need to keep buses clean and the ever increasing cost of manpower, it is usually worth its investments except perhaps for very small agencies.

8. **Storage Tanks for Fuel and Oil.** Storage tanks for fuel and / or oil are needed, if these operations are done by the agency itself. The suggested method is to have these tanks underground. There are also advantages of storing fuel and oil in large tanks. Although such tanks are costly, scale advantages may be apparent because large tanks enable the agency to buy at

the best bulk discount and through competitive bidding. However, the size of the facility has a limit and it is always wise to provide contingencies for the worst. So if fuel use makes it necessary to have say a 12000-gallon capacity, it is probably wise to have two 6000-gallon tanks to allow for possible tank breakdowns, even though this practice may increase the total cost per gallon stored.

9.   <u>Overnight Bus Parking Facilities</u>. Overnight parking is necessary to avoid theft or damage to the buses when parking them at the curbs of urban streets. It is also important to have an overnight parking to avoid blocking the urban streets with parked buses, a practice that is strongly undesirable not only by the local authorities and residents but also for the image of the bus agency itself.

Overnight parking space is usually combined within the same area where maintenance is held. Obviously the cheapest method is to provide outdoor parking space for the buses since the cost of construction and upkeep of a covered area is usually high. However, a more careful look at the matter may provide a different view.

Outdoor parking is harder on paint and other exterior parts, causes more wear and incurs expense due to vandalism. In cases of (usually older) buses without oil-sealed axles, lubricants do not serve their purpose and fail to keep friction at a minimum when buses are kept outside in the cold. This factor is particularly important for the first few kilometres each day and obviously more so in colder climates.

Sometimes even the construction of a less expensive, aluminium (or steel) shelter may be used as an adequate alternative to a fully covered parking space.

In calculating the space requirements for a bus parking facility a minimum of 50 sq.m. per bus should be provided to allow for parking and easy entry/exit manoeuvres in the area.

TECHNOLOGICAL ADVANCES IN URBAN BUS DESIGN

In this final section we consider it appropriate to give in a summary form what can be considered as the most realistic possibilities for improved technology to be applied in urban buses in the near future. Some of this technology is already here and applied in a limited scale and/or on a trial basis. Other technological advances are still at an experimental stage but may well be in actual application in the foreseeable future.

Optimization of the Diesel Engine and the Transmission

Fuel consumption of urban buses is greatly influenced by the special operating mode of these vehicles, which comprises the following phases: full-throttle acceleration, travel at constant road speed, braking and stop. As distances between stops diminish, overall consumption is increasingly influenced by the amount of fuel used in the acceleration phase. This fact has been taken into account in industry's efforts to optimize this drive cycle with a view to both reducing the fuel consumption and improving the efficiency of the bus engine. The following improvements have been investigated and are being gradually introduced in buses in recent years:

Improvements on the engine:
- Improved fuel injection system (injection nozzles, injection pressure).
- Matching of torque curve to the specific operating conditions.

Improvements on the automatic transmission:
- Matching of torque converter.
- Lowering of "headshift" point.
- Reduction of losses at idling speed and of losses through friction.
- Optimal choice of gear ratios and of number of gears.

Improvements on the vehicle:
- Optimal choice of rear-axle ratio.
- Reduction of rolling resistance and drag.

The above improvements have resulted in a reduction of about 15% in the fuel consumption of city buses without reducing performance (M.A.N., 1985).
Reduction of driver influence on the driving

201

"style", offers additional potential for fuel saving. "Intelligent" control systems which can register and process fuel consumption characteristics are being investigated. Such engine-transmission management systems will enable the driver to program his bus for optimal fuel consumption or for top performance, whichever is desired.

Regeneration of Braking Energy

Urban buses, which operate in stop-and-go mode, are braked very frequently. Fuel consumption can be reduced by partial regeneration of braking energy. There are various types of systems. For example, one well known system uses a mechanical accumulator (flywheel) which accumulates energy during braking and gives it back to help the engine during acceleration. Another system utilizes a pressurized gas accumulator.

Both systems demand a continuously variable transmission. During the braking phase, the vehicle's kinetic energy is transmitted via the continuously variable transmission from the driving wheels to the energy accumulator, raising the pressure in the hydraulic storage tank or increasing the rotation speed of the flywheel, as the case may be. During the acceleration phase the above process is reversed, thus "giving back" the energy that otherwise would be lost during the braking phase.

The energy accumulators should be kept as small as possible in order to minimize weight and keep accumulator losses as low as possible. A two-axle bus should not need an energy accumulator capacity larger than 200-300 Wh. Energy savings of 20-30%, depending on operational mode of the vehicle, may be possible.

Alternative Fuels

Alternative fuels such as methanol, LPG, LNG etc have already been used in urban buses with mixed results.
The main advantages include:
a.   Exhaust gases are free of sulphur and soot, as well as smoke, thus making these fuels environmentally more acceptable.
b.   There is not such a great dependence on fossil fuels.
Disadvantages include:
a.   Because of the "closed" system (under pressure or low-temperature) the fuel system is more so-

phisticated and the lower calorific value of these fuels makes a fuel tank of roughly double volume necessary for a given operating range.
b.   Fuel consumption in relation to calorific value is, because of the Otto combustion system, higher than that in the case of diesel combustion.

Buses using such alternative fuels are already in full operation in Vienna, Berlin, Auckland, Los Angeles and other cities.

Electric Buses

Electric drive systems have long equipment lives, require little maintenance and do not have polluting emissions. Against these advantages is the disadvantage of higher initial costs. "Electric" buses may be of three main types.

The first type concerns the normal trolley buses operating in many cities and taking their energy from overhead wires, a fact that creates, flexibility and visual obstruction problems.

The second type is the battery electric bus taking its power from batteries. This technology is still under development. Its main problems are the weight of the batteries and the small "autonomy" of the bus before recharging them.

The final type is the so called dual energy bus, operating with two completely independent drive systems, one diesel and one electric. In areas where the diesel operation is environmentally unacceptable (e.g. tunnels, CBD's etc) the bus is switched to electric operation. In all other areas it operates as a normal diesel bus. The main advantage of such dual-mode buses is on the flexibility they offer with respect to the protection of the environment, while they do not have the disadvantages of the electric mode buses, mainly the frequent recharges of their batteries, as in the case of the all electric bus, or the overhead wires in all their network of lines as in the case of trolley-buses. A large fleet of dual-energy buses is planned for the city of Seattle in the US, while cities around the world are considering the same option.

Automatic Guidance Systems for Buses

Automatic guidance is an effort to make buses match the efficiency of Light Rail Systems, in terms of speed and capacity. They give the possibility for otherwise normal buses to become "track guided", thus dramatically improving their line capacity characteristics like any other rail system. There are two alternative forms of bus guidance.

A. Mechanical or Track Guidance

Mechanical guidance systems necessitate specially equipped buses and tracks. Relevant equipment on the bus consists of a rigid feeler arm with a feeler roller, bolted to the steering knuckle (see Figure 6.19). The guide curbs on the road, can be of metal or concrete. The curb rails and the roadway form a trough in which the bus drives. This trough gives the bus a protected right of way. The feeler rollers are pressed against the curb rails and follow their course.

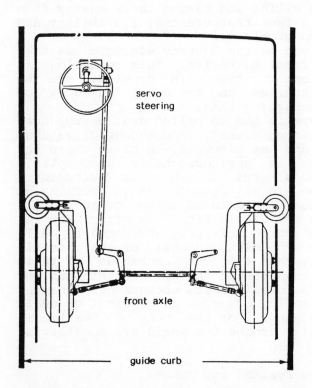

servo steering

front axle

guide curb

Figure 6.19: Diagrammatic representation (left) and actual photograph (right) of a bus track guidance system with feeler arm and guide curb.

The bus following a track guidance system is steered along the course of the "guide" curbs solely by the feeler device. A setting device on the feeler arm allows track width to be adjusted and feeler roller wear to be compensated. This track guidance system makes a marked reduction in bus lane width possible. The resulting savings in construction costs are particularly significant for such works as tunnels, bridges etc. The most well known such systems are developed and already in trial operation by both M.A.N. and Mercedes in the Federal Republic of Germany.

Problems arise with mechanical guidance at junctions. Here the following possibilities exist:

a. Normal junctions without guidance system. Here the bus is driven, like any normal bus, by its driver on the driving wheel.

b. "Active" points. These are guidance structures resembling rail crossings. They are, however, complicated and should only be used where a central control room is responsible for setting the points.

c. "Passive" points. Here the bus driver determines the direction he wants to follow and directs the vehicle until the feeler roller touches the guide rail on the appropriate arm of the junction. A control system regulates the adhesion pressure on the guide rail. Steering right or left is done by the driver through a switch on the instrument board.

A version of the track guidance system doing away with the curblike guidance tracks and using only a central, very light, track in the form of a 4 cm "crack" in the roadway, is the GLT (for Guided Light Transit) system developed by GN of Belgium and soon beginning operation in Rochefort, Belgium.

The greatest advantage of the GLT system is its simple and not obstructing guidance structure. This advantage is particularly important for the junctions, which, because of the very light "track", can be negotiated easily by all vehicles.

B. Electronic Track Guidance

This is done by a pilot cable buried in the roadway, through which an alternating current flows, generating an electromagnetic field fed by an emitter at the roadside. The equipment on the bus consists of antennas, a supplementary hydraulic servo-steering system and the electronic controls. For safety reasons the entire system is usually of dual-channel (redundant) design. This system in diagrammatic form is shown in Figure 6.10.

The two steering channels alternate constantly. Each of these two functional groups of the active system of electronic steering unit can steer the vehicle independently.

A simulation computer and a fail-safe monitor, guarantee safe and reliable operation. All conceivable errors and failures, even fracture of the pilot cable, can be so monitored and corrected as to completely eliminate danger.

The great advantage of the electronic guidance is the simple and not obstructing solution for the guidance, which now does not require any impeding structures on the road surface. This fact greatly simplifies switches and crossings. Both "active" and

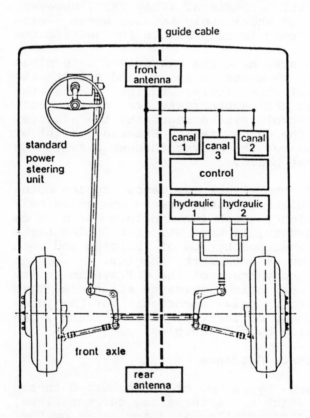

Figure 6.20: Diagrammatic representation of the electronic track guidance system.

206

"passive" junctions are possible in simple form, e.g. by switching the current in the control centre from one pilot cable to another or by the driver's switching to different frequencies in the pilot cables.

Some Concluding Remarks

The advances in technology, which were briefly described above, show that the bus can be much more than just a vehicle "swimming" along in the general traffic stream and having stops which are nothing more than just a post on the edge of the sidewalk. The developments already in the horizon show that it is well worth exploiting the unused reserves of the bus as a means of mass transport in urban areas. The components of the whole system, i.e. the "vehicle", the "roadway/bus stop" and the "operational control", can be improved so as to form a comprehensive package from which each public transport authority can tailor a system fitting perfectly into its overall transit concept.

The bus has the great advantage over rail transport that each individual measure or action, that is planned, can be immediately put to practical use, allowing a system to be built up stage by stage. In times of economic uncertainty, when difficulties are encountered in financing large-scale public investment, the appeal of public transit operations can be considerably increased for a relatively modest capital investment by upgrading the bus to a "bus transit system".

The above real possibilities are worth examining seriously according to the specific needs of each urban area. Needless to say, that, for the bulk of the normal day to day operations for public transport in the majority of urban areas, the internal combustion (thermal) buses, as we know them to date, will continue to dominate the scene for many years to come.

7 Guidelines for the operation

The "operation" of a bus system entails the use of a number of rules and the implementation of decisions that aim at the best possible utilization of the human and other resources of the operating agency, and providing an efficient service to the public. The items, that are of interest and can be said to determine the whole quality operation, are:

- the occupancy rates of the buses
- the frequency of the schedules
- the average waiting times at bus stops
- the reliability of the timetables
- the hours of operation
- the number of transfers
- the safety record.

In addition, a major element of the operation is the fare policy. This affects the overall levels of patronage, their distribution in time during the day and the overall perception of the bus system in the eyes of the travelling public as an alternative to other modes.

BUS OCCUPANCY

Bus occupancy is defined as the average number of passengers per bus for a given period of time and for a given part of the network. Usually, the peak periods of operation are considered, because these are the ones most likely to exceed the predetermined limits of occupancy. The idea is that, if the (average) bus occupancy over a certain part of the network and for a given time period exceeds the desired limits, then more buses should have to be scheduled, i.e. the frequency of service should be increased. If the situation is left without such actions, then the resulting congestion and the overloading of buses would result in passenger dissatisfaction and possible change of mode, bad image for the system, great ware and tare of the rolling stock, greater environmental pollution by the overloaded engines, and reduced safety.

The usual way to express the occupancy rate of a bus, is to use the ratio of the total number of passengers to the number of seats (or seated passengers). For example, an occupancy rate of 1.25 (or 125%) means that there are standees equal to the 25% of the seats, an occupancy rate of 1.00 (or 100%) means that there are no standees and all seats are occupied, and so on.

Suggested limits as to the occupancy rates according to the type of bus route, are given in Table 7.1. These are suggestions based on existing practice on several European bus networks but can and should be adjusted to suit specific local conditions.

To be able to monitor occupancy rates regularly so as to establish whether the limits are exceeded, it is necessary to measure the occupancy with an easy and reliable method. In chapter 3 some bus passenger counting methods were mentioned, and these can be used for determining bus occupancies too. However, if the agency does not have a more permanent programme for surveys and counts, as it was contemplated in chapter 3, a very simple method for determining the bus occupancy rates is as follows.

One or two observers (depending on the frequency of passing buses) count the number of standees per bus for a certain time period (usually the highest 30 minutes of the peak, or the whole 2-hour peak). The average number of standees per bus for the time period examined, added to the number of seats and divided by the same number of seats, is the occupancy rate. An adequately organized agency would normally keep records of bus occupancy rates per line at its busiest points. If the limits suggested in Table 7.1 (or whatever ones the agency establishes) are exceeded for more than say 30% of the time (i.e. 2 days a week or 10 days a month), then action should be taken to increase the frequencies of the schedules (or to use bigger buses).

Table 7.1

Suggested upper limits of bus occupancy rates

Type of line	Indic. length one way line	Maximum average occupancy rate(*)for time period:		
		30 highest minutes	peak hour (total)	off-peak
Urban feeder	1.5 kms	2.00	1.75	1.10
Urban local	2 kms	2.00	1.50	1.00
Urban long distance	3-4 kms	1.75	1.25	1.00
Suburban	5 kms	1.25	1.00	1.00
Inter-urban	>20 kms	1.00	1.00	1.00

(*) Ratio of total to seated passengers.

SCHEDULE FREQUENCY - AVERAGE WAITING TIME AT BUS STOPS

The schedule frequencies are directly influencing the average waiting time at bus stops and this is why they are examined together. The frequency of a bus service depends primarily on the level of passenger "demand" for the service. The procedure for calculating the bus timetables and schedules has as a major step the determination of the bus frequencies based on the demand characteristics of the line (see for example Ceder, 1986 for a detailed description of the various alternative methods).

In cases where the existing demand does not "guarantee" a certain acceptable level of bus frequency, a minimum should be kept irrespective of whether there is demand or not. This is necessary in order to provide a minimum of accessibility to a given area and also to provide a picture of the "reliability" of public transport for the travelling public. This also helps to avoid getting into a "vicious circle" with respect to ridership, i.e. as the frequency drops, passengers will be further discouraged from using the service, thus resulting to more cuts in frequencies etc. So, if at the end of a service evaluation process (see chapter 4), the line is found not to be worth keeping, then it can be stopped altogether but, if it is kept, it must maintain a minimum of an acceptable frequency.

Table 7.2 shows the suggested minimum bus frequencies in the above sense. These minimum frequencies vary according to the type of bus route, the time of day and the size of the urban area. As long as the published timetables are followed fairly exactly, the waiting times at bus stops can be kept small (of the order of 5-10 minutes). Schedules with frequencies smaller that 6 or 7 minutes are not memorized and thus the average waiting time at the stop is taken simply as half of the frequency. The frequencies suggested in table 7.2 are again meant to be indicative. They should be adjusted taking into account local conditions and practices.

Table 7.2

Suggested minimum bus frequencies (in minutes between successive buses)

Type of line	Peaks			Off-peaks		
	Population (000's) :			Population (000's):		
	5-20	20-60	>60	5-20	20-60	>60
Urban feeder	20'	20'	15'	(a)	(a)	(a)
Urban local	30'	20'	15'	60'	50'	30'
Urban long distance	30'	30'	20'	60'	50'	50'
Suburban	40'	40'	30'	120'	90'	60'
Mixed (urban+suburban)	30'	30'	30'	90'	60'	60'

(a) Minimum frequency to depend on that of the main bus line.

RELIABILITY OF BUS TIMETABLES

The term "reliability" is used to express a measure of the adherence of buses to their predetermined (published or unpublished) timetables. It is usually expressed as the percentage of "punctual" bus arrivals to a certain stop with respect to the total number of arrivals (e.g. 90% punctual arrivals).

Punctuality is a notion that needs further definition. A bus is considered to be "punctual" if it arrives within a given time interval from its scheduled time of arrival. An acceptable such interval is usually between 0 and 5 minutes either before or after the scheduled time.

The acceptable reliability percentage varies according to the frequency of buses. The higher the frequency (i.e. the smaller the time interval between buses), the less important is the question of reliability. On the contrary, as frequency decreases, reliability should get higher.

For urban areas a reasonable standard is that bus lines with frequencies lower than two buses per hour should have a reliability of more than 90%. This means that buses should be expected to arrive within 0 to 5 minutes from the scheduled time of arrival in more than 90% of the cases. For frequencies of more than two buses per hour, the reliability factor could drop to 80%.

The reliability of bus schedules is a serious element of the analysis of the service provided and is one of the factors determining a successful operation. Two of the major causes of a reduced reliability are the traffic congestion and the inadequate (or even non existent) supervision. Both causes can be manipulated to a great extent by the planning authorities or the operator. The first, by giving buses priority over the rest of the traffic (see chapter 8) and the second, by employing and training appropriate numbers of personnel.

HOURS OF OPERATION

The period of operation of a bus service can have serious consequences on the operating costs of the agency but also on the service offered to the public. Depending, for example, on the labour legislation of each country or area, an extension of a bus service for one hour in the evening, beyond the normal 7 or 8-hour shifts, can add from 30% to 100% or even more to the operating cost per bus-kilometre during these hours. Although extending the hours of operation can add substantially to the operating costs of the agency, this may well be worth, especially for the early morning hours when people travel for the journey to work.

The hours of operation in the morning will have to be established according to the size of the urban area (influencing the average travel time from home to work), the socioeconomic characteristics of the areas served, and the possibilities of the agency itself. For the evening hours of operations, again the pattern of travel to and from the areas served by buses will have to be examined.

Unless these factors are evaluated (and this can only be done locally for the specific area under consideration), there is no meaningful suggestion that can be given concerning the hours of operation.

NUMBER OF TRANSFERS

The number of transfers required from one bus to the other for somebody to reach his/her destination is a factor seriously affecting the choice of mode. As a general rule, travellers do not like having to change buses. This may be acceptable in the case of relatively long journeys from a local feeder line to a "central" one with greater speed and capacity provided that there are proper transfer facilities and short waiting times involved.

Normally, people do not accept more than one transfer. If more than one transfers are necessary, the great majority of "non-captive" passengers will choose another mode. This must be kept in consideration when planning (or reorganizing) the network of bus lines. As a general rule of thumb, an "orthogonal" type of bus network increases the number of transfers, as compared to a radial one (see also chapter 5).

An indicative number of the level of transfers, that may be acceptable within a bus system, would be one transfer for up to 15% of the trips and two or more for up to 5% of the trips. These figures apply only in the case of a bus (or bus-like) system being the only mode of public transport in the area. When other modes operate, e.g. rail or metro lines, the number of transfers between buses and these high capacity lines will inevitably be higher than the figures mentioned above.

A tricky point, concerning the number of transfers, is how to measure them. Normal statistics kept by bus agencies do not include this type of information. Nevertheless, if one is planning to reorganize the network of bus lines or is to introduce a new mode of public transport in the area (e.g. a new LRT line), the number of transfers before and after the change could provide a helpful measure of comparison.

The most common method of measuring the number of transfers is through on-board questionnaire surveys. A sample of buses per line (of the order of 10-20%) is included in the survey and people are asked 2 or 3 very simple questions (e.g. their origin, their destination and whether or not they are going to use more than one buses). Questions about the number of transfers can also be asked within other wider scope surveys such as for example household interview surveys and on-board O-D surveys.

SAFETY OF OPERATIONS

Finally, the question of safety for passengers and personnel is discussed here. This is a self-evident objective. A small number of accidents for a certain amount of travel may be considered as "normal", i.e. within statistically expected limits. However, if the number of accidents starts rising and exceeds a certain acceptable level, the bus agency must take specific steps to investigate and reduce the accident causing factors.

The most common indicators that can be used to express the safety level of a certain bus transport operation, are:

a. The total number of accidents per 100,000 vehicle-kilometres run. As "accidents" are meant here all accidents involving humans (passengers or pedestrians) and property. Values of 0.45 to 1.8 accidents per 100000 vehicle-kilometres (on a yearly basis) are usually considered as "normal" figures.

b. Another possible indicator is the number of accidents involving passengers, per million passengers carried. Here the "normal" levels are between 4 and 10 accidents per million passengers.

The low values of the above indicators have the meaning that anything below them indicates a very high level of safety, while values above the upper limits indicate that the system is "unsafe".

FARES AND FARE POLICY

Some General Remarks

The system of fares and the agency's fare policy are perhaps the most important single elements of the bus operation that affect the travel behaviour of passengers.

Traditionally, the fares charged have always occupied a central position from the business management and market economy points of view as well as for the operating results and the demand for transport. The principle that the fare structure is not only a metre of costing but also involves evaluation of the market, whereby the passenger ascribes a certain advantage to the transport service, is generally accepted. In many countries the bus fares are centrally regulated, so as to achieve wider social and economic objectives, but in general it can be stated that the overall aim is to ensure optimum utilization of the existing operating capacity and operating performance within acceptable revenue levels. This means that not only the effect of fare changes on the number of passengers but also the effect on revenue is of particular interest. What applies in other sectors of trade and industry also applies to bus transport, i.e. with a given combination of operating and transport area structures, agency size and costs, the maximum revenue is achieved at the fare at which marginal costs and marginal revenue are identical. It is not the purpose of this book to go into a lengthy analysis of the economics of fare structures and costs of a bus agency. The interest reader is referred to other more specialized references (see for example CUTA, 1985, chapter 9, Talley, 1988, Nash, 1982). What will be attempted here is a presentation of generally accepted principles and practices regarding fares, all in line with the emphasis of this chapter in "operation".

The Importance of Cost Analysis

The analysis of the cost structure of the agency is the starting point for establishing the fare structure and levels in a given operation. In doing so it is advisable to establish not only the total costs of the existing operation but also the marginal costs, i.e. the costs of producing an additional unit of "output" (in this case a passenger or passenger-kilometre). An approximate estimate of the marginal costs can be obtained by breaking down the different types of costs into fixed (i.e. not changing with the amount of output produced) and variable costs.

Variations in the degree of capacity utilization lead to better or worse utilization of seats without any substantial change in the costs of the operating capacity. It is generally assumed that the fixed costs, i.e. those not dependent on the change in seat utilization, account on average for about 95% of the total costs, provided that the change in seat utilization is within certain limits.

Variable costs are those incurred when the operating capacity is transformed into transport output, e.g. additional ticket collection costs, the small increase in fuel costs, taxes on revenue etc. These are usually extremely low, and can be equated with the marginal costs. If the marginal costs vary over a relatively wide range, fare graduation based on the marginal costs can be recommended. If the differences in the marginal costs are very small, this procedure is virtually impossible when fixing a fare structure, which is then determined only by the demand elasticity.

Form and Limits of Fare Differentiation

It can be derived from the above considerations that a bus operator is not compelled to fix a standard fare for all services, but he can differentiate the fares and take the demand elasticity into account. The short-distance urban bus agencies, whose cost structure is characterised by a high proportion of fixed costs, as already outlined, can increase the utilization of their capacities by fare differentiation. The aim will be to increase the number of passengers and also the revenue. Fare differentiation charges the costs of the different transport services according to the demand elasticity, by seeking to sell transport services at higher prices, the less elastic the demand, and at lower prices, the more elastic is the demand (see also next section).

There are several forms of fare differentiation. There is for example "spatial" differentiation, i.e. when the fares are graduated according to distance,

217

or "temporal" differentiation, when they are differentiated according to time of day, i.e. fares are
reduced during slack periods and increase during peak
periods. Spatial differentiation is often practised,
sometimes in conjuction with socio-political considerations, whereas the temporal one is hardly ever
used. In contrast with other branches of the economy
in which prices are increased when demand is high,
urban transport undertakings are more likely to offer
lower fares in the form of discounted season tickets
during peak hours. (However, most transport agencies
add surcharges on the normal fares, in the form of an
excess fare for travel on night services.

Another form of fare differentiation is based on
the quantity of travel, i.e. passengers who buy a
mutliple-journey ticket or season ticket receive a
discount in comparison with passengers who make only
occasional use of the transport service.

Finally, fares can be differentiated if the
transport services are intended for specific purposes, e.g. for school children, apprentices and students, who are travelling to school or their work-
place and whose fares differ from the normal fares.

Fare Levels and Demand Elasticity

In examining the options for a fare policy the
bus agency must have a good understanding of the "demand" for bus travel in the area. When considering
"demand", the first thing realised is that the demand
for transport services must always consist of "derived requirements". In other words, the demand for
transport services arises in conjuction with the pursuit of productive activities or consumption. The
extent of the "need" for transport is thus determined
by many factors only some of which can be controlled
by the bus agency. One of them is certainly related
to the fares, i.e. the price at which the transport
service is offered. Thus a crucial factor in evaluating a fare structure is the reaction of passengers to
fare changes, i.e. the elasticity of demand after an
increase or reduction of fares. The price elasticity
of demand plays an important role in determining the
market position and thus the profitability of the bus
agency. Unfortunately, the research on the relationship between demand and fare changes, in general, is
far from being complete in the case of short-distance
passenger transport. Opinion polls often give widely
varying results and are sometimes even contradictory,
as evidenced, for example, by the many public opinion

polls concerning "free" travel. Unlike business in other sectors of the economy, transport agencies cannot take a uniformly reacting demand as a basis. Price elasticity is not the same for the various types of passengers, on different route sections and at different times. Hence, accurate measurement of price elasticity, as can be done in other branches of the economy, is virtually impossible, in the case of urban transport.

However, there are considerable possibilities of empirical calculation. The transport agencies have long been trying to establish the effect of fare changes on demand by means of statistical surveys. On the basis of the data obtained from these surveys, they are generally able to estimate the trend in transport services for one to two years, if normal economic conditions prevail. It can be deduced from most of these experiences that progressive percentage fare increases lead to a decline in the number of passengers. Assuming that the number of passengers would fall by 2-3% even without any fare increases, because some passengers would desert public transport for reasons other than fare increases, experience so far has indicated that a mean fare increase of up to 5% would not trigger any demand reaction, i.e. small fare increases do not cause any re-appraisal of attitudes. This is attributable inter alia to the fact that, normally, travelling costs are generally small in comparison with income: the proportion of fares in income, e.g. for travel to work, has declined over the last few years in Europe. It has often become so small that the passenger does not even look for a cheaper alternative. In Greece, for example, it is estimated that only 2.5 to 4% of the income of a worker's household is spent on public transport for journeys to and from work.

An accurate analysis of demand in the case of fare changes would have to be based on various factors, such as the fare, motor car ownership, timetables, parking policies, working hours and so on. However, these factors can generally be assessed only inadeaquately in practice because of the lack of suitable statistics. An analysis of statistical results in a large number of towns and cities in the Federal Republic of Germany over eleven years (UITP data for 1969-1980) revealed a mean fare elasticity of 0.27-0.33%, i.e. a mean fare increase of 10%, for example, during this period led to a 3% fall in demand. Experience has also shown that different passenger categories react differently to fare changes.

Season-ticket holders generally react less strongly to a fare increase than those who use public transport only occasionally. If the fare structure is not modified, the demand of the different groups can be determined and an insight into the various reactions to fares thus obtained. The fare system and the types of fares also to some extent enable the regular passenger not to desert public transport completely, even if he has a car available.

Experience has also shown that there is less reaction to a fare reduction than to a fare increase, as evidenced by the fares for off-peak periods. A fare reduction must be substantial, if it is to lead to an increase in demand.

To summarize, it can be stated that general methods of estimating the price elasticity of demand are possible and are being practiced by many bus agencies. It is recommended that the urban bus transport agencies base their fare decisions on concrete information and estimations of the price elasticity.

FARE SYSTEMS

In the following a distinction is made between fare systems and types of fares. By the "fare system" is meant the general structure of the fares in an area, while the term types of fares refers mainly to the way the fares are paid for, by passengers.

Flat Fares

In the flat fare system the fare is charged regardless of the distance covered. The flat fare offers a number of widely known advantages, particularly in connection with fare collection in the vehicle. It permits rapid cash transactions, which are particularly important on large vehicles and for one-man operation, and generally simplifies fare collection. It also permits easy inspection of passenger's tickets and checking of ticket stocks.

The chief disadvantage of the flat fare is that it does not take into account the opportunities offered by fare differentials in attracting short distance passengers. The flat fare generally appears logical, where the journey lengths of most passengers are similar. This becomes particularly clear if the transport area is confined and the residential areas are generally sited "concentrically" round the town centre.

The wider the difference between the mean journey length and the "most frequent", the greater may be the adverse effect on short-distance passengers, while long-distance passengers enjoy correspondingly advantageous fares.

The flat fare is applied less frequently today in its true, classical form and more in combination with other fare systems. For example, there have been different variants on the flat fare, such as the route-related flat fare or, in particular, the flat fare with a preceding short stage.

The route-related fare can be used if the journey length structure of the catchment area does not allow general application but permits it in certain cases of specific routes.

The most important variant of the flat fare is its supplementation by a short distance fare. This avoids the disadvantages for short-distance passengers, who have to pay the same fare as passengers travelling longer distances. The short-distance fare is generally charged in town centres or for a specific number of stops in the entire transport area. Basically, such a fare includes elements of the stage fare and it may also resemble the zonal fare. In this case we are dealing with a combined fare. Its use is often restricted to certain times, e.g. the period after the morning peak.

Distance-based Fares

In this case the amount of fare is determined basically by the distance covered. A distinction is drawn between kilometric, stage and zonal fares.

a. **Kilometric fares.** The dependence of the fare on the distance covered is reflected most strikingly in the kilometric fare, which is determined by multiplying a fixed rate per km by the number of kilometres covered. A minimum distance (minimum fare) is assumed. Some agencies charge fares strictly according to the distance covered, while others grant discounts as the length of journey increases by reducing the price per kilometre. Kilometric fare systems, in which the rate per km rises as the length of journey increases, have also been used but they are not recommended. In this case the economic justification is usually extremely low utilization of seat capacity, e.g. on route extensions in insufficiently populated areas or for topographical reasons.

In applying the true kilometric fare system collection difficulties (triangular table) have to be borne in mind. Even if the kilometric fare is simplified by forming groups to achieve coarser graduation, fare collection may still be difficult because the most frequent journey length is always relatively short in the local transport sector and it would take too long to collect fares. Hence, the kilometric fare is suitable for urban transport only under certain conditions and is not used very much today.

b. **Stage fares** are calculated on the basis of the distance covered by the passenger in the form of the so called "stages". The stage is a section of a route consisting of one or more distances between stopping places and serves as a basis for fare calculation. For this purpose the transport network is divided into route sections of roughly the same length. Depending on the fare policy for short-distance passengers, longer or shorter stages are fixed in town centres than in the less densely populated suburbs or surrounding areas. The distance between two stage points is generally between 2 and 3 km. The point of stage change must be easily recognizable and quite specific.

The stage fare represents an attempt to combine fairness to the passenger and consideration of the actual costs for the agency with acceptable fare collection times. The system should not only take into account the varying demand for transport services for short and long distances, but should also be advantageous to the agencies as regards the method of fare collection.

The different possible fare structures permit flexible fare calculation. If the graduation is too extensive, the disadvantage that additional fares make collection difficult must also be tolerated. Despite its advantages compared with the flat fare, the stage fare may be an obstacle to rationalization efforts of local transport undertakings if it provides for too many different fares.

c. The **zonal fare** is simplified in relation to the stage fare since it divides the transport area into zones whereby the town centre generally forms the inner zone around which the outer zones may be arranged like a belt. The transport area can also be divided into adjacent zones. If transverse and ring routes exist, their lengths must be delimited by dividing the zones into sectors.

The distance and fare scales are formed in a similar way to the stage fare system, i.e. basically one distance and one fare stage. A disadvantage for the passengers who travel only a short distance in two adjacent zones is that they have to pay the fare for two zones. Hence, long journeys inside a zone may be cheaper than short journeys which cross a zone boundary. An attempt is made to offset this disadvantage either by introducing of the so called overlapping zones or by introducing fare scales applicable to two zones.

As with the stage fare, an upper fare limit can be fixed by not making provision for further graduation from a certain number of zones onwards. Grouping of several zones is also possible.

Combined Systems

The combination of the previous three systems is also a possibility. As it is often difficult to delimit flat and distance-based fares in practice, the question arises as to when one may refer to combined forms and when not. A fare system should not be designated as "combined", if the majority of passengers are handled according to one or the other fare system. For example, a combined system does not exist if the system is basically a stage fare, but a flat fare is fixed, e.g. for children. A system can be regarded as combined however, if the basic fare is a flat fare, whereas the concessionary fares are based on a distance-related fare system.

The justification for such a combined system is that the basic fare is to facilitate fare collection on the vehicles, while the concessionary fare does not require special collection if the tickets can be purchased in advance. In this case the fact that the fare system may become less comprehensible is tolerated.

In general, combined systems may increase confusion about the system and should be avoided.

TYPES OF FARE

Some Basic Definitions

There are three types of fares: <u>basic</u> or normal fares, <u>reduced</u> and <u>supplementary</u>.

The type of <u>basic</u> fares includes the fares that are used by majority of passengers and whose price constitutes the basic fare policy of the agency.

The question whether the single or multiple journey ticket constitutes the basic fare of an agency is determined by the frequency of utilization; if the number of journeys with multiple-journey tickets exceeds that with single tickets, the former is regarded as the basic fare. In this case the single tickets are regarded as supplementary fares, which are justified by the greater fare collection time compared with multiple-journey tickets. <u>Supplementary</u> fares are also adopted for night travel on account of the higher costs, or because of the higher speeds on express services or as a protective fare for overlapping long-distance routes.

<u>Reduced</u> fares are those which offer a concession. Here it is good to distinguish between fare reduction for operational reasons and those done in the public interest, in other words between commercially viable discounts or "political" fares. The former are known as **fare allowances** and the latter as **fare concessions.** The concessionary fares which are given in the name of the social policy of a local or central government, include in particular the heavily discounted season tickets for children, schoolchildren, students and apprentices. The demand is repeatedly put forward by the agencies that fare concessions in the public interest should be granted only if the loss of revenue is refunded by public authorities. This demand, however, has been met only in a few cases. Recently, however, several countries have started to reimburse the so called "public service obligations" at least for the excessively high discounts.

Fare Allowances

The fare allowances are granted as quantity or period discounts because the agency envisages higher revenue in this case, without any increase in expenditure. The main types of allowances are as follows:

a.   Multiple-journey tickets

Fare allowances as a quantity discount take the form of multiple-journey tickets. The multiple-journey ticket is a transferable ticket for a specified or unspecified number of journeys. The first group includes ticket booklets and multi-journey tickets, which are generally used with flat fare systems. The second group (i.e. tickets for an unspecified number of journeys) includes the strip ticket, which is used mainly when operating a distance-based fare system.

b.   Season tickets

The season ticket is issued for a specific period (e.g. week, month, year) for an unlimited number of journeys as a pass, or for a fixed number of journeys with or without a cancellation obligation. Season tickets are available to everyone (with quantity discount compared to single tickets) and concessionary season tickets for specific groups of persons (employees with a limited income, schoolchildren, students etc) to whom a quantity and social discount is granted. A distinction is also drawn between route, section and network season tickets. As a rule, season tickets are non-transferable. If they are transferable under certain conditions, a surcharge is levied. The most widely used season tickets are generally those issued to ordinary passengers with varying discounts according to the period of validity.
Season tickets can take various forms as they are not tied to fare collection. They can be based on stages and zones, routes, the entire network and specific times. They provide the agency with considerable rationalization opportunities by simplifying ticket-issuing and fare-collection procedures, while operating times are reduced and travelling speeds are increased.
If the possibilities of unrestricted use and independence from fare collection are properly

225

utilized, the pass undoubtedly includes certain elements of freedom from the constraints associated with conventional fare collection on the various forms of transport.

c.   Season tickets for slack periods

In recent years there has also been substantial increase in the use of season tickets for certain times of the day. Their introduction is attributable to the utilization of the generally low level of activity of the transport operation in periods between traffic peaks at weekends and during the summer months.

d.   Pensioners' tickets

These are really concessionary tickets given in the interest of public service. They are introduced for both socio-political and economic reasons. The transport undertakings are usually chiefly concerned with greater use of vehicles outside peak hours. Hence if pensioners' tickets are to be considered a true concession for public service a pre-condition is that they must be valid for use in peak hours. However, this pre-requisite has not been met in many countries with the result that the economic aspect of the offer has been falsified.

e.   Special offers

There are finally fares that constitute special offers. These are based on off-peak periods, (e.g. evening and night hours, special shopping hours etc) or special categories of passengers, (e.g. families, or sporting events, exhibitions, excursions, etc) and may refer to single or season tickets.. A whole range of special fares, sometimes of greatly varying characteristics, has been introduced by transit agencies around the world. These special offers have been met with varying success. Good results have been reported in the case of network tickets. It is reported that cheaper return tickets lead to loss of revenue without attracting a real increase in demand.
A variant of special offers has developed in connection with the Park and Ride systems. These schemes were usually introduced in cooperation with retail

trade associations or advertising companies. In principle, all special offers of this sort are based on the fact that the passengers travel into the city centres by public transport from a parking area outside the city centre. These measures have enjoyed a varying degree of success, but this is obviously due to the site of the parking areas in relation to the city centre and the speed at which the public transport vehicles travel to the city centre. Some undertakings have established that despite the offer of a free parking place and free transport the Park and Ride system has generally been rejected, while in other cases, where the site of the parking areas was more favourable, the system obviously enjoyed greater popularity.

Free Travel

The ultimate fare policy is "free" travel. This can take two forms. Completely free, i.e. paid for by the general budget of the local and/or central government, and "free" in the sense that passengers do not pay in the bus but all households in the area pay a monthly fee to support their public transport services. These two types of "free" travel will be referred to in the following as type A and type B free travel respectively.

Completely free travel (type A) on local and regional transport services has been the subject of public discussion since the mid-sixties. In the Federal Republic of Germany, for example, it has been discussed on a much wider scale, since the so called "Rote-Punkt-Aktionen" ("Red Point Demonstrations") in various German cities during the summer of 1969. Experience acquired with type A free travel includes short-term experiments in large cities in the USSR after the First World War and in the beginning of the 70s in Rome but also in several cities and towns in the US (UMTA, 1977). In Athens, Greece type A free public transport exists in all major cities for the period 5-8 am since 1984.

Advocates of free travel of either type justify their demand by arguments on various levels, but in particular by social, transport and financial considerations.

Free travel, especially type A, is justified in social policy terms by the argument that short-distance (i.e. urban) public transport should be available free of charge in exactly the same way as roads and parking areas, to make the individual more mobile and independent of his place of abode and work.

The transport policy objectives of those in favour of free travel is the anticipated greater attractiveness of short-distance public transport, especially in city centres, and the resulting readiness of motorists, especially car commuters, to switch or return to public transport. This argument is based on the fact that introduction of free travel makes the vehicle owner more aware that he is incurring disproportionate costs by using his car. Marked effects on demand are anticipated above all during commuter traffic periods in city centres with the high network and timetable densities of public transport.

An interesting case of free transport is the one that provides payment by <u>all</u> households of the area through a monthly fee. The justifications for this, type B, free travel can be summarized as follows:

a. It secures the financing of public transit operation with an equitable form of payment (the non-users are also paying as a compensation for the disproportional loading of the network that they cause when they use private cars or taxis).

b. It provides the financing from local taxes, i.e. from the people who use the system and not from universal taxes i.e. from people all over the country (as in the case when the central government subsidizes all or parts of the service).

c. It is a strong inducement for using public transport in the congested urban areas.

Of the disadvantages, the following two are the most commonly cited:

a. It will be politically very "costly" to impose a monthly fee on the households, especially for those who do not use (or use very little) public transport at present.

b. It may create an excess demand for public transport which may deteriorate the existing levels of service.

A fuller analysis of type B free travel and a case study for Athens can be found in Giannopoulos (1980).

SOME CONCLUDING REMARKS

A critical part of the operation of a bus system concerns the systems of fares charged which must comply with an overall policy regarding fares. A certain system of fares must be evaluated with both social and economic criteria. Social, in the sense that it must not overcharge the persons using public transport, especially those who do not have any alternative means of transport (captive riders), and economic, in the sense that it must provide the agency with sufficient income to provide an economic and financially secure service in the long term.

An analysis of the various fare policies shows that substantial differences may exist in the fare concepts of the various agencies. As regards the types of fare, two general groups can be distinguished. The flat and the distance-based fares. In order to choose between these, two considerations play an important part: firstly, the limits of the scope for fare differentiation and, secondly, the anticipation that cost savings during operation may be so high that they outweigh the economic advantages of a differentiated fare structure. This probably explains why flat fares are preferred not only by agencies with a small network but also by large agencies with a large volume of traffic. Flat fares have been introduced in some towns not only for operational reasons, but also, and sometimes exclusively as a result of political initiatives, the associated loss of revenue being tolerated.

When there is a fare increase the main question with either flat or distance-based fares is their end result in terms of revenue. This seems to be less important with the flat fare system than with the distance-based fare; this is because in the distance based fares potential short-distance passengers regard only a low fare corresponding to the short journey as appropriate, while the long distance passengers tend to accept that their fare should be higher. This is confirmed by the fact that fare increases in recent years led to a movement away from public transport, particularly in the short-distance sector. So it may be questionable whether the resulting loss of revenue due to loss of passengers was always outweighed by the fare increases, especially for the short journeys. Experience shows that overall fare increases may produce additional revenue, even in the case of the flat fare, if they do not exceed a specific amount. Certain techniques and models have been developed to help test alternative policies in this sense the most recent one being described in Daskin et al, 1988.

The costs of fare differentiation are generally negligible. Additional administration and settlement costs would be incurred only with an extensively differentiated price structure, which would not be feasible in practice.

However, distance-based fares are not as compatible with automatic machines as the flat fare and the whole process of fare calculation and collection is more difficult with the distance-based fare than with the flat fare. Inspectors are required with both systems, but inspection is more costly in the case of distance-based fares. To summarize, it should be pointed out that both the flat fares and distance-based fares have advantages and disadvantages, which can be quantified only with difficulty and inaccurately in some cases.

Consideration of the types of fares also reveals the great importance of the multiple-journey tickets, which often form the basic fare of many agencies because of their great popularity. They are used by agencies operating both standard and distance-based fare systems. Such quantity discounts may be granted for purchase in the vehicle or in advance and for whole-day or off-peak use.

Season tickets are also important but their importance in the fare structure varies from country to country. The discounts granted to specific categories of passengers often include public interest elements, which should be refunded by public authorities. A full settlement of the so called "public service obligations" is striven for in many cases, but the general principle is now generally accepted.

To conclude, the formulation of a proper fare policy is a complex matter that requires both experience and careful analysis of a multitude of data. It should therefore be made with extreme caution and within the overall operational objectives of the agency as well as the social objectives of the supervising agencies.

SOME PRINCIPLES OF BUS TRANSPORT FINANCING

In the same context that fares and fare policies influence the whole bus operation one should also mention the basic principles and alternative ways of bus transport financing. Again the material in the

next sections is meant to be at an introductory
level. It is aimed at giving some basic facts and at
pointing to the interrelated nature of bus transport
operation and financing.

Introduction

The whole question of financing public transportation is becoming of increasing importance to planners, politicians, and transport operators all over
Europe and in most of the world. For urban public
transport in particular the problems of financing and
the difficulties involved are much more pronounced
and difficult to solve. The reasons are well known
(see for example Webster, 1984) and can be summarized
in the much higher cost of providing public transport
infrastructure in urban areas, in the immense costs
and difficulties of public transport operation in
these areas with all the congestion and complexity of
the networks, in the highly complicated and largely
unknown side effects and repercussions of the solutions applied to urban public transport problems etc.
Urban public transport financing is therefore at the
moment perhaps the most pressing issue facing politicians and operators in almost all urban areas of
Europe. In this context bus transport financing forms
a major element.

The need for financing comes from the increasing
deficits of public transport operators both for the
operation of the system and for its expansion and
acquisition of the necessary fixed assets. Accordingly two types of financing are usually distinguished
for "capital" and one for "operating" deficits. The
former refers to money supplied to cover expenditure
on large capital items such as workshops, bus terminals, urban railway lines, rolling stock etc. Some
of these elements of "capital" expenditure, such as
for example rolling stock replacement, are sometimes
classified as "operating" expenses, a fact that creates some confusion. "Operating" financing is aimed
at covering the "gap" between "earned" revenue[a] and
total operating cost.

Most urban public transport operators are suf-
fering increased deficits both on capital as well as
on operating expenses. As a result, only a handful of

---

[a]. That includes fare box revenue, grants for
carrying concessionary passengers advertising and
other miscellaneous revenue.

231

operators remain in purely "private hands". The great majority or urban public transport operators is publicly owned or in "mixed" ownership situation, where the public (usually the local authority) owns part of the shares while the rest are in private hands. Thus the question of financing of urban public transport operators is usually closely associated with the type and form of subsidies given to them by the public authorities in order to maintain a socially acceptable service.

In the context of this book the whole topic of financing of urban public transport is seen as providing some answers to the following set of interrelated questions:

a. What are the main sources of finance and what conditions are usually attached to them.
b. What are the aims, motives and, in general, the justification of financing urban public transport operators, i.e. in the current state of economic deficits for the majority of them, what is the justification of subsidizing them.
c. What are the effects of providing the financing, on the performance of urban public transport operators.

Sources of Urban Public Transport Finance

SUBSIDIES. By far the most common source of urban public transport finance is subsidization by the local, national or federal government. Funds in this case come obviously from local, state, or general taxation, depending on the political and statutory situation in the country concerned. Subsidies are given for either or both capital and operating expenses to fully cover the deficits or part of them.

With regard to subsidies a number of points have emerged the most important of which are briefly mentioned and commented upon in the following:

A. The institutional framework of granting subsidies

The ways in which funds are raised in the various countries, reflect the degree of decentralization achieved in each country and the overall government policies applied at each particular period of time. For example, concerning "operating" subsidies, in the Federal Republic of Germany - a very decentralized country -the majority of public transport operators depend on the local authorities for financing their operation. In France, the set up for financing of urban transport is described in Annex 1.

In other countries operating subsidies are supplied by the local, regional or central government in similar ways and to varying degrees. For "capital" subsidies the most usual body of finance is central government. In a recent survey carried out by the TRRL (Bly et al 1980) only in Finland, amongst the 16 countries surveyed, there was no central government aid for capital expenditure. On the other end of the scale in Belgium, five of the major urban transport undertakings have set up a service financed by the government to plan and carry out major infrastructure projects. The government pays for both labour and materials although the individual companies contribute to track and overhead lines. In Greece, too central government finances all capital expenditure of all three Athens public transport operators.

Since considering of a claim for subsidy always brings many different interests to light and requires a large amount of information and constant monitoring of the results, recommendations have been made (ECMT 1974) for setting up an effective supervisory body which would form a kind of buffer between the operators, the central, regional or local government, and the users. Such an institutional structure exists already in Athens where the three public transport operators are "supervised" by an organization called OAS which approves and distributes their operating (and to some extent the capital) subsidies.

Finally it is worth noting that some countries, such as the United Kingdom and possibly Norway, have a "mixed" system whereby local governments have discretion to allocate the transport grants given to them by central government.

B. The management and "control" of the subsidy and its use.

In general, operating subsidy in most countries appears to entail less rigorous scrutiny than capital subsidy where the project or programme involved can be more easily defined and may involve a greater lump sum. However, the two countries which have a particularly high level of operating subsidy and where central government bears the whole deficit of the urban transport undertakings, the Netherlands and Belgium, according to Bly, 1980, have a highly developed system for scrutiny of accounts and impose a

233

wide range of conditions. Conditions in the Netherlands include the maintenance of service levels, fare rises restricted to the rise in the cost-of-living index, the granting of priorities for buses and the discouragement from the use of private cars. In Belgium, government representation is required on the boards of managers, and fares and wage rates for public transport employees must be agreed by the central government.In the United Kingdom the individual councils will often determine fare and service levels.

Apart from these formal and specific conditions related to either operating or capital subsidy, there are other more general controls, which are applied in some countries before the payment of either operating or capital subsidy is made. Fares are frequently regulated by central or local government, particularly where statutory or other government price controls are in force. In Switzerland, fare rises can necessitate a referendum while in Norway any general change in fare levels requires Parliamentary approval.

Again, when no direct legislation exists, the "management" and control of a subsidy is better to be left to the "intermediate supervisory body" mentioned earlier.

C. Timing and preferred type of the subsidies.

A subsidy can be given either in advance (ex-ante) or after the end of the period for which it is given (ex-post). At the same time it can be a "capital" subsidy or an "operating" one or both.

Capital subsidies have for long been considered as far superior to operating subsidies in terms of efficiency. Whilst the very aim of the former is to build for the future, in some cases the latter ultimately leads only to the survival of an absolute state of things, and so it handicaps any real future development.

Whilst this statement may appear satisfactory at first sight, it nevertheless involves some serious hazards. A capital subsidy may in fact be quite inefficient; what, for instance, is the use of creating new infrastructures if there is no genuine need for them? Would it not be better, in some cities to subsidize existing railways rather than build a new underground system at great expense?

There is a growing impression that existing transport infrastructure is not being used to its best advantage and that urban transport problems could be overcome at much lower cost, not by the creation of new infrastructures, but by the achievement of better organization and management of the transport facilities already available. Therefore, despite appearances, an operating subsidy might also prove highly effective.

The real crux of most discussions, however, about the form of a subsidy concerns the relative merits of ex-ante and ex-post subsidies. Generally speaking, there is a clear preference for the ex-ante type, because of the incentive it provides for more efficient management on the part of subsidized operators, who are obliged to "make do" with the ex-ante subsidy to balance their accounts at the end of the year. Ex-post subsidies, by contrast, are held responsible for the mentality that if loses will be offset by a corresponding subsidy, there is no incentive to raise productivity and there is little inclination to give the due weight to the financial implications of management decisions.

In reality of course the situation is not as simple as the above distinction implies, and there are several arguments also in favour of the ex post type of subsidies. For example:

a. If a subsidy is fixed ex-ante, the operator must, of course, strive for financial balance at all costs; there is a risk that this constraint will lead to a marked deterioration in the quality of the service provided, with all the effects that may be produced, on time, on demand and on the urban transport undertaking's financial position. Moreover, in a monopoly situation such as this usually prevailing in urban transport, an ex-ante type of subsidy does not seem calculated to bring about a structure and climate conducive to innovation. By contrast, the ex-post subsidy gives scope for wider freedom of experiment. Ex-ante subsidies involve the risk of sacrificing long-term to immediate interests.

b. In practice, there is often no alternative to the ex-post subsidy for urban transport. The growing wish to intervene in this area, which political authorities and supervisory bodies display, makes ex ante subsidies all the more unacceptable by reason of the apparent difficulty, at least in the short term, of creating new institutional structures to channel the influen-

235

ces of the various parties concerned in the provision of a subsidy.

The above points simply highlight some of the most important questions relating to subsidies. Some additional points are:

- The need to consider urban transport subsidies in a broad context which also embraces private transport, the main problem being to minimize a city's total transport costs.

- The need to treat the question of subsidies to transport operators as part of a general transportation package and an overall urban transport policy. Subsidy is only one of the instruments available to public authorities, and a satisfactory answer to the difficulties facing urban transport will be sought in vain if attention is confined only to this single issue.

- The need to look at the problem of transport subsidies in a far wider context than the transport sector alone. There are at least two kinds of option: those relating to transport as such (public transport or private transport, and so on), and those covering a broader range (transport or other fields of activity).

Relatively little damage may be done by distorting the users' choice of mode through a wrong decision about subsidies; but there are infinitely greater hazards, when the provision of subsidies to urban transport is discussed for the question of fundamental choices to be disregarded or evaded. The failure to speculate whether the money, proposed to be spent on subsidies to urban transport, could not be more usefully allocated elsewhere invites the risk of creating formidable distortions where the economic and social optimum, in terms of the welfare of the community, is concerned.

BANK LOANS

Financing through normal bank loans is a type of financing that almost ceased to exist in recent years for urban transport. The reasons are the ever increasing deficits and the downward trends in patronage that are common to many urban public transport operators through Europe.

Basic loans are, however, usually given if there is a guarantee for them by some public or other authority. In Greece, for example, this is the way in which the government usually covers the deficits of the public transport operators in both Athens and Thessaloniki, i.e. via long term loans from the government owned post office savings bank. It is obvious, of course, that this form of financing is based on the government's ability to influence independent institutions such as banks (even if they are government owned) to carry the burden of non-profitable and not so economically sound investments in the interest of general social policy.

INTRODUCTION OF SPECIAL TAXES OR TAX CONCESSIONS
Second to giving subsidies, the practice, most commonly exercised to revenue support for public transport, are fuel taxes and various other taxes originally earmarked for highway building funds, a policy which reflects the view that the balance between public and private transport should be changed in favour of public transport for the benefit of the community. In general, however, highway funds diverted to public transport tend to be used more often for capital projects (for example in Sweden these are used for new Metro systems). In Switzerland the revenues from car parking can be used to finance public transport, while in France a transport levy (versement de transport) is raised at up to one per cent of total payroll costs on all employers with more than nine salary or wage earners in urban areas over 100,000 (1.5% in towns which are building new Metros and 1.9% in central Paris). The proceeds of this levy are used as compensation for reduced rate workers' tickets and concessionary fares, and for capital projects and service improvements. The introduction of special taxes seems therefore a widely accepted and practiced form of public transport financing and also perhaps the most accurate, because funds are raised among the local population which benefits from the public transport services in question and not from the general tax payer.

Taxes concessions to public transport operators are usually given by several governments as a way of reducing their costs. For example, some such concessions are refunds of excise duty on fuel, exemption from sales taxes, zero-rating for VAT etc.

OTHER WAYS OF RAISING FINANCE
In a recent publication of the US Department of Transport (UMTA, 1982) on alternative ways of financing urban public transport, no less than 23 techniques are mentioned which have been tested. Some of them are indeed adapted to the U.S. situation, but

others could well be applied (and in some cases have been applied) in Europe.

For example, the following techniques can be mentioned:

a. "Special Benefit Assessment" tax. This is a tax on all properties within a designated geographic area to pay for all or part of the cost of specific public improvements made within that area.

b. "Negotiated Investments". This is a commitment by a land developer to contribute to the cost of public improvements necessary to support his new development. The developer's commitment is usually offered in exchange for revisions of existing land use regulations needed to accommodate the development.

c. "Tax Increment" Financing (TIF). A "Tax Increment Finance District" is established in the area most directly benefitting from the improvements, and a "base year" assessed property value is determined. Property taxes collected on the base year value within the district are distributed to pre-existing taxing jurisdictions as usual; however, taxes collected on any increases in property values above the base year value are dedicated to financing the public improvements within the district.

d. "Transit Impact" fees or requirements, more generally. These are imposed on developers to mitigate the impact new projects have on the transportation system. The fees or requirements are established by local ordinances as a condition for obtaining building permits, and have been justified on the grounds that, since the new development will exacerbate peak-hour traffic on transit problems, the developer should pay for necessary mitigation measures.

e. Employee Income Tax. This is the opposite of the "employer's tax" applied in France and is a flat-rate percentage tax deducted from wages or pay-checks of all employees working within a designated geographic area, regardless of residence location. The "employer's tax" is also included in the list but is not mentioned here, as it is already known in Europe.

f. Peak Hour Surcharge. A peak-hour surcharge is a higher fare charged to commuters who travel during peak hours, usually 6-9am and 3-6 pm.

g. "Land Banking". Land banking is the advance acquisition (by the public transport operator) and

238

holding of land for planned future uses. It permits operators to purchase desirable properties before inflation and land speculation create exorbitant prices. UMTA has provided funding for land banking through its "Advanced Land Acquisition Loan Program" which loans 100% of land costs at attractive interest rates of properties to be used for transit purposes within ten years. Purchases can be made before plans for future facilities are finalized.

h. Leasing/selling Development Rights. In the process of constructing certain new facilities, transit agencies sometimes acquire land or land rights, not of immediate transit use. A financial return may be gained by leasing or selling the air or subsurface rights of such land.

i. Certificates of Participation. A certificate of participation, sometimes known as an equipment trust certificate, is a certificate (much like a bond) which serves as evidence that an investor owns a percentage of interest in a piece of equipment or property. Certificates of participation allow the cost of the equipment or property to be spread among many investors. Each investor owns a percentage of the title to the equipment or property and "leases" his share back to the municipality or transit authority.

j. Interest Arbitrage. This is the process of privately investing funds, borrowed at low interest rates, in financial instruments returning a higher rate of interest.

k. "Safe Harbour" Leasing. The "safe harbour" provisions of the US Economic Recovery Tax Act of 1981 and the 1982 Tax Act permit transit agencies to "lend" anticipated bond proceeds or other funds to a private corporation for the purpose of purchasing rolling stock; the corporation leases the equipment back to the transit agency (the lease payments usually equal to the debt service payments, owed by the corporation to the transit agency), but can then take accelerated depreciation deductions associated with that equipment providing a "shelter" against its total taxable income - the transaction easing the transit agency's cash flow problems, and the corporation gaining a net tax saving.

PRICING AT TRUE COST

Finally the most straightforward way of financing urban public transport should be mentioned, and that is to raise the fares so that they cover the true cost of operation. From a purely theoretical point of view, pricing at true cost, when contrasted with subsidies, is much preferable, because it gives operators a strong incentive to improved operation, efficient management and cost effectiveness, in general. This view is supported by the fact that almost all investigations so far show that fares are a steadily diminishing factor in the choice of mode by passengers, whilst they are very sensitive to such aspects as speed, comfort, and frequency.

In practice, however, pricing at true cost is met with serious difficulties. These are chiefly of political nature, but also difficulties can be found on purely economical grounds. According to this argumentation, one of the aims that public transport subsidies are intended to achieve is to remedy defects in the price mechanism which, in present circumstances does not operate, so as to make private motorists bear all the costs which they impose on the community, and thus to bring about equal terms of competition. The levying of congestion taxes or parking fees on private motorists, for instance, may be envisaged as alternatives to subsidies for public transport or pricing at the cost. However, although a pricing system based on the true costs to the community may be attractive and efficient, it is nevertheless beset by a host of well known difficulties, when it comes to applying it in practice.

In conclusion, as regards sources of finance, it appears that there are a number of alternatives. Which one of these, may be the most advisable or appropriate for a particular case is largely dependent upon the political and social strength of the decision making authority. A recent survey shows that by far the most common type of financing is subsidies, followed by special taxes. It may be true after all that the sociopolitical advantages of subsidies, when compared with alternative forms of finance, more than outweigh their economic defects, and for this reason we will look into them in some more detail in the following.

JUSTIFICATION OF SUBSIDIES

The motives and arguments which are usually being advanced in support of subsidies are fairly well known and have been discussed rather extensively in the past. They have nevertheless been classified here in four categories and are presented in the following in summary form in order to give a complete picture of the subject tackled in this section.

a. Macro-economic justifications
    The main objectives of subsidies to public transport operators under this heading include:
    -   to fight inflation: by preventing an excessive rise in fares, a subsidy holds down the general price index and avoids triggering off an inflationary, price/wages spiral
    -   maintenance of full employment: a subsidy enables some inflationary imbalances to be warded off, thus helping to avoid slumps which lead to unemployment.

b. Micro-economic justifications
    The main arguments in favour of subsidies, in terms of economic efficiency, are related to the following points:
    -   Distortion of the price mechanism: Subsidies to public transport would be a powerful corrective, mechanism equalizing the terms of competition between modes of transport, some of which are privileged by pricing systems which do not fully reflect the costs they impose. Subsidy would prevent distortion of users' choice between public and private transport by offsetting such handicaps. Thus, a subsidy to public transport would be more than a counterweight for what the community gives private motorists indirectly, and a fair reward for what public transport contributes in the form of extraneous benefits.
    -   Economies of scale: Because it tends to be indivisible, it is a characteristic of urban transport that its returns increase with the scale of production. Hence a subsidy, by leading to lower fares, particularly for certain groups of users, would attract greater patronage, thus making for substantial economies of scale to the benefit of users and the community.

241

- Innovation: Because of their high costs and low short-term profitability, radical technical advances usually need official support in the form of subsidies. Thus, one aim of subsidies to public transport may be to encourage operators to introduce new services and apply new technologies.
- "Option" facility: the fact that public transport is almost permanently available to the community would in itself justify a subsidy. Public transport is in practice a "safety-valve", a potentially available option, always on tap even for those who seldom, or never, use it.

c. Social justifications
Subsidies would be a very good method of providing help, via the transport sector, to certain social groups or particular sections of society, e.g. the old, the young or other deserving groups. The reduction of their costs of consumption by subsidy would increase their purchasing power.

d. Other justifications
Subsidies, channelled through transport, may indeed be used to tackle problems in areas such as safety, reliability, prevention of pollution, urban planning, environmental improvement, or even education, national defence, etc. The distinguishing feature of subsidies given in pursuit of aims such as those is that the benefits accrue not only to transport users but also, and often mainly, to taxpayers generally.

The Effects of Subsidies

In 1978/79 the Transport and Road Research Laboratory of the U.K. undertook a survey and analysis of the effects of public transport subsidies on behalf of the European Conference of Ministers of Transport (ECMT). The survey was repeated in 1984 using a larger data base (Bly, 1984). It is from this work that most of the documented information on the subject, is shown below.

Effects on fares, patronage and veh-kms. Subsidies have been correlated with changes in fares and increases in both patronage and veh-kms. As subsidies are increased to cover an extra 1% of cost, fares

seem to be reduced by 0.4 to 0.9%, while the amount
of service operated, as expressed by the veh-kms run,
seems to be increased by 0.14 to 0.30%, but not necessarily in the same year.

As far as patronage is concerned the relationships are less clear and not uniform for all the
urban areas considered. It would appear that subsidies might affect patronage trends indirectly via
their effects on fares and whatever elasticities of
patronage towards fares exist in each country. It
appears that patronage is much more affected by factors such as the distribution of land uses, car
ownership etc.

Effects on costs and productivity. The extent to
which increasing subsidy might have been responsible
for encouraging increases in costs, rather than being
merely a response to them, is a matter of some con-
troversy.

The study made by TRRL suggests that roughly
half of the subsidy increases have been taken up in
increased unit costs. Some of this may well have been
used to cover cost increases arising for reasons totally unconnected with subsidy. However, analysis
using time lags between changes in subsidy and
changes in the various cost and productivity indicators suggest that for several of the indicators there
is a tendency for the changes in subsidy to precede
the changes in costs and output per employee, although the evidence is not conclusive. If the interaction is in this direction, at least in part, then
this suggests that subsidy is being used in a way
which increases unit costs and reduces output per
employee.

It may be that subsidy is being used to provide
additional services which are, on the whole, more
expensive than average. Since relatively little of
the subsidy seems to be used to provide additional
vehicle-kms, however, the extra services would have
to be expensive indeed to account for the net increase in costs, and, in any case, the analysis of
the TRRL data suggests that increases in services are
in general bought at a marginal cost well below the
average cost. The conclusion is that several uneconomic services seem to be maintained by subsidies.

The Prospects for the Future

In the above the biggest part has deliberately
been taken in describing ways of financing urban pub-

243

lic transport and more particularly subsidies. The reason for this lies in the belief that current trends of increasing subsidies are very much indicative of the prospects for the future which are discussed briefly in the following.

In the last 15 years the percentage of operating costs covered by subsidies shows a rather uniform trend in most European countries. According to the TRRL survey mentioned previously, there was a rapid rise in subsidies in all European countries in the late 1960s and early 1970s, but there has been a general tendency for the growth to slow down and in several countries for the subsidy to decline as a fraction of cost, in more recent years. Table 7.3 shows these trends. At the same time the TRRL survey notes that there is also a very wide variation of subsidy levels, from zero subsidy in some countries in the earlier years to subsidies which cover almost three quarters of the operating cost (e.g. Belgium, Italy, Netherlands, Greece).

It appears therefore that, with few but notable exceptions, the trends are for greater differences between operating costs and revenues which will need to be filled with greater and greater subsidies or other ways of financing.

The sense in which we mention the term "difference" is that, including the amounts of money payable to the public transport operator by way of compensation for concessionary fares or even for keeping fares below their proper economic level for reasons of social policy. Unfortunately, in several countries there is still some amount of confusion as to how much is due to the operator as compensation for a certain social policy and what is proper subsidy.

In the author's opinion, the current trends will continue in the future and we will see increasing magnitudes of both real subsidies and the overall differences between operating costs and revenues. It is very much a question of the policies followed by each particular government, whether the amount of "concessionary" contribution will increase or decrease in future. Inevitably it will be the "social" nature of public transport in urban areas that is likely to prevail and therefore an increasing amount of "unprofitable" public transport lines will have to be kept operating and financed by means of subsidies or otherwise.

Table 7.3

Proportions of urban areas at different levels of subsidization

Subsidy range as a % of operating cost	Percentage of towns with level of subsidy in each range			
	1971	1976	1981	1986
0 (in profit)	19%	9%	5%	6%
0-10	26	7	10	18
10-30	35	14	16	20
30-50	14	33	26	20
50-70	7	25	36	30
over 70%	-	13	7	6

Source: TRRL survey (Bly, 1984) and more recent data collected by the author.

It would appear, therefore, that the outlook for urban bus transport financing in the future will evolve along two main lines.

First, increasingly drastic measures will have to be taken in order to reduce public transport deficits and improve public transport operation.

Secondly, at the same time financing will have to come more and more from local taxation, since covering it through subsidies, as seems to be the practice today, is likely to be met with more and more opposition and political costs, since subsidies come from general taxation.

An investigation of the application of a "public transport" tax to all households in the greater Athens area (Giannopoulos, 1980) at the same time the abolition of the existing system of tickets in public transport revealed a number of advantages, while the resulting monthly contribution by each household barely exceeds the cost of 100 trips per month by household (i.e. 2.8 trips per day). However, it seems that we are still a long way from political approval for such a "transport tax" and, for the years to come, public transport operators will continue to be financed through one of the ways described in this section and (principally by subsidies), while at the same time being under increased pressure to reduce operating costs and cut down on capital expenses.

8 Bus priority measures

INTRODUCTION

Bus priority measures have been in existence ever since the growth of urban road traffic made the operation of urban buses problematic and reduced the capacity and level of service of existing bus lines.

The nature of bus priority has changed over the years from the implementation of simple schemes, for example short length parking restrictions or an exemption from a turning prohibition, to the use of comprehensive schemes involving wide-scale transportation improvements to whole areas, e.g. pedestrianisation, traffic engineering measures, road closures and new road building. In these latter measures, improvements to public transport services and the application of bus priority are an integral part of the overall plan.

The subject of this chapter therefore is not something novel. Of the many references in this field, two are particularly recommended. One, written in English and published by the British Transport and Road Research Laboratory (TRRL, 1976), is the study of Bus Priority systems by the NATO Committee on the Challenges of Modern Society. The other, written in French, is a study on bus lanes having the form of a

manual, by a team of consultants on behalf of the Paris Public Transport Authority (RATP, 1977).
The term "Bus Priority Measures" is used to express a wide range of actions such as:

a. Various simple bus priority measures, including traffic regulations giving priority to buses (for example when leaving bus stops), parking restrictions near bus stops and on bus routes generally and traffic management measures specifically applied to bus routes to facilitate the passage of buses.

b. Priority at traffic signals (e.g. automatic adjustment of the start and finish of the green periods to favour approaching buses, redesign of signal programmes in area traffic control schemes to give special weight to bus flows).

c. With-flow bus lanes (i.e. reserved for buses travelling in the same direction as general traffic).

d. Contra-flow bus lanes (i.e. reserved in an one-way street, for buses travelling in the opposite direction to the general traffic).

e. Reserved bus lanes on freeways (sometimes reversible for tidal-flow operation), priority access to freeways and other facilities (e.g. toll booths).

f. Bus-only streets (i.e. normal streets converted to pedestrian and bus use only).

g. Busways (segregated roads for buses only).

The most prominent of these types of measures are examined in greater detail in the following.

PRIORITY AT TRAFFIC SIGNALS

The first, relatively simple, form of comprehensive bus priority measures are those that give priority to buses at signalised intersections. This is done by adapting the signal timing and phasing to decrease the delay to approaching buses. This is usually done in one of the following three ways (or combinations):

a. <u>Interaction of on-coming buses with the lights</u>. This type of priority can be arranged by mounting a radio transmitter on the bus, and a detector on the control box of the signals. When an approaching bus is detected, the signal phasing is adjusted to ensure that the green period will not end until the bus has passed. Alternatively, if the signal is red against the bus, the green phase will be recalled as soon as practicable. Where this has been tried in practice, not only appreciable reductions in bus journey times through the junctions have been observed, but the variability in journey time has been reduced so helping buses to maintain regularity (TRRL, 1976). A possible disadvantage of this system may be the delays caused to other vehicles, including buses, on the non-priority phases. For this reason, the sites for this treatment must be carefully selected so that substantial benefits can be obtained.

b. <u>Priority to buses at pre-calculated signal plans</u>. This case has been particularly connected with area-wide traffic control systems. Normally the signals in such schemes operate according to one of a number of fixed-time programmes, depending on the time of day or on the level of traffic, as indicated by the output from a number of strategically-placed detectors. Several methods are available for determining the best signal settings in each of the various signal programmes, the most well known of which are TRANSYT, and SIGOP. All of these methods originally derived their optimum settings by minimising delays to vehicles rather than to persons. In other words, buses were given no greater weight than private cars. This is no longer the case in later modifications to these programmes giving "priority" to buses. For example, BUS TRANSYT allows new sets of signal timings to be deduced which give preference to buses in accordance with their greater passenger-carrying capacity. Signal programmes derived from the BUS TRANSYT method have been applied to a network of about 100 signals in the central area of Glasgow, UK, where surveys showed that buses saved between 5 and 10 per cent of their journey time across the area when this method was used (as opposed to the normal TRANSYT method), while the delay to the other vehicles using the system was not measurably different (TRRL, 1976).

c. The last technique to be mentioned here is known as "gating". The idea behind this method is to limit the number of vehicles gaining access to a particular area so that once through the "gate" the vehicle can travel much more freely. The "area" in question may be a freeway, a stretch of an all purpose road or it may be a whole area of a town. In holding vehicles back at the "gates", buses would be likely to suffer as much as other vehicles, so it is common to allow them to bypass the queues at these points by means of bus-lanes, special bus-only roads or by other devices depending on the local circumstances. Techniques of this type have been applied to a number of towns with mixed results; generally, buses have saved a few minutes of journey time while other vehicles have usually gained as much time from the reduced congestion on the particular area as they have lost in gaining access to it at the "gates". This technique has also been criticized as being a "negative" rather than a "positive" measure and may be quite unpopular once known to the public, i.e. that traffic is deliberately blocked at some points.

"WITH-FLOW" BUS LANES

General Characteristics

With-flow bus lanes are one of the most common types of bus priority measures. As the name implies, they are reserved lanes for buses travelling in the same direction with the rest of the traffic. This type of priority is applied mostly to important roads in town centres and to main radial roads.

There are some positive and negative points about the use of bus lanes "with-flow". Starting with the disadvantages one could note:

A. For curbside bus lanes (see section on bus lane location):

a. They require continuous and vigorous enforcement, since non-priority vehicles will be attracted to the curb lane because of its free-running conditions or for loading and unloading and may also try to stop or even park in the lane.

b. They cut off access by commercial vehicles to curbside properties (where the priority is restricted to peak hours only this tends to be less of a problem).

c. They complicate drivers as to their actions when they reach intersections.

d. They cause difficulties in the operation of taxis, which should normally not be allowed to stop for passengers while using the bus lanes.

e. There is sometimes an increase in traffic congestion and hence in the journey times of non-priority vehicles. If the non-priority traffic uses neighbouring streets to avoid the street in question, there may be a spread of congestion (with associated environmental problems) to these streets, as well as an increase in journey time for those diverting.

B. For median bus lanes (see section on bus lane location):

a. Bus passengers are required to cross lanes which have moving traffic in order to reach the buses; this can be both dangerous and inconvenient.

b. The streets need to be wide enough to accommodate the normal traffic lane (which is approx. 3m wide), the reserved lane (approx. 3m) and the median pedestrian refuge (approx. 1.5m).

c. Where only one solid centre median island exists, and the median bus lane operates with two-directional flow of buses, then either buses must be adapted for left-side passenger loading and unloading or separate loading islands must be installed, unless buses do not load or unload passengers at any point along the lane.

d. As in the case of curbside lanes, there may be increases in traffic congestion and hence in journey times of non-priority vehicles, both on the street containing the priority lane and possibly on adjacent streets also.

251

Compared to the above disadvantages the main advantages of with-flow bus lanes are that the disruption of normal traffic is minimal and that (if properly planned) they can act effectively as "queue jumping" devices at traffic signals and other bottlenecks.

Normally a "bus lane" is totally reserved for buses and no other types of vehicles are allowed to use it. However, if the flow of bus passengers is rather low, the bus lane can frequently be justified by allowing other easily recognizable types of road users to share the facility, for example taxis, car pools and van pools. In some countries bicycles are also allowed to use with-flow lanes. Application of the results of theoretical investigations to real-life situations suggests that bus lanes can only be justified in many cases during peak periods. Even though this complicates the signing of the lanes, it has the advantage that in off-peak hours loading and unloading operations can be accommodated more easily than when bus lanes operate during the whole day.

Conditions for Installation - Expected Benefits

Specific guidelines, as to when a "with-flow" bus lane should be installed, cannot be given. The need for and the design of such lanes depend very much on what the implementing authority hopes to achieve from their use.

If the objective is to minimize travel times for buses "at all costs" with little or no regard to the other traffic, continuous bus lanes up to the junction stop line should be provided, while at the same time prohibiting right or left turns (whatever the case may be) for normal traffic, so as to avoid dangers of accidents. Such "complete" priority schemes for buses require the existence of high numbers of buses and passengers. Depending on the local conditions and bus loading practice, a "reasonable" limit, above which such types of bus lanes might be justified, could be 20 buses per hour loaded at 95% of their capacity, or 30 buses per hour at 85%, or 60 buses per hour at 80%.

If the objective is to minimize travel costs in terms of time and money for all modes of travel in the street, while helping the most efficient form (i.e. the bus), then the design should not reduce appreciably the capacity of the intersections. This can be achieved by stopping the bus lane at some distance (usually 50-80m) before the stop line of the

252

signalized junctions, so that the space between the junction and the bus lane (which is called the "setback") can be used by other vehicles, so as to maintain the capacity of the junction. The optimum length of the setback varies for different levels of saturation and bus passenger flows. Table 8.1 shows suggested setback lengths.

The justification for a "with-flow" bus lane in economic terms depends on the traffic flow through the junction and the bus passenger flow. It appears (TRRL, 1976) that a bus lane with a setback is almost always justified, when the degree of junction saturation exceeds 90 per cent (i.e. when the flow of traffic through the bottleneck in the absence of the bus lane is more than 90 per cent of the capacity of the bottleneck). The benefits increase with increasing degree of saturation. Below 90 per cent of junction saturation level, higher bus passenger flows are required, before a net overall benefit is obtained (e.g. 60 buses per hour at 80 per cent of junction saturation as opposed to only 20 buses at 95 per cent of saturation in one case studied).

If a setback length, for whatever reason, is not provided, then, at medium and high levels of junction saturation, not all the traffic originally using the road in question can pass through the junction, when the bus lane is installed and then the justification for such a lane in economic terms depends very much on:

a. the ease and ability of diverting to other routes,

b. the effect of diverted vehicles on the speed of traffic and

c. the number of passengers receiving the priority.

On the other hand, this design (i.e. without setback distances) increases the advantage to buses, since no traffic can queue in front of them. Calculations relating to a few hypothetical situations (described in TRRL, 1976) have indicated that, at very high degrees of junction saturation, bus flows of the order of 100 per hour (occupancy of 60 passengers per bus) are required to justify such a lane on economic grounds and even greater flows (up to almost twice this level, depending on the severity of factors (a) and (b) above) are required at lower levels of saturation.

Table 8.1

Suggested "setback" distances[a] for with-flow bus
lanes at signalized intersections.

Veh. flow through int/ction (% of capacity with no bus lane)	"Setback" distances per sec of green time for:	
	Low occupancy of bus (60%)	High occupancy of bus (90%)
25 %	0.5 m	0.5 m
50 %	0.6 m	0.7 m
75 %	1.2 m	1.6 m
100 %	2.3 m	3.5 m

(a) Distance before stop line where bus lane stops.
Source: Based on data from TRRL (1976)

As a conclusion the design and the resulting
benefits from with-flow bus lanes obviously depend on
the local conditions and especially the length of the
lane, the degree of congestion, the bus passenger
flow etc. Where benefits have been measured, they
have ranged from almost nothing, or even disbenefits
in some cases, to time savings of several minutes for
buses. A saving of 2-3 minutes in bus travel time
over the length of a typical lane seems to be an average achievement. Such savings can, however, be estimated to be worth quite a lot in reduced operating
costs and passenger travel time. Unfortunately there
is little evidence of changes in modal split arising
from bus priority. In most cases the time savings are
too small for an observable shift in modal split to
be expected, though, where the benefit to buses is
really substantial, there is some evidence of increased patronage.

Our general conclusion is that the with-flow bus
lanes should not be expected to have any "spectac-
ular" results. They do help, if properly placed, and
can have a useful promotional effect in that they
emphasize to the public that the Local Authority has
faith in public transport and is willing to invest in
this way towards its future.

Delineation of a "With-Flow" Bus Lane

Once the decision has been made to implement a
with-flow bus lane, the detailed layout of the lane,
including provision of adequate and clear signs and

carriageway markings, can be drawn up. Figure 8.1 shows in a perspective way the signing of a with-flow bus lane and other information to aid in designing a proper layout. Typical widths of a with-flow bus lane range from 2.7 to 3.5 meters. The particular signs used to delineate the reserved lane vary in different countries. Figure 8.2 shows some examples. In cases where enforcement is not (or cannot be) effective, "physical" separation of the lane should be considered. This can be achieved by simple curb-like structures having a typical cross-section as shown in Figure 8.3 and made of concrete or plastic material. The obvious advantages of physical separation, as regards the enforcement of a bus lane, are somewhat reduced by three disadvantages:

a. In the case of a single bus lane, buses cannot overtake each other, so the position of bus stops for the different bus lines becomes critical. Also, when there is a break-down of a bus, the delays to other buses can be considerable.

b. The construction and placement of the curb-like separation makes it difficult for service vehicles to load and unload at the curb side (see also specific comments in the section "placement of bus lanes").

c. The chances for accidents (mainly vehicles hitting the separation) are increased but the rate of accidents tends to diminish ,as time passes and drivers become more familiar with the arrangements.

Physical separation should be considered with extreme caution and, when it is implemented, it would be recommended to allow for a setback distance before junctions.

CONTRA-FLOW LANES

General Characteristics

Contra-flow bus lanes are almost as common as with-flow bus lanes. Such lanes allow buses to travel in the opposite direction to that of normal traffic, usually (but not always) in an one-way street system.

Perhaps the greatest advantage of a "contra-flow" bus lane, compared to a "with-flow" one, is that it is easily (almost automatically) enforced.

255

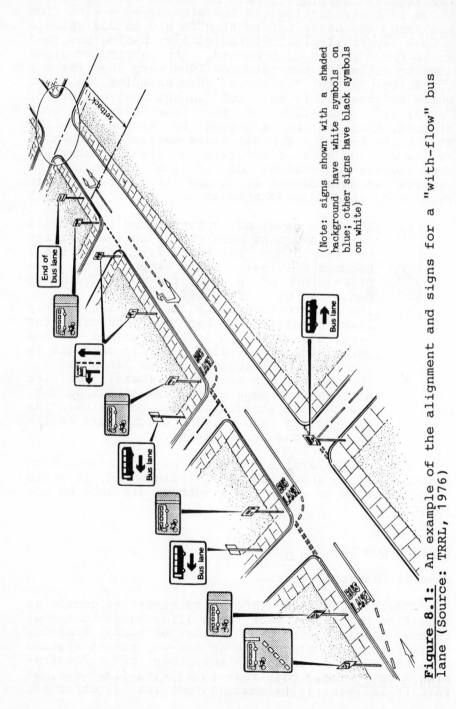

(Note: signs shown with a shaded background have white symbols on blue; other signs have black symbols on white)

Figure 8.1: An example of the alignment and signs for a "with-flow" bus lane (Source: TRRL, 1976)

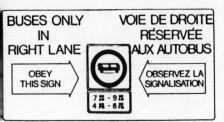  

Start of bus lane   Along the bus lane   End of bus lane

Black lettering and symbol on white ground, green circle

Advance warning   Along the bus lane   End of bus lane

Black lettering on white ground, white diamond on black ground

White lettering on a blue ground, time limit has black letters on white ground

Figure 8.2.: Examples of bus lane signs from different countries (TRRL, 1976).

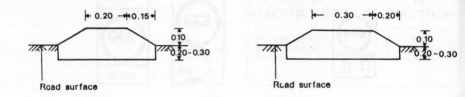

Notes:
Material: Prefabricated light concrete slabs or hardened plastic.
Adherance to road surface by constructing like a normal kerb,
or by nailing it on the road surface (in the case of plastic).

Figure 8.3.: Typical dimensions of "physical" separation barriers for bus lanes.

The ease of enforcement in itself makes "contraflow" bus lanes more efficient and can cause a serious improvement in service.

Contra-flow lanes usually restore to buses the situation which existed prior to the implementation of the one-way system. Thus, one objective of contraflow lanes is to shorten bus routes (compared to the situation of one-way streets only) and give buses unhindered passage, thereby saving running time and operating costs. Another objective is to allow buses to pick up and drop off passengers, at points of greatest convenience to them, so saving passengers walking time; moreover, the presence of buses in areas of greater pedestrian activity encourages higher bus usage.

Of the disadvantages one can note:

- Contra-flow lanes may complicate some of the junctions in the one-way system, the main purposes of which may have been to simplify the main intersections in an area and to increase their capacity.
- Installation of a contra-flow lane often re-introduces traffic conflicts, which the one-way system had eliminated, and therefore signal control may have to be re-introduced (if it had been eliminated) or the phasing (if signal control is still required with the one-way system) may have to

be more complicated than in the absence of the contra-flow lane.

- Signal progression, which can be highly efficient in one-way streets, has sometimes to be compromised in order to give buses reasonable progression in the opposite direction.
- Finally, the problem of loading and unloading of delivery vehicles may be more difficult to solve and may create more safety hazards than in the case of "with-flow" lanes.

Calculations of the benefits to bus passengers and the losses to other road users in typical situations suggest that contra-flow lanes can often be justified in economic terms, even when the flow of buses is quite small. The benefits to buses depend mainly on the reductions in route length and passenger walking distance and the losses to other vehicles depend mainly, on the extra delay at the junctions due to the presence of the lane. Even in extremely unfavourable circumstances, where the cost of installation is high, the reduction in route length is small and there is substantial extra delay to other traffic, a bus flow of only about one bus per iemna: is sufficient to justify the provision of the lane, according to the calculations made in TRRL (1976).

One significant difference between with-flow and contra-flow lanes is that the former may operate during certain hours only, whereas the latter almost invariably operates for the full 24 hours. Consequently signing of contra-flow lanes is simplified but because of the potential accident risks to pedestrians, and the danger of traffic emerging from side roads, well-positioned and adequate signing is even more essential than for with-flow lanes.

The costs of implementing contra-flow lanes tend to be greater than for with-flow lanes because of the extra junction complications and the provision of extra signalized pedestrian crossings. Maintenance costs are also higher because of "tracking" (buses travelling continually in the same lateral position make grooves in the lane). Tracking appears to be more of a problem with contra-flow lanes than with with-flow lanes, perhaps because buses are more confined in the lane due to the presence of opposing traffic or, sometimes, due to solid curbs.

The benefits, on the other hand, tend to be a little larger than for with-flow lanes and generally contra-flow lanes amount to approximately 4 to 5 minutes saving in riding time (for an average length lane) with an additional saving of a few minutes in walking time for each passenger boarding or alighting in the lane section, though this walking-time saving is rarely measured.

On the safety side, there have been a number of problems mostly involving pedestrians, but these have usually been sorted out by:

a. restricting the locations at which pedestrians can cross the road to one or two places where traffic signals can be used

b. preventing pedestrians from stepping out into the lane at other places by means of pedestrian barriers or railings. There has been a tendency for the accident rates to increase initially (as it is also the case with the with-flow lanes) and then to fall, as drivers and pedestrians become accustomed to the new situation; in most cases, the final accident rate for an one-way pair of roads, one of which includes a contra-flow lane, is lower than that for the original two-way pair, though the road containing the bus lane usually has a higher accident rate than the one without the bus lane.

In conclusion, the overall attitude, concerning contra-flow bus lanes, is that they can provide buses with considerable improvement in terms of travel times, proximity to the centres of activity etc, and thus increase their patronage. Their main drawbacks are that they complicate intersection control, which the one-way street system was aiming to reduce, and they tend to increase accidents at least in the beginning.

Delineation of a "Contra-Flow" Bus Lane

Existing contra-flow lanes are generally between 2.7 and 3.5m wide, with a maximum width of 4m in some American examples. As with the with-flow lanes, the beginning and the end of the priority lane presents the greatest problems in design. The introduction of one-way streets almost always simplifies junction design, sometimes to the point where the junctions contain only merging or diverging movements, with no crossing of traffic flows, so that traffic signals can be eliminated. Where contra-flow bus lanes exist, a more complicated junction design or signal phasing is required.

The signs associated with contra-flow reserved lanes indicate the presence of the lane to three distinct categories of users:
- normal traffic moving in the opposite direction
- traffic entering or crossing the street from side roads
- pedestrians

Figure 8.4 shows an example of the delineation of a "contra-flow" bus lane. The types of signs shown in Figure 8.2 are also valid for a contra flow lane.

PLACEMENT OF BUS LANES

Typology of Urban Streets and Cases of Bus Lane Placement

The term "placement of bus lanes" refers to the position of the bus lane with respect to the rest of the street, i.e. the curbs, the road furniture, other objects on the sidewalks such as trees, lamp posts etc. Also a crucial area that needs to be studied in detail are the arrangements of the junctions and the bus stops. In discussing the placement of a bus lane it is necessary to distinguish between 4 types of urban streets.

1. Principal road axes with excellent geometric characteristics. These are road axes with a minimum of 2 lanes per each direction, a median separation and side streets for the local trips (see sketch below).

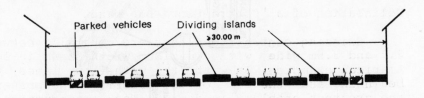

Parked vehicles   Dividing islands
>30.00 m

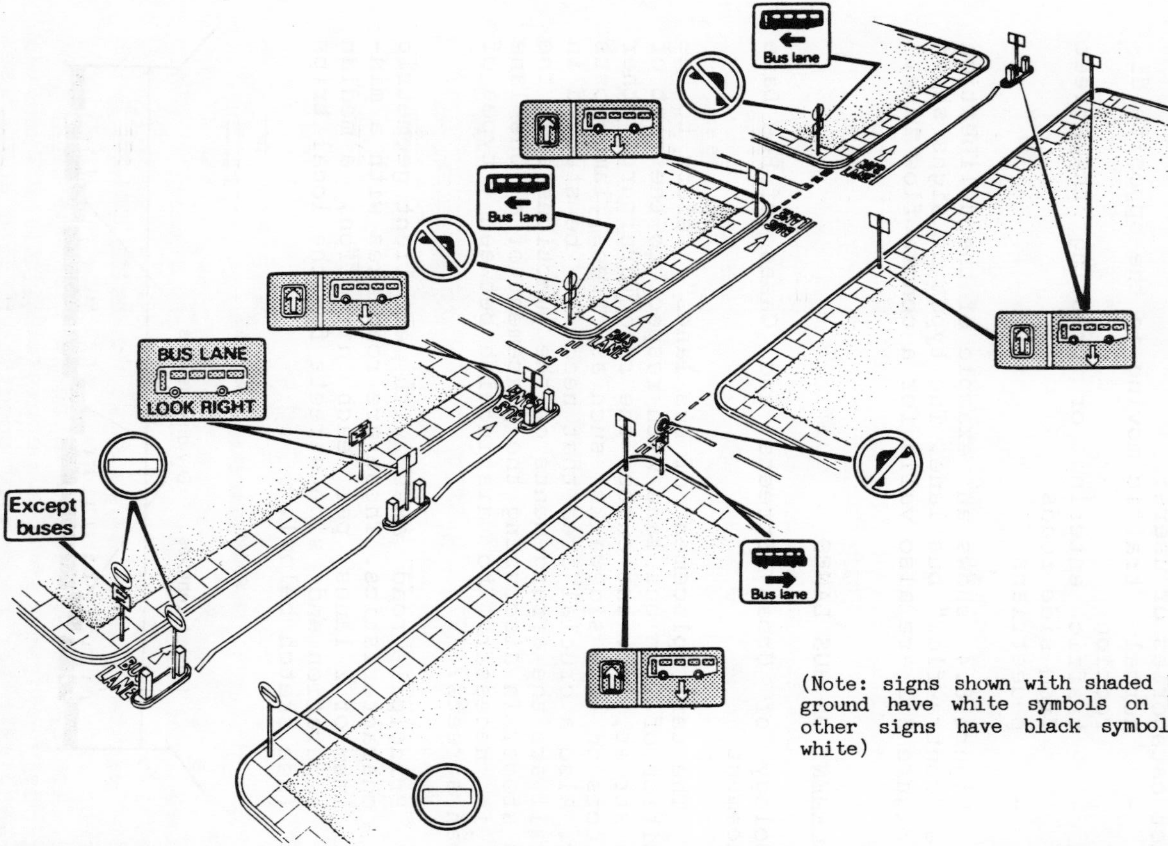

(Note: signs shown with shaded background have white symbols on blue; other signs have black symbols on white)

Figure 8.4: An example of "contra-flow" lane signs and lay-out (from TRRL, 1976).

2. Principal road axes of a "conventional" type. Here the pavement is not separated by a dividing island and there are no side streets. The total width of the pavement remains over 25 meters (including the sidewalks) and there are usually sidewalks of substantial width (3.00 to 5.00m). A typical cross-section of such a road is shown below.

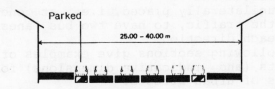

Parked

25.00 – 40.00 m

3. Secondary roads with good characteristics. These are fairly large secondary roads or distributors with one lane in each direction and usually one more lane of parked cars on either side. Typical widths are between 15.00 and 25.00 meters, including pavements (see sketch below).

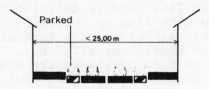

Parked

< 25,00 m

4. Narrow secondary or local roads. The rest of the streets can be classified in this category which has typically widths below 15.00 meters (see sketch below).

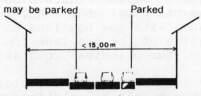

may be parked   Parked

< 15,00 m

The placement of a bus lane can easily be accommodated in the first two types of streets. In the last two a bus lane could be fitted only, provided that parking is not allowed on the sides of the street and this prohibition is strictly enforced. For the last two categories of streets the case should be seriously considered for conversion to a bus-only street, if other necessary conditions also apply (see section below).

263

With respect to any type of street a bus lane can be:

    a.   covering the whole street, i.e. in this case we have a bus-only street,

    b.   bilaterally placed with respect to the rest of the traffic, i.e. one bus lane in each side,

    c.   centrally placed, i.e. at the centre of the street and

    d.   unilaterally placed, i.e. at one side of the traffic, to have two bus lanes, one for each direction.

The following sections give examples of bus lane arrangements (and indicative dimensions) for the various types of urban streets.

"Bilaterally" Arranged Bus Lanes

A bilateral system of bus lanes, i.e. one bus lane on each side is in effect a system of two separate with-flow bus lanes if the street is two-way and one with-flow one contra-flow if the street is one-way. Each bus lane is situated between the pavement and the traffic lane and is delineated as suggested earlier for the with-flow or contra-flow bus lanes in general. Typical widths of the lane are from 2.75 m to 3.50 m. There should normally be a narrow safety strip of 0.20 to 0.30 m between the edge of the lane and the curb. Thus the suggested total width until the curb comes to 3.00 - 3.80 m.

For a bilateral arrangement of bus lanes, obviously the total width of the street must be 4 lanes and over. Typical arrangements are shown in Figure 8.5. Figure 8.5A shows the range of dimensions of such an arrangement while Figure 8.5B a typical arrangement of the bilateral bus lane, which consists of 4 traffic lanes with one bus lane on each side and physical separation of the bus lane from the rest of the traffic (i.e. for principal road axes of the conventional type).

Deliveries to the shops are obviously seriously hampered, but two possible solutions may exist. The first can be applied if there is enough space available on the side walks. In this case one can create special lay-bys for the delivery vehicles. These lay-bys are 2.7-3.0 m wide with variable length (according to available space) and are placed between the bus lane and the side walk. If space for lay-bys does not exist, then delivery vehicles should be allowed to use the bus lane and/or stop on the pavement but

264

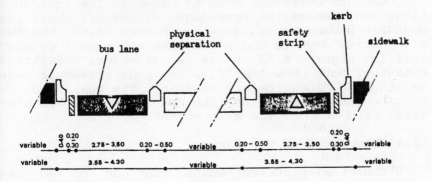

A : General Arrangement

kerb

safety
strip

physical
separation

bus lane

sidewalk

| variable | 0.40 0.20 0.30 | 2.75 – 3.50 | 0.20 – 0.50 | variable | 0.20 – 0.50 | 2.75 – 3.50 | 0.20 0.30 | variable |

| variable | 3.55 – 4.30 | variable | 3.55 – 4.30 | variable |

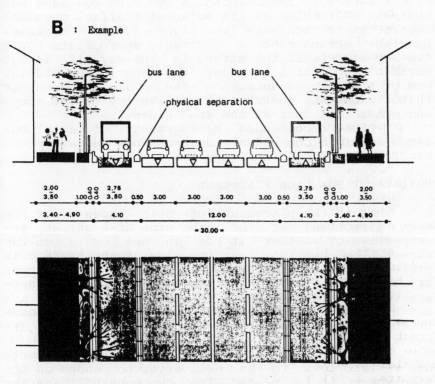

B : Example

bus lane   bus lane

physical separation

| 2.00 3.50 | 1.00 | 2.75 3.50 | 0.50 | 3.00 | 3.00 | 3.00 | 3.00 | 0.50 | 2.75 3.50 | 1.00 | 2.00 3.50 |

| 3.40 – 4.90 | 4.10 | 12.00 | 4.10 | 3.40 – 4.90 |

= 30.00 =

Figure 8.5.: Typical "bilateral" bus lane arrangements. (A): range of dimensions. (B): typical arrangements for a principal axis of the "conventional" type. (Source: RATP, 1977).

265

only during certain hours of the day (obviously off-peaks) when there is no strong traffic flow.

Special attention must be given to the intersections and pedestrian crossings. Figure 8.6 shows two possible arrangements. Note in Figure 8.6B the two alternative ways to end a bus lane and permit turning traffic. Figure 8.6A shows a mid-block pedestrian crossing. Note how the "flow" of pedestrians is made to stop and "look" before crossing the bus lane, by putting the crossing on the bus lane a little off-sited from that of the main street.

Axial Placement of Bus Lanes

The axial placement means that one or two bus-lanes, one for each direction, are placed in the middle of the pavement. Figure 8.7 shows the typical arrangements. For the two bus lanes a total width of 6 to 8 meters is recommended. Since each bus lane has the same direction as its adjacent traffic, physical separation is necessary (see figure 8.7A). The axial bus lane arrangement is obviously appropriate for a two-way street. If the street is one-way, it is not advisable to put a two way bus lane in the middle. One of the main advantages of the axial placement is that it does not obstruct the deliveries to the shops and other land uses at the road sides.

Typical recommended arrangements of axial bus lanes at mid-block pedestrian crossings and at intersections are shown in Figure 8.8.

Unilateral Bus Lane Placement

This is the placement of both lanes (one for each direction) at the one side of a street, irrespective of whether it is an one or a two-way street. The bus lane near the side of the traffic is preferable to have the opposite direction to that of its adjacent traffic lane. In addition physical separation is recommended. Typical arrangements are shown in Figure 8.9. Possible arrangements for pedestrian crossings and intersections are shown in Figure 8.10.

The unilateral bus lane arrangement poses serious restrictions to the deliveries to shops on the side where it is placed. The two possibilities for facilitating deliveries to shops, mentioned earlier for the bilateral arrangement, are also valid here for the side under consideration. For the opposite side there is no noticeable obstruction.

266

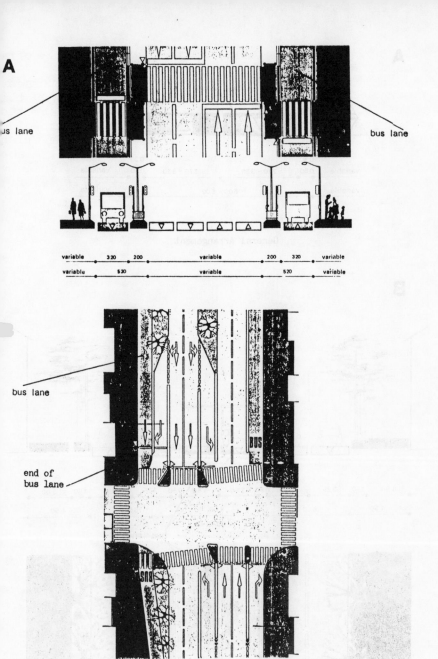

Figure 8.6.: (A): Examples of pedestrian crossings and (B): intersection arrangements in the case of a <u>bilateral</u> bus lane. (Source: RATP, 1977).

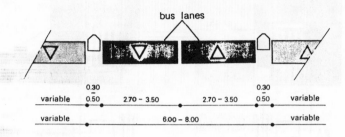

A

bus lanes

General Arrangement

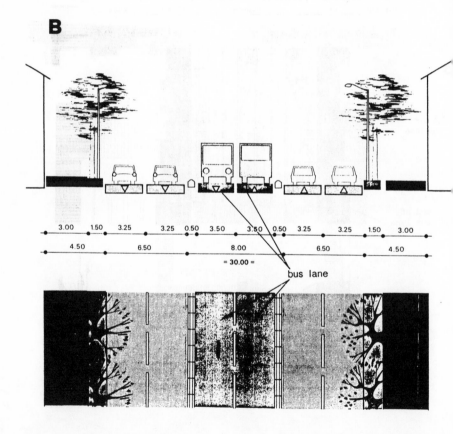

bus lane

Figure 8.7.: Typical _axial_ bus lane arrangements. (A): range of dimensions. (B): Typical placement on a 6-lane principal road axis. (Source: RATP, 1977).

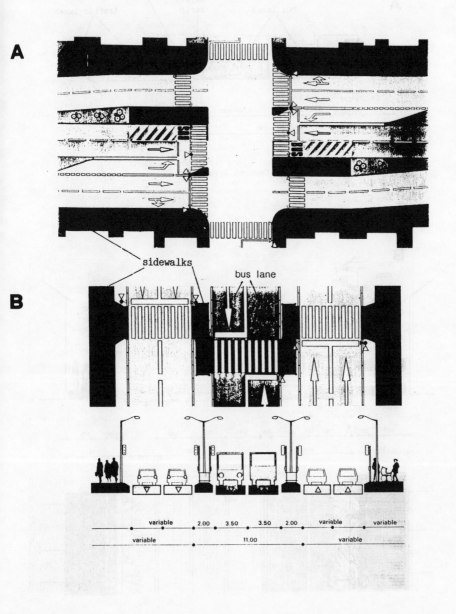

Figure 8.8.: (A): <u>Axial</u> bus lane arrangements at intersections. (B): Mid-block crossings which can also be arrangements for bus stops (Source: RATP, 1977).

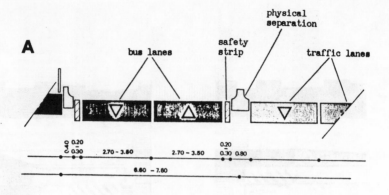

A

bus lanes

safety strip

physical separation

traffic lanes

General Arrangment

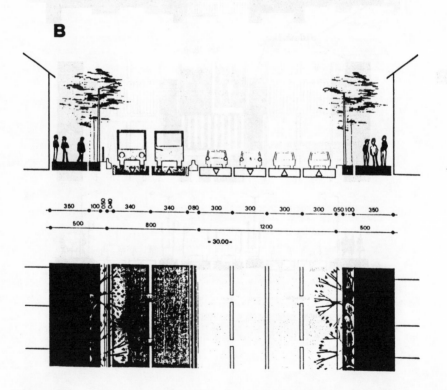

B

Figure 8.9.: Typical <u>unilateral</u> bus lane arrangements. (A): Range of dimensions. (B): Typical placement on a principal road axis (Source: RATP, 1977).

270

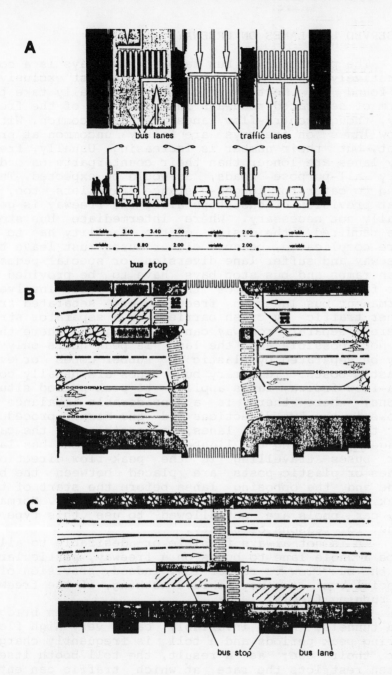

Figure 8.10: **Unilateral** bus lanes. (A): Examples of mid-block pedestrian crossings. (B): Intersection arrangements. (C): Bus stop arrangements (Source: RATP, 1977).

RESERVED BUS LANES ON FREEWAYS

The provision of bus lanes on freeways is a comparatively new form of bus priority almost exclusively found in North America. They generally take the form of separated roadways in the centre of the freeway, though contra-flow lanes are not uncommon. With-flow lanes on freeways are fairly uncommon at present, but their number is increasing. Usually, freeway lanes are longer than their counterparts on ordinary all-purpose roads, as would be expected. They tend to cater for longer-distance travellers too, so that provision of bus stops along the freeway is generally not necessary. Where intermediate bus stops are required, the design of the facility has to be more complicated, because either buses must leave the freeway and suffer lane diversion, or special pedestrian ramps and bus stop bays have to be provided on the freeway. Because of the higher speeds involved, permanent bus lanes on freeways are separated from other traffic by crash barriers or a separator strip where a separate roadway can be provided. Where this is not possible and the lane is peak-hours only it may be separated by plastic or rubber cones or even plastic posts. Temporary bus lanes are usually contra-flow freeway lanes applied to peak-period situations, where there is a considerable imbalance of flows in the two directions and the normal procedure is to convert two lanes, if possible, of the carriageway carrying the lighter flow into one bus lane for buses travelling in the peak-flow direction. Cones or plastic posts are placed between the bus lane and the opposing lanes before the start of the peak period and removed immediately after it. Normally, car pools are not allowed to use this type of lane, for reasons of safety.

It is not always feasible or desirable to allocate a whole lane to buses on a freeway, particularly if the bus flow is rather low. Indeed, provision of a special bus lane may achieve nothing, if the freeway is running freely.

Another way to give buses priority is in bridges and tunnels, which invariably carry very high flows during peak periods and a toll is frequently charged for their use; as a result, the toll booth itself often restricts the rate at which traffic can enter the facility and causes long queues, but, once payment is made, travel over the bridge or through the tunnel takes place at relatively high speed. A way of giving buses (and/or car pools) priority over other traffic is to allow them the exclusive use of certain approach lanes at the toll plaza.

BUS-ONLY STREETS

Bus-only streets are streets which have been set aside for the exclusive use of buses _and_ pedestrians. They generally exist in downtown areas, and may be created either by banning all other traffic (except emergency vehicles and possibly other authorized vehicles) from the street, or by admitting buses to a previously pedestrianized street or area.

The various aims behind the creation of a bus-only street are:

a. to improve the environment,

b. to speed up buses by removing other traffic from the street,

c. to assist pedestrians to move about on the road more easily and safely,

d. to create sufficient carriageway space so that buses can stop and wait, if necessary without hindrance to other buses (bus termini are often located in bus-only streets, so that the street becomes a mini bus-station).

Though some authorities regard bus-only streets as an inferior form of pedestrianized street, many others regard them favourably because of the increased accessibility to public transport which they offer. They can provide the bus with a distinct advantage over private traffic in its ability to pick up and set down passengers at the very points where shopping or business activity are at their highest level. On the other hand, the pedestrian is obviously more restricted in a bus-only street than in a completely pedestrianized street and the danger of accidents is still present, though much can be done in the design of bus-only streets to improve amenity and safety to pedestrians, e.g. wider pavements and speed restrictions on the bus. In many cases taxis and vehicles requiring access to premises fronting onto the street are allowed to enter. It is not usually possible to provide wall-to-wall paving in such streets, nor flowers, shrubs and kiosks to the same extent as in fully pedestrianized streets, though nevertheless careful design can produce a very pleasing environment.

273

Despite these criticisms, bus-only streets are generally highly regarded by local authorities, by public transport operators, by pedestrians, by shop-keepers and by the public in general.

From the point of view of bus operation and service offered to the public, bus-only streets are an excellent arrangement. Their designation, however, must be made after a full traffic study to see the wider effects of re-assigning the traffic to the rest of the road network, the effects on available on-street parking spaces and the accessibility of the land uses along the streets that are to become bus-only streets.

Invariably the conversion of a normal street to a bus-only street is combined with parallel widening of the pavements, installation of new street furniture and general upgrading of the street environment for pedestrians.

The deliveries to the shops are made either from side streets or during specific hours of the day when the delivery vehicles are allowed to enter the bus only street just as it is done for pedestrian streets.

Intersections with other streets are single level crossings and can be controlled in a way depending on the traffic flow of the crossing street.

BUSWAYS

The term "busway" is used to indicate a continuous road (usually specially constructed) segregated from the rest of the road network and exclusively used by buses. Busways are undoubtedly an extreme form of bus priority and in existing urban areas they are relatively uncommon because, once a town is built, it is very difficult to find a continuous strip of land in the right place to provide the right-of-way for a busway. Even when new towns are planned and built, provision of such a facility is rather expensive, because, to be fully segregated from the normal road network, the busway must be sunken or elevated for an appreciable proportion of its length in order to accommodate the intersections. However, sometimes the opportunity may be taken to provide a busway which will go nearer to houses, shops and workplaces than conventional public transport services normally do, and in some cases routes can go nearer to workplaces and shops than cars are permitted to go, so giving the bus an advantage over private cars. Furthermore, as car ownership increases, congestion on the ordinary street system will eventually inhibit some private trips, but the busway will remain free from congestion at all times. This will give powerful encouragement for the use of public transport.

A well-known busway with 19 kms of segregated track in the form of a figure-of-eight has been built in Runcorn, U.K. This "new" town with a population of more than 50,000 was built in the '60s. On most of the track, junctions were planned grade-separated, but away from the town centre there are several at-grade junctions controlled by traffic signals which give immediate clearance to buses on the busway.

A similar busway of 10 kms and again a figure-of-eight has been designed by the author for Brega new town (pop.50,000) in Libya (Giannopoulos, Zekkos 1980).

9 Marketing and public information systems

INTRODUCTION

Marketing, and Public Information, which is in fact part of the marketing function, are two tasks that a modern Bus Transport Manager, of any sizeable bus agency, cannot ignore. Despite the huge sums of money that are spent world-wide on public transport, these two areas of an agency's activity have been relatively neglected until fairly recently. At present, they have become an important field for research and development, and an increasing number of public transport agencies are applying modern techniques of Marketing and public information.

The objective of Marketing is to provide the manager with answers to questions such as :
- What type of service is desired and needed ?
- Who desires and needs it ?
- How can it be provided best ?

The objective of a Public Information System (PIS) is to make sure that the available services are as widely known as possible to the travelling public. In this way it complements marketing. In fact, a good PIS is part of the marketing mix which is a concept defined in the next section.

In other words, Marketing aims to maximize the service to the public in terms of meeting its needs. It also aims to increase the utilization of the transit facilities in order to spread costs and increase revenues. Public Information forms part of modern marketing but it is examined separately here, because of its wider scope and significance.

This chapter looks at both marketing and public information systems at a rather elementary level. The aim is to provide managers with basic knowledge and techniques that will enable them to appreciate the potential of these systems and to even apply some of these methods in simple cases. For larger agencies, both marketing and public information should be the subject of a specialized department staffed appropriately (see also organization charts in Chapter 2), or giving a contract to an outside consultant.

THE MARKETING PROGRAM

Definitions and Objectives

Marketing has been defined (Institute for Urban Transportation, 1971)as the "science" that deals with the discovery and exploitation of opportunity. Consistent with this definition, the marketing of a bus transport agency must be geared to discovering the opportunities to serve the public and taking advantage of these opportunities in terms of maximizing the patronage.

In the process of "exploiting" the available opportunities, various combinations of "product" (i.e. types of services offered), place (i.e. the coverage of the area), price (i.e. fares and fare policies) and promotion techniques (i.e. public information systems) have to be combined with the general aim of meeting consumer needs. These are also the four most widely used factors that form the so called marketing mix introduced by McCarthy and also known as the four p's. In general, the marketing mix can be defined as the set of controllable variables that the agency can use to influence the buyer's response. Many other variables may be qualified as marketing mix variables. Through the marketing mix, management has the opportunity to exercise its creativity in meeting market opportunities and increase the patronage for its buses.

It can be said that a first basic objective of a successful marketing program is to discover the various "segments" of the (bus transport) market. Dif-

ferent kinds of people, travelling for different reasons, with various requirements and constraints on
their time and money, are the different "segments"
that need to be discovered.

A second basic objective is to find and propose
the types of service that will serve these segments
best. Also the price at which these services should
be sold and the fare strategy to be followed.

A third objective would be to supply the elements that will form the guidelines for the public
information campaign, which the management of the
firm will later utilize to attract more segments of
the market to the buses, as part of the overall marketing mix of the agency.

In general, all parts and functions of the bus
agency should be aimed at meeting various consumer
objectives or needs through an appropriate marketing
mix.

Meeting the above objectives is admittedly a
difficult task. Even under the best of conditions,
accurately determining (and meeting) the needs of
consumers or potential consumers of a bus transit
service, is likely to be a tough proposition. Questions of costs, difficulties in determining the
needs, and lack of flexibility due to legal constraints, make the full satisfaction of the above objectives of marketing rather difficult in the real
world.

Developing a Marketing Strategy

Three broad alternative marketing strategies are
possible:

   a.   Undifferentiated marketing.
   b.   Differentiated marketing.
   c.   Concentrated marketing.

An "undifferentiated" marketing strategy can be
defined as the one that markets one product and attempts to appeal to the entire market with one marketing program.

A "differentiated" marketing strategy is that,
in which a firm still appeals to the entire market,
but it separates or segments the market into different classes and appeals to these segments with different marketing programs.

A "concentrated" marketing strategy would not
appeal to the entire market. Instead, it would concentrate its efforts on a large share of a particular

279

market segment. As with the differentiated strategy, the firm aims at a segment of a large market. The "concentrated" strategy is particularly recommended if a firm's resources are limited and, since the resources of small-scale bus transit firms are typically quite limited, the concentrated strategy appears to be most sensible for small to medium sized agencies.

The type of marketing strategy that an agency will choose, depends on various factors that relate both to the resources and size of the agency itself and to the "external environment" in which it operates. For example, cost can be a serious limiting factor, as is the structure and extent of the services offered by the agency. Also, factors such as car ownership and usage, and the average income and age distribution of the population served, are usually among the factors that have to be considered.

The main factors to be considered in selecting a marketing strategy, are the following:

a.   The costs and, more generally, the resources that will be associated with the strategy to be followed. Since these resources are usually limited, a "concentrated" marketing strategy may be the more reasonable one to follow, as already indicated above.

b.   The degree to which the "market" for public transport (i.e. mainly the population of the areas served) is homogeneous in terms of its socioeconomic characteristics that determine its "transit usage" behaviour. Generally the population is treated as homogeneous, but in a number of situations it may not be so. In the latter case more effort should be directed into defining the homogeneous parts of the total population. The problem is always to define the various "segments" and isolate the ones that can be served advantageously within the cost constraints and the overall goals of the bus agency.

c.   The degree to which the service provided by the agency is homogeneous. This is usually so. However, special techniques such as express buses, local buses, charters (e.g. for schools), dial-a -bus etc, differentiate the service offered, and these have to be taken into account in choosing the marketing strategy to be followed.

280

d. The competition exercised by other modes of transport. Normally, a bus agency will not, and should not, be in a competitive position with any other mode of public transport. In cases when such situations arise, steps should immediately be taken to avoid competition and promote co-ordination among the various different public transport modes operating in the same area. However, the agency should see itself in competition with private cars (and to some extent with the taxis). There, a **competitive marketing strategy** should be followed, so as to try and attract customers from these modes of transport.

If a concentrated strategy is finally adopted, a first "target" should be the non-users of bus transport who could be changed to potential users. Finding such "segments" of the market (i.e. potential users), to which then the marketing effort would concentrate, is a special task in itself which will be addressed in later sections. It is also recommended to "combine" the services offered with the desires and needs of these particular segments of potential users, so as to present "packages" of transit service. For example the specific recreation and social requirements of the people can be tied in with the bus agency's services to transport them there, and marketed as a complete "package". For example, campaigns such as "Going to the football on Sunday? - Buses so and so will take you there", may produce positive results.

Of the other two types of marketing strategies, i.e the "undifferentiated" and "differentiated", the first is perhaps the simpler to carry out with less preparation in advance, because it appeals to the whole of the population indiscriminately. However, it obviously involves greater commitment of resources (and considerable "wastage") than the concentrated strategy. The second type of strategy is the most difficult and cost intensive of all but also the most effective, since it appeals to the whole population but with a different approach, according to the particular characteristics and needs of each segment.

Data Collection and Research Needs

The definition of potential market segments, as well as the needs for other information, can only be met through research into the market served by a given transit agency. Some information, such as patronage and revenue figures, should be gathered on a routine basis and normally do not require special effort. This regular, so to speak, information collection has been described in Chapter 3. In addition to it, the more complicated marketing research efforts are likely to require the services of outside professional help. Other information, on the city itself or the population, can be found by consulting the city planning agency (if such an agency exists) or the Census Bureau.

In general, it can be said that, although some market research techniques are quite complex and require highly skilled staff of researchers assisted by a computer, in several cases assembling original and otherwise unavailable information needed for small-scale transit agencies will not require the high degree of sophistication necessary in probing a bigger market.

Probably the best marketing data collecting device in terms of simplicity is a simple questionnaire consisting of direct, undisguised questions. Like any questionnaire, it must be pre-tested on a small-scale basis to make sure that the questions are properly worded and not misleading. Relatively little skill is required in order to use such an instrument and, unless the questionnaire is used in an attempt to study the psychology of consumer motivation, it is generally not necessary to hire expensive, specialized outside personnel to interpret the data.

However, designing a good questionnaire is an art and that is where specialized help should be sought. Also the sample selection technique, that will determine who will answer the questionnaire, is a delicate and specialized task that may require outside help. The interested reader can seek more information on such questionnaires on specialized publications such as Institute for Urban Transportation (1971), Parten (1966), Babbie (1979) and UMTA (1986).

Another useful source of information that may be forgotten is the complaint department. Any well-managed transit property should have a systematic procedure for handling complaints. A simple analysis of the problems that crop up regularly can give clues to needed service improvements.

Another source of information may be the telephone information service, offered by many agencies as part of the agency's public information effort. An analysis of the requests for information may reveal marketing opportunities that would otherwise be neglected. For example, several hundred calls over a

period of a month or two, asking how to reach an athletics ground, give a sign that service should perhaps be provided, if it is not offered, or that promotional efforts should be directed towards the benefits of using the ground and how easy it is to get
there by bus. The inquiries may also be an indication
that the maps, schedules and other types of public
information are not sufficiently clear.

DETERMINING THE MARKET SEGMENTS

General Guidelines

The success of a marketing strategy depends primarily on the meaningfulness of the segments to which
it appeals. It also depends on the quality of the
promotion campaign that will be developed to appeal
to these segments.

The concept of market segmentation is a powerful
tool which enjoys widespread use among business firms
in general. For most producers of goods and services,
the meaningful market segment is the smallest unit,
for which it is worthwhile to tailor a separate marketing program in terms of the product and the necessary promotion.

Once the market has been segmented, the management can spot marketing opportunities more easily
than if the market is treated as a single, large
unit. Also the allocation of the marketing budget and
the adjustments to the product, place, price and
promotion elements of the marketing mix can be more
easily done.

In determining the market segments, the following general guidelines should be kept in mind (Institute for Urban Transportation, 1971):

a. **Measurability.** This refers to the ability
    to find information on the market segment,
    that is of value. Information may already
    exist on certain consumer characteristics
    (for example census data) or it may require
    a fresh and separate research effort. The
    danger here is in using certain informa-
    tion, primarily because it is available
    rather than because it is pertinent to the
    task at hand.

b. **Accessibility.** After segmentation is ef-
    fected, the agency must determine the
    degree, to which it can effectively focus
    its market efforts on the various segments

283

of the market; in other words, whether these segments are "susceptible" to public transport use. An example of a segment that is not "susceptible" to transit is salesmen who cover the entire urban area carrying their samples. This segment is obviously not accessible to a marketing effort.

c. **Substantiality.** Each segment must be large enough to warrant separate "cultivation" in terms of service and promotion.

Methods of Market Segmentation

The traditional marketing bibliography contains several methods or models of market segmentation. Here we will present and discuss two of them, adjusted to the transit agency situation and its main product which is transportation service.

A. Segmentation Based on "Influencing Factors".

This first method employs the so called "**segmentation factors**" in order to determine the groups of the population that will form the "segments". These factors are typically socioeconomic and demographic characteristics of the population and trip characteristics, such as purpose of trip, time of day, duration of trip etc.

The most commonly used socioeconomic factors are:

- car ownership
- income
- age
- sex
- education
- physical condition
- geographical location
- availability of a car

Other possible factors may be used, but those listed above are objective in nature, and data on them are most likely to be found. All of the demographic factors may affect the way a person views public transport, the degree to which he needs it, the degree to which it may serve him, the price he is willing to pay and the promotional approaches that may be used to attract his attention.

Ownership of a car is perhaps the single most important factor in determining transit use. However, this factor must not be taken simply as a matter of whether or not a family owns a car. The important element is use of a car. As a case in point, the housewife in a single car family is likely to have limited possibilities of using it, at least for some days of the week.

Income is also a critical factor and is often used as a substitute for factors that are more difficult to define, such as social class and level of education. It also has a close tie-in with car ownership. The main difficulty associated with this factor is that there are not usually available statistics on income levels in the various parts of the city. In the type of market research effort discussed here, the levels of high, middle and low income could be established by some simple but objective method with the co-operation of local or regional planning agencies. A reliable basis for defining and interpreting income classes would be the one that best reflects local conditions of wages and prices. Income statements (provided that existing legislature permits their use) can be another method to find and analyse income data.

Age is another obvious divisional element. As a general rule, "young" people are those under 16 years of age and old people are those of 65 or over; everyone else is in the "middle age" group. Age is important for several reasons. Older people tend to be less confident of themselves, more easily confused and, perhaps, less patient than younger persons. If retired, they may have certain transport needs that can be cultivated and utilized into a clearly distinguished market. Older people also tend to drive less, and their car ownership level, as well as their income, is lower than that of the rest of the population. People in the middle age groups tend to have higher incomes, higher likelihood of owning a car and a regular need for working and shopping trips. The younger people tend to be without their own personal car transportation, their personal incomes tend to be limited, and they have a variety of public transport needs for recreation, work and school that may be unlike those of other age groups.

The distinction made by sex is important because men are more likely than women to own and to know how to operate a car. In their later years, women are less likely to wish to drive, even if they know how and have access to a car. Apart from that women are the major shoppers in a family and, unless working at a regular job, they have generally different travel patterns than men.

Different levels of education also indicate the kinds of promotional appeals that can be made to different parts of the population. As an example, a highly sophisticated advertising campaign geared to a more educated group is likely to fail if used in an area where most of the population has failed to finish high school.

"Physical condition" refers to whether or not persons are physically handicapped. The handicapped persons who are relevant to the transit situation are those who have difficulty in moving about, and they cannot easily utilize conventional transit services. If transit in general is to serve those with serious physical handicaps, special kinds of service and special vehicles may be needed.

Location is simply the geographical location of a person or group of persons in an urban area. Locations with accessibility to public transport are likely to induce their residents to use a bus, thus making them potential targets of a marketing effort (possibly improving also the conditions of transit in their area).

As regards the trip characteristics, trip purpose has an important bearing on determining the segments of the market for transit. Trips are usually divided into the following types: work, school, shop, recreation or social and personal business. However, this distinction which is usually made for trip modelling purposes can be simplified for public transport marketing. What is important here is the flexibility to alter certain characteristics of the trips. So a useful distinction could be:

a. "Inflexible" Trips, i.e. trips that are constrained in the sense that it is difficult or impossible for the trip maker to alter the time and/or destination of his travel. Meeting a time schedule is critical to this type of trips, which include journeys to work, school and similar purposes. The destination points of these trips tend to be concentrated. For this type of trip, it is essential that the mode of transportation used is dependable and that it goes close to the places people want to reach.

b. "Flexible" Trips, i.e. trips in which the traveller usually has considerable freedom as to when and where he will travel. Transport flexibility is generally associated with reaching many possible trip destinations. Unlike work and school trips, the destinations for many of the so called flexible trips are not likely to be highly concentrated. Trips in this category would include those for shopping, recreation, social, or personal business. Such trips offer potential opportunities to bus agencies because they are likely to occur at off-peak times, permitting the agency to utilize better the available capacity. On the other hand, the multiple destination points required for such trips may make it difficult for the service to meet consumer needs conveniently.

By dividing the trip purposes into the above two broad categories, it is possible to focus on the critical factors of dependability and flexibility. Dependable service is primarily the responsibility of the operations segment of the agency which must make sure that service runs on schedule. Flexibility is related to the coverage of the city the important traffic generators and destinations reached, the ease of transfer between routes and the overall convenience of the service.

In the methodology of segmentation described here, the combinations of demographic information describing portions of the population are further classified according to flexible or inflexible trips. For example, trips by low-income young females, with a college education and access to a car, living on the north side of the city are classified into "flexible" and "inflexible" trips and then modified by estimated constraints on time, energy and money. Many segment categories can be derived simply by figuring out various combinations of demographic factors and the general nature of their trip; estimates of the number of persons involved can be derived from available information. Speculation on the time, energy and money cost of making a trip by transit, and the availability of time, energy and money possessed by potential consumers will provide clues to the product, price and promotion, necessary to attract these segments. Experience of the area and, of course, some good knowledge of marketing techniques will help to determine the final segments.

The type of methodology described here may seem too general or too abstract. Nevertheless, it provides guidance and a place to start; it can be improved upon with experience and is a logical and reasonable way to proceed.

B. The "Trial and Error" Approach.

This second method for market segmentation is to try a, so to speak, "trial and error" approach. Some sort of general marketing program, addressed to a broad range of population, is first implemented and its results are monitored and tested so as to show its appeal. Then this information can be used to better tune the marketing program and define the segments.

The basic premise of this method is that, by providing in practice a marketing mix certain to have a fairly broad appeal and then dropping back to find segments that actually utilize the service, the manager can find valuable clues leading him to discover other useful segments. Therefore, according to this approach the market is divided into segments after an initial marketing action is taken.

This action typically focuses on two or three broad categories of trips that are best served by the bus system, stressing dependability in performance and flexibility (in terms of service area). Promotional work and pricing are manipulated in conjunction with the service, to build image, inform the public and encourage use.

After the service is geared up and operating marketing research is utilized to find the segments that are being served in terms of demographic, trip purpose or other meaningful segmenting factors. Based on this research, transit management can determine what segments are satisfied and get clues on segments that are not being satisfied. Decisions can then be made on the elements of the marketing mix that must be adjusted to reach new segments or to expand the grip of the transit enterprise on the segments of the market that do utilize the service.

In the successful utilization of this method, special attention should be paid to guaranteeing dependability and image building in the initial stage, by use of well trained personnel, well maintained vehicles, and convenient schedules. Routes should be designed carefully in order to provide for maximum coverage of key residential areas and places of economic and social activity. Transferring, where necessary, should be made as convenient as possible.

SOME FINAL REMARKS

Having defined the segments to which it will appeal, a concentrated marketing approach can then proceed most effectively to appeal to these segments and tailor the service to meet their requirements in the best possible way. In doing so, the management must also take account of certain points that will help it focus better the whole strategy on the objectives of marketing stated previously. These points are discussed in the following.

A. Recognizing that Transit is not an End in Itself.

Public Transit, and transport more generally, is not an end in itself but the means to an end. It is needed only because the traveller desires something else. The bus passenger is not interested in the bus ride itself[a], except as it permits him to go to work or shop or whatever purpose he has in travelling. This fact is important in the marketing strategy, because it may be far easier to sell a destination than the bus ride as such. Use of transit can best be promoted as a means to an end, provided it is a better alternative than some other means of travel (or than not making the trip at all). The agency must therefore explore many "destinations" that are attractive to various segments of the market, especially if demand can be stimulated at off-peak times or on routes that are not enjoying sufficient patronage.

B. Taking Account of the "External" Factors

Another important element associated with the previous one is the fact that the basic needs that exist among the segments may not be met by transit alone. For instance, elderly people are often lonely and feel a strong need for companionship. The availability of transit service convenient to older people can provide an opportunity for them to reach areas where companionship might be expected. Similarly, younger people will be induced to take public transport in order to reach sites of athletic or other outdoor events and so on.

In trying to sell a "companionship" destination, it can be successful only if some social institution exists at the end of the trip that satisfies these needs of the transit passenger. Churches, clubs and other social institutions for the elderly, as well as athletics grounds and so on, are examples of such

---

[a]. Except, of course, in special cases such as city touring for example.

institutions. It is not outside the province of the transit firm to appeal to, and deal with various organizations to help promote needed service. Indeed, it is part of the community relations effort to deal with outside institutions to help complete the package of overall social, recreational and other services that should be available in a modern community.

C. Promoting Under-utilized Capacity

One of the major efforts of the marketing program should be to take advantage of the usually under-utilized capacities of the transit system. Many investigations of market segments and adjustments of the marketing mix are aimed at generating off-peak traffic. During the off-peak most transit systems have manpower and vehicles that are not being fully utilized. This period is ideal to sell special services and charters, so as to induce people to use the available capacity thus making demand more uniform in time and the whole operation more effective.

D. Maximizing Service Self-support

The marketing program has also the task of finding which services are self-supporting. The informational feedback of the data collection system used in marketing and the constant monitoring of that system should reveal profitable or self-supporting parts of the transit operation. Why these services are profitable or self-supporting should be determined and the successful technique or conditions should be transferred, wherever possible, to other services offered by the agency.

At the same time, it is the obligation of the management to identify loss making services and to find the needed alterations to make these services either profitable or less costly or more genuinely useful in serving the needs of the people. Even a publicly owned transit operation geared to public service, rather than profit, as a major objective should take all reasonable steps to minimize cost and maximize revenues as long as the principal goal of service is preserved.

By concentrating intelligently on the goal of self-supporting service it may be possible to operate profitably in the long run. At the same time, failure to provide adequate service to the public can only cause transit to fail both socially and economically and worsen the situation in the long run.

PUBLIC INFORMATION SYSTEMS FOR PUBLIC TRANSPORT

The Need for Public Information

As it has already been stressed above, public information and promotion of the services, that are offered by the public transport (or bus) agency, is an integral part of the marketing mix. Even in the absence of a marketing program, a Public Information System is an indispensable part of any well organized agency. Its purpose is to make known to the public, irrespective of whether somebody travels by bus or not, the transportation services offered, as well as the advantages of using the system, compared to other modes of transport.

Information is necessary for those who already use public transportation as well as for those who would like to use it. It is characteristic that even regular passengers of a bus line may not know more than one or two lines of the system. In Sweden, for example, a recent survey (TFB, 1984) among public transport passengers in two regions, Upsala and Jonkoping, revealed that a relatively small percentage of public transport users knew more than 2 bus routes. Of the total number of users asked, 40-60% took the bus only occasionally, 56-66% were familiar with 1 or 2 routes, while a full 25% in both areas said that they were not familiar with any route. The percentage of those familiar with more than 5 routes was 0-5%.

Efficient information can therefore help the users to choose faster and more convenient connections, thus making the system more appealing to them and through them perhaps to new users. In line with this observation, there are indications that improved information can lead to new passengers, especially during the off-peak periods when they are needed.

For the non-users of Public transport the need for improved public information, and therefore awareness about the public transportation system, is perhaps even more pronounced. Carefully designed signs at stops, terminals and on vehicles, as well as maps, diagrams, boards and other means of conveying information about the system as a whole can lead to increased public awareness and induce more people to use it.

General Design Principles

Perhaps the best way to present the overall scope and importance of a PIS for bus transportation, is to refer to the basic principles that should govern its design and implementation.

First, the system should be designed and implemented as a complete system with the true meaning of the word, i.e. covering the entire journey from the time that the potential passenger is planning it until the final destination has been reached. The main steps of a complete journey and the kind of information that should be provided are diagrammatically shown in Figure 9.1. In this figure the types of the necessary information are shown, as well as the means of providing it to the public. For example, before the trip, information is needed as to which bus line or lines are the best to take, where are the bus stops, what are the timetables, how long will it take and so on. The means to get this information are usually maps, timetables, or information by telephone. Then, at the bus stop, the passengers need to know when the bus comes, what other buses use this stop, where they go etc. The information needed for the rest of the steps in a complete journey is self-evident as shown in the diagrammatic presentation of Figure 9.1.

Secondly, the information supplied by the system must be comprehensive in its coverage of all the different types of journeys and modes of transport available in the area. Special attention must be given to the transfer points (terminals), where this information is crucial. Where the different types of journey and/or modes of transport are within the same administrative jurisdiction, it should not be too difficult to provide this type of comprehensive information. Where the various types of journeys (e.g. urban, regional, interurban etc) or modes of transport (bus, rail, light rail) are under different jurisdictions, then there is usually a serious problem of co-ordination and update of information. Whatever the structure is, any effort should be made to provide as complete as possible information for the urban and regional transport services in the area.

A third point of importance is that the system of information must be uniform and consistent. This means that designations, symbols, colours and names should be used in a consistent and uniform way throughout the system. If, for example, a particular destination name is used in the timetable, then the

BEFORE THE TRIP

INFORMATION NEEDED	SOURCE OF INFORMATION
Which bus should I take?	Route map
Where is the bus stop?	-"-
When does the bus go?	Time-table
How long will it take?	-"-
	Telephone information

AT THE BUS STOP

INFORMATION NEEDED	SOURCE OF INFORMATION
Where does the bus stop?	Bus stop sign
What route does the bus take?	Route description
Where do I have to change buses?	Route map
Which bus is that coming now?	Sign on the bus
	Terminal personnel, driver

DURING THE TRIP

INFORMATION NEEDED	SOURCE OF INFORMATION
Where, on the route is the bus presently?	Route description
When do I get off?	Announcement of bus stop
	Driver

WHEN CHANGING BUSES

INFORMATION NEEDED	SOURCE OF INFORMATION
Where is the bus stop for my connecting bus?	Information board
What's the quickest way there?	Local map

THE END OF THE TRIP

INFORMATION NEEDED	SOURCE OF INFORMATION
How do I get from the bus stop to my goal or to the connecting bus stop?	Local map
	Route map
	Terminal personnel, driver

Figure 9.1.: Diagrammatic representation of the information needed in a "complete" Public Information System for the passengers (source: TFB, 1984)

same name must be used on the bus if a bus stop has a name on its sign, then the same name should be called out on the bus and so on. This is important, not only for the passengers to know where they are but also in helping to create a mental image of the transportation system for its users. The consistent use of designations and names is also convenient for the personnel, the chances of misunderstanding between personnel, as well as between personnel and the public, being in this case reduced. Uniformity and consistency in design, symbols, type-face, colours etc, also give the company a distinct image and indicate to the public that this particular information pertains to public transportation. They may also reduce costs in connection with the production of the information material (signs, boards, pamphlets etc).

Finally, a number of more specific points merit attention. The most important information items in terms of creating a mental image of public transportation are the name of the stop, the route number and the name of the final destination. A name for a bus-stop is necessary for indicating where to get on or off the bus and to enable communication with personnel and other passengers. Naming the stops is a standard practice in connection with rail traffic (e.g. subways), but unfortunately not on bus routes. It follows that, if a name is used for a bus stop, the same (or an expression containing the same) name should be utilized in timetables, route maps, bus-stop signs and announcements on-board the bus. The route number relates to a particular geographical route. The name of the destination should be a well-known place. Leaving out the destination name is not recommended. Those who are not familiar with the route number have only the destination name (if it is properly chosen) to go by. The route number itself does not actually say much by way of information. In general, route numbers and destination names reinforce one another.

PRINTED INFORMATION

The main tools for disseminating printed information about the system are the route maps, the printed timetables and the various informational pamphlets hat give general information about the operation of the system (fares and fares structures, area covered, hours of operation etc). There is a wide variety of designs and ideas to make these types of printed information simple and easy to understand as well as aesthetically attractive. It is not possible in the limited space available here to give even a summary description of the multitude of designs. The interested reader who would care to write to the various public transport agencies in major cities around the world, would receive plenty of examples of pamphlets, maps etc, on which to base his own designs.

In the following we give some of the basic elements and principles for design for printed information. These elements come from a number of sources around the world, but basically they draw from Greek (Giannopoulos, 1986) and Swedish experience (TFB, 1984).

Route Maps

Route maps are a well-known way to show the network of routes, the terminals, the transfer points and the bus stops of a bus network. As the size of the network (i.e. the number of lines) increases, it becomes increasingly difficult to show all the lines in one map or to make the map easy to read and understand for the travelling public.

The alternative to having one single map covering the whole area would be to have maps for sections of the city or maps for individual routes or groups of routes along the same broad corridor. Both of these alternatives but mainly the second could offer more easily digestible information and may be easier to use.

The main disadvantage of a route map covering the whole area arises from the difficulties that an average traveller usually has to read and understand it, since most people, especially the less educated ones, are not familiar with maps. A divided route map, showing only a few routes at a time, may be easier to read, but it looses on informational content, as it cannot show the totality of the network and thus help the passengers in choosing combinations of routes to reach their final destination.

Another important point is that the route maps should show the actual geographic background, i.e. the actual network of streets (and buildings) of the area. If the map becomes complicated and rather confusing by showing this background then a more simplified version of this background should be shown. A good example of such a simplified background can be usually found in maps showing the Subway lines of the big metropolitan areas around the world.

The recommended contents of a route map are the following :

a. The designated bus routes.
b. The terminals and transfer points.
c. The fare zones (if such zones exist in the fare system).
d. The names of the bus stops (or those that have a name).
e. The marked out symbols and names of final destinations.
f. The names of different parts of the city.
g. Major street names and popular destinations, as well as those of well-known places and buildings.
h. The scale and an indication of the North with an arrow.

Colour-printing improves the legibility of a map considerably and is highly recommended. The background should be printed in a softer tone than the route map itself, in order to create a better contrast effect. It is almost impossible to draw a map in the same format as the pocket-size timetables for urban areas, except if it is a very small area. Therefore, the map must often be distributed separately, or designed as a foldout for the pocket-size timetable. An example of a bus route map, used in Sweden is shown in Figure 9.2. This is based on a background map of the area which helps a better orientation of the prospective passengers.

Timetables

A timetable is a list of the times when buses will depart from all, or the most important, stops of the bus route network. For an urban situation it is virtually impossible to give times of departures from every bus stop. However, every effort should be made to give times of departure from major stops and/or at transfer points, and terminals. This need must be taken into account when making the schedules, so that provision is made to "anchor" the schedules from the above mentioned specific points along the network.

The most important prerequisite for a coherent timetable is to have a well-organized "pattern" showing the movement of buses. The number of exceptions from normal service and the alternatives available should in principle be as few as possible. Too many exceptions lead to misunderstandings and to a general feeling of uncertainty causing people to doubt whether they have understood the timetable correctly.

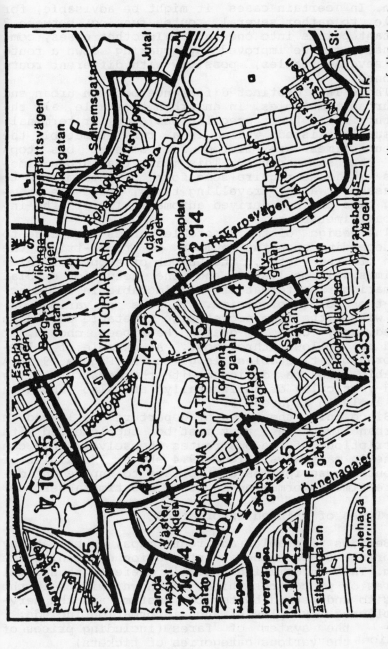

Figure 9.2 : An example of a bus route map. (Note how the map shows the names of the stops, the names of the main streets, and the terminal points for the routes).

The general outline of the written timetables should be according to the passengers'need for information. In certain cases it might be advisable, for example, to gather several routes running between 2 important points into one table. In other cases, comprehension can be improved by breaking down a route into several tables, possibly with different route sections.

There is a distinct difference between urban and interurban timetables. In an urban timetable, all the departure times from specific bus stop (or terminal) are usually listed, while in a rural timetable the departure times are listed for several bus stops along the same route. This means that urban timetables will also require some form of information to the passenger about travelling times, while the travelling time can be derived automatically in the interurban timetables.

The design of the timetable varies from case to case depending upon the number of round-trips, the length of the routes, the number of stops for which the times will be listed and the need for special information. The format of the timetable is influenced by the choice of design. The use of various designs within the same pocket-size timetable should be avoided, and, once a design has been chosen, it should be followed throughout. An example of a layout for urban timetables is given in Figure 9.3. A timetable can be designed with the departure times listed vertically or horizontally as also shown in the example in Figure 9.3.

Since only the times of departure are listed in the urban timetables, they must be supplemented with a description of the bus routes themselves. This can be done in many ways. Figure 9.4 shows 3 examples of bus route descriptions appropriate to supplement departure time information in urban bus timetables.

Other Types of Printed Information

Besides timetables and route maps, a bus agency can print other general information concerning its system. This information usually refers to special features or procedures which, if known, will help the public to understand better the system and the services offered. Examples of such information include:
- the system of fares (including prices of the various categories of tickets)
- procedures for obtaining the special monthly or tourist passes

TIM	MON-FRI				SATURDAY				SUNDAY		
4				50							
5	05	20	35	50							
6	05	20	35	50		20	35	50			
7	05	20	35	50	05	20	35	50			40
8	05	20	35	50	05	20	35	50	00	20	40
9	05	20	35	50	05	20	35	50	00	20	40
10	05	20	35	50	05	20	35	50	00	20	40
11	05	20	35	50	05	20	35	50	00	20	40
12	05	20	35	50	05	20	35	50	00	20	40
13	05	20	35	50	05	20	35	50	00	20	40
14	05	20	35								
15	05	20	35								
16	05	20	35								
17	05	20	35								
18	05	20	35								
19	00	20	40								
20	00	20	40								
21	00	20	40								
22	00	20	40								
23	00	20	40								
00											

departures horizontally

departures vertically

Bus departure from Times Square

6	7	8	9	10	11	12	13	14	15	16	17	18	19	20	21	22

Mon-Fri 15/5—31/8

6	7	8	9	10	11	12	13	14	15	16	17	18	19	20	21	22
														15	15	15
	18	18	18	18	18	18	18	18	18	18	18	18	18			
	38	38	38	38	38	38	38	38	38	38	38	38	38	45	45	
	58	58	58	58	58	58	58	58	58	58	58	58				

Saturday 15/5—31/8

6	7	8	9	10	11	12	13	14	15	16	17	18	19	20	21	22
								15	15	15	15	15	15	15	15	15
		18	18	18	18	18	18									
		38	38	38	38	38	38	45	45	45	45	45	45	45	45	
58	58	58	58	58	58											

Sunday 15/5—31/8

6	7	8	9	10	11	12	13	14	15	16	17	18	19	20	21	22
			15	15	15	15	15	15	15	15	15	15	15	15	15	15
			45	45	45	45	45	45	45	45	45	45	45	45	45	

Figure 9.3: Examples of urban timetables.

- descriptions of how to reach specific points in the urban area by bus
- other information

Figure 9.5 shows two examples of lay-outs for information on fares and on "how to get there" from a recent pamphlet of the Public Transport Authority of the Greater Thessaloniki Area, Greece.

The information is typically printed on pocket size fold-ins or small pamphlets and be distributed free of charge. Putting a price, even small, in this material will reduce its readership dramatically . Also the more colourful and "appealing" these pamphlets are, the more attractive they will be and the more chances they will have to be read.

In order to be effective, the material should comply with the following general principles :

a. It must contain one only or may be two major themes of information which will be clearly marked in the title (e.g. **Fares in Greater Athens**, or **The Monthly Pass** etc).

b. It must have a simple and easy to understand layout without lengthy descriptions and preferably with many sketches, drawings etc.

c. It should contain names, addresses and telephone numbers that someone could con-

tact, if more information is desired.
In drawing pamphlets or fold-ins for additional
information to the travelling public, and in view of
the above requirements, it is recommended that the
help of professional people in the fields of graphics
and printing is employed.

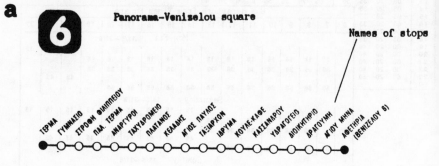

a

6   Panorama-Venizelou square

Names of stops

ΤΕΡΜΑ ΓΥΜΝΑΣΙΟ ΣΤΡΟΦΗ ΦΙΛΙΠΠΟΥ ΠΛ. ΤΕΡΜΑ ΑΜΑΡΓΥΡΟΙ ΤΑΧΥΔΡΟΜΕΙΟ ΠΛΑΤΑΝΟΣ ΚΕΛΑΔΗΣ ΑΓΙΟΣ ΠΑΥΛΟΣ ΤΑΞΙΑΡΧΩΝ ΙΔΡΥΜΑ ΚΟΥΛΕ-ΚΑΦΕ ΚΑΣΣΑΝΔΡΟΥ ΥΔΡΑΓΩΓΕΙΟ ΔΙΟΙΚΗΤΗΡΙΟ ΔΡΑΓΟΥΜΗ ΑΓΙΟΥ ΜΗΝΑ ΑΦΕΤΗΡΙΑ (ΒΕΝΙΖΕΛΟΥ 6)

b

33

Town Hall   National Bank   Shopping Mall   Sun Square

Name of stop   30.35.36.41
Museum   30.31.34.35
                40.52.54.55

Lake

                                            B connecting metro line A

St.Sophia   Central square   Connecting bus route numbers

University 32.34.40   32.36   31.32.35.36
St.George   34.38   37.40   38.40.42

Anabella   40   Rough indication of the route

            C Panorama

            D
            E   Travel time information

Relevant information

Figure 9.4.: Examples of bus route descriptions

300

LINE 10	PANORAMA - New RR Station

Number of buses : 13 Average length : 7.6 kms
Starting time : 4.45´ Frequency peak hour : 5´
Ending time : 1.56´ Average Frequency : 7´

<u>Routing:</u>

Direction 1: Panorama, St. Katherine's ....etc.
Direction 2: New RR Station, Museum, ...etc.

<u>Area</u> : National Theater - White Tower
<u>Buses</u> : Via Mela street : 1,5,6,12,15,33
    via King George street: 7,10,11,31,59,61

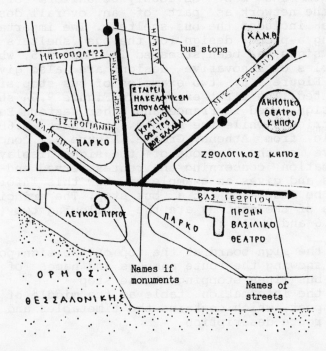

Figure 9.5: Examples of general information on routes, travel time and "how to get there" (used in Thessaloniki, Greece).

301

INFORMATION AT STOPS AND TERMINALS

Bus Stops

The items of information recommended to be displayed at a bus stop are the following :

a. the name of the stop,

b. the route numbers it serves (i.e. the numbers of the buses that stop there),

c. the description of the routes (i.e. their stops and terminal points),

d. the times of departure of the buses (if the stop is a major one or a transfer point) and

e. possibly a map of the whole system of lines on a city map background.

The description of the stop in terms of its name and the route numbers must be the same as the one appearing in the maps, timetables, pamphlets and other written material concerning the system.

The sign of the bus stop is part of the information system and must obviously be uniform for the whole of the network as part of an overall design which also includes the bus shelters. The importance of adopting a proper design for the bus shelters and bus stop signs has been stressed in chapter 5, where some examples of innovative designs are also given. Here, in Figure 9.6, two examples of bus stop signs are presented. The first example in Figure 9.6A shows types of signs used in France and other Western European countries, while the second in Figure 9.6B is an example from Athens, Greece. Figure 9.7 concentrates more on the lay-out of the signs displaying the information concerning the routes served and the timetables and gives an example of how this information can be displayed at a bus stop. The principal components of the setting are the following two (see Figures 9.6 and 9.7A) :

- the sign board at the top of the sign post, showing the route numbers and names of the bus lines stopping at the stop

- the information table at the middle of the post, which contains the timetables and the route description

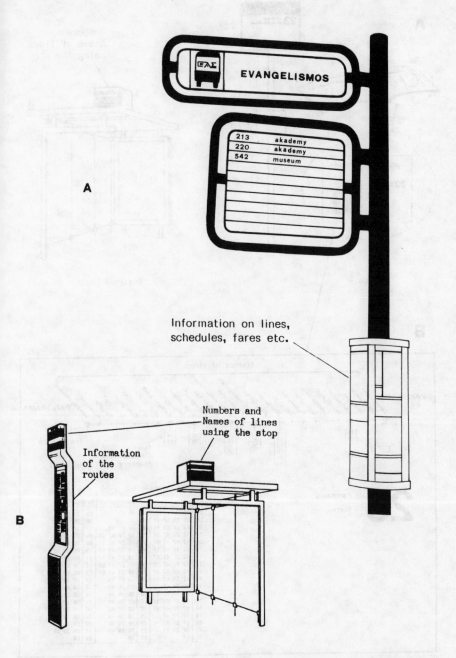

Figure 9.6: Two examples of bus stop sign posts and the points of display of the information. (A):Athens, Greece (B): France (design by J.C.Decaux).

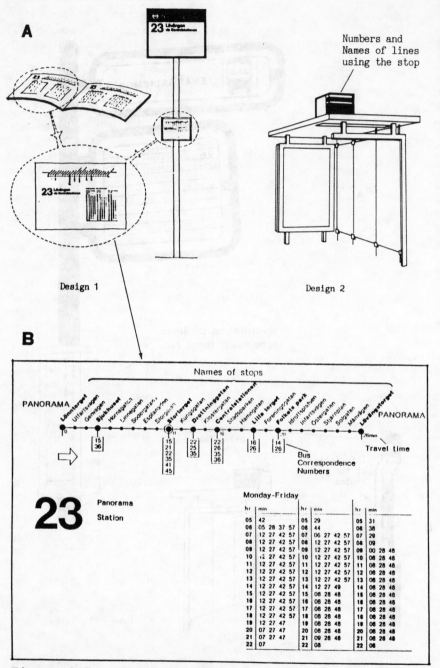

Figure 9.7: An example of the comprehensive information that can be displayed on a bus stop sign post (Source: Adapted from TFB, 1984)

304

An important point in laying out the information at bus stops is the size of the letters to use so as to achieve maximum legibility. The size will depend on the reading distances for :

    a.   persons on the opposite side of the street to read the stop signs (distance approx. 15m),

    b.   persons inside the incoming bus to read the name of the bus stop from a distance of approximately 8-10m and

    c.   persons standing near the sign at a distance of say 2-3m to read the information table.

For these distances, and taking into account the reading abilities of persons with slightly impaired vision (see Figure 9.10), the suggested sizes of the letters for the top board sign of the stop are:

Bus Stop Name	:	50 mm
Route Number	:	90 mm
Main Destination	:	36 mm
Secondary Destination:		27 mm

Terminals

As Terminals are meant here all bus terminals. These are usually at the end of bus lines or groups of bus lines, and are especially important when combined with railway stations (subway or suburban rail), airports, ports and so on. In these areas there are several bus lines originating or terminating and therefore the information on the bus system is both pertinent and of utmost importance.

In Terminals there is both the space and the scope to display additional information about the system, i.e. in addition to that displayed at simple bus stops. The additional information may include the following:

    -   Route maps of the whole system or its parts.

    -   Fare information.

    -   Local maps with indications as to where to find the bus stops.

    -   Information about other modes of public transport in the area, e.g. taxis, interurban buses, suburban rail etc.

    -   Other relevant information.

The information is usually displayed in aesthetically pleasing boards, strategically placed at points of maximum pedestrian flows. An example of the lay-out of such a board is given in Figure 9.8.

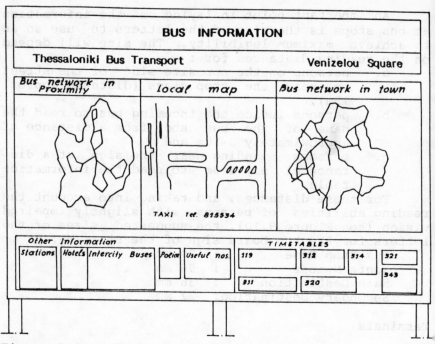

Figure 9.8: Example of a lay-out of a bus information board for terminals.

INFORMATION CARRIED ON THE VEHICLES

The information that is carried on the vehicle can be distinguished according to whether it is on the exterior of the bus or in the interior.

Exterior Signs

A. Contents and Position

The exterior signs of the buses usually contain up to three principal pieces of information :

    a.   the route number,

    b.   the destination name and (if applicable)

    c.   some additional information or clarification, such as for example an intermediate destination or major stop, or a brief description of the route and the type of service (e.g. whether it is an express line or local bus and so on).

306

The route number should be placed in 4 positions (see Figure 9.9A) :
- the front
- the back of the vehicle
- the right side next to the entrance door
- the left side of the vehicle, preferably near the back

The name of the destination can be placed in two positions : at the front, and/or at the right side by the entrance door, in both cases together with the route number.

The additional information is put either on the main sign in the front of the vehicle, together with the route number and the name of the (main) destination, or separately on a special sign usually hung on the inside of the right side of the windscreen.

B. Overall Design Criteria

The principal design criteria for the exterior bus signs can be outlined as follows :

a. The characters for the names must be large enough so that all lettering of the front sign is legible at a distance of at least half a block away from persons with average or slightly impaired vision. Route numbers should be even more pronounced. The following dimensions are suggested:

Front sign :

route number	25 - 30 cm
main destination	10 - 12 cm
additional information	8 - 10 cm

By the entrance:

route number	15 cm
main destination	6 cm
additional information	4 cm

Route number at the back and left side :	15 cm.

b. Type faces should be selected on the basis of legibility rather than contemporary style or tastes (see also comments on next section on legibility,

c. The recommended type of writing on the front and entrance signs is negative print with high contrast (see next section on legibility) and well illuminated.

d. The front sign display should have a storage capacity for the numbers and names of a number of routes at least equal to the double of the existing routes to allow for future expansions.

307

e.   Colours can be used as an element of marking
        certain words and sometimes as a way to reduce
        the number of words required. For example, the
        word "express" in an express bus service can be
        written in red.

C. Display Design

    All displays of the exterior signs must have the
possibility to change their information according to
the route that the bus is scheduled in. There are the
following potential designs:

1.   Manual Roller Curtain

    This is the most common design and has the best
legibility at the lowest cost. The driver manually
turns the roller curtain to the appropriate destination.
    The advantages of this system are that it :
    -       is inexpensive
    -       is reliable with a minimum of maintenance
    -       has relatively large character capacity
    -       has unlimited graphic variability
    The disadvantages include :
    -       limited storage capacity for different
            routes
    -       very slow and cumbersome in changing
            destinations

2.   Automatic Roller Curtain

    This system consists of the conventional roller
curtains powered by synchronized motors controlled by
the driver.
    The advantages of this system include:
    -       large character capacity
    -       unlimited graphic variability
    -       relatively quick in changing the displays
    The disadvantages include :
    -       limited storage capacity
    -       moderately expensive
    -       high maintenance costs

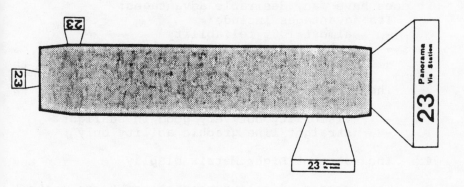

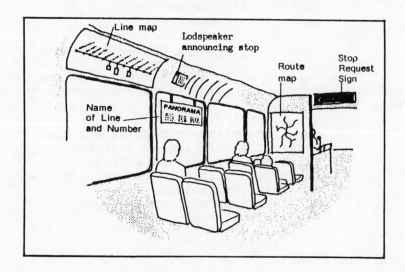

Figure 9.9: Example of the types of information (A): on the exterior and (B): on the interior of a bus.

3.   L.E.D. (Light Emitting Diode)-usually 13-Segment
      Display

      This type of display is usually very costly but
it does have many desirable advantages:
      Its advantages include:
      -    almost 100% reliability
      -    unlimited storage capacity
      -    very low maintenance costs
      -    very quick changing of destinations
      The disadvantages include :
      -    very high initial cost
      -    visibility not very good in sunlight
      -    straight line graphic ability only

4.   Incandescent Light Matrix Display

      This screen displays characters by the control-
led combination of lighted bulbs in a whole matrix,
giving a dot formation appearance.
      Its advantages include:
      -    unlimited route storage capacity
      -    contoured graphic ability
      -    very quick changing of destinations
      The disadvantages include:
      -    poor legibility
      -    poor contrast in sunlight
      -    moderately expensive

5.   Incandescent 13-segment Character Display

      This system has approximately 3 incandescent
bulbs per segment to give 13-segment character display.
      Its advantages include:
      -    good visibility in daytime and night-time
      -    very quick changing of destinations
      -    unlimited destination storage
      -    good reliability and low service cost
      The disadvantages include:
      -    straight line character shapes only
      -    high initial cost

Interior Signs

      Inside the vehicle, a variety of information
such as route maps and instructions are recommended.
The various suggestions are shown in Figure 9.9B.

Standardized symbols should be used for instructions as much as possible, to facilitate comprehension for passengers with language difficulties for example. Furthermore, a graphic description of the route should be displayed in the vehicle, for example over the window opposite the exit. It should be the same as the route depicted in the timetables.

It is considered essential that the bus stop name is announced on the bus. This is seldom done, despite the fact that passengers seem to prefer it. Bus stop announcements, along with route maps, make it possible for the passenger to know where he is and to prepare himself to get off in time. Even regular passengers appreciate bus stop announcements, since they may be absorbed in reading or discussion or it may be difficult for them to recognize their surroundings at night or in bad weather. A variable sign showing the "next stop" can also be used in addition to calling out the stops. This is important for people with impaired hearing.

As regards the stop request sign this is also considered essential. Once a passenger presses the bell for the next stop, this sign lights up, usually in bright red, so that other passengers intending to get off the bus can see as well as the driver (through a similar light on his instrument panel) that the stop bell has been pressed. After the stop, the light turns off again. Besides being a reminder the stop request light helps to avoid irritation from repeated bus stop requests.

A NOTE ON LEGIBILITY

Since most printed information (as well as that displayed on bus stops and terminals) has to be read quickly and often from a distance, **legibility is of primary importance.** The following comments will help to understand better the importance of this notion and to choose the appropriate size of letters to use.

When reading a normal text, there is no difference in legibility between the most common character types. However, when reading from a distance, or for those with bad vision, straight and sharp contours are considered the best. A good type to use is, for example, the Helvetica Medium type or other similar character types, shown below:

Helvetica Medium

This character type has recently become the most common in information displays. It is therefore recommended to use the Helvetica Medium type of letters in public transportation information. A bold-faced type (i.e. darker) is easier to read at a distance than a lean-faced type.

For reading from greater distances, Figure 9.10 shows the relation between print size and reading distance, with respect to different vision abilities. The line for "slightly impaired vision" (1:160) is a reasonable line to use. The ratio for "impaired vision" (1.5:100) implies unrealistically large signs.

The low-case letters in a consecutive text produce better legibility than the capital letters. Capital letters are more legible when used in single words, for example on signs, especially when the words are short. For longer words the first letter is better to be a capital and the following letters lowcase.

The distinction between "positive" and "negative" texts is also important. Positive is a text with black (or coloured) letters on a white background, while negative is a text with white letters on a black background.

A positive text is more legible than a negative one when the characters are of normal size (i.e. less than 12 pica). A negative text is more legible when the characters are large and when a single word is used. This latter comment applies especially in the case of electric signs which are illuminated from behind, such as for vehicle signs with "rolling-band" text.

As regards colours, their use adds importance in some words but it does not seem to have any particular effect on legibility. The important thing is to have good contrast between the colours used.

Finally, the legibility of a sign requires not only a certain text size, colour and contrast, but also a certain type of illumination. The need for proper reading light increases with age. Dim reading light leads to dullness of vision, low contrast sensitivity and bad colour perception. Reflections, for example, in protective glass on timetable displays, or shiny signs reduce legibility markedly for those with visual defects.

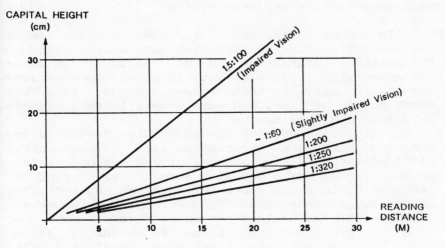

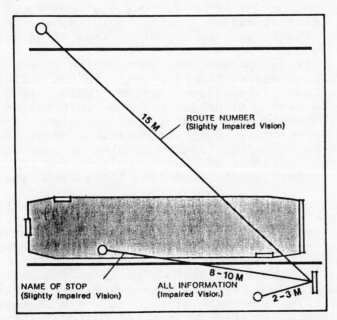

Figure 9.10: (A): Relation between reading distance and size of letters in PIS signs. (B): Requirements for legibility according to the type of information displayed.

OTHER MEANS OF INFORMATION DISSEMINATION

Telecommunication Assisted Systems

In recent years, public transport systems around the world are increasingly using more modern means of transmitting information to the public. These means are especially important, when it comes to notifying changes in services that have to be out in a very short period of time, and more generally to a dynamic information dissemination.

Today all modes of transport have developed and are using some form of remote (i.e. telecommunications assisted) demand management and customer information system. For a detailed account of current telecommunications and computer application, including buses, see Giannopoulos, 1988. For buses telecommunications assisted systems may be used for:

- providing information to potential customers about the timetables, cost and other relevant information in order to motivate them to travel
- providing and continuously updating information at the various stations about the time of arrival of the vehicles, the causes of delays, the expected times of departure etc
- giving passengers information about the progress of the trip while in the vehicle.

Telephone information systems were among the first to be used. Although printed information and signs may seem to be adequate, there is always a need for a more personal, oral information. Many people may also have difficulties in reading or understanding printed information. This applies, for example, to many older people and to those with impaired vision.

A number of telephone bus information centres, which also give information about all public transportation systems in their areas are now in operation in Europe and the US and their number is expected to increase in the next few years.

Ideally these telephone centres are equipped with computerized systems that give all necessary information in a matter of seconds. A most notable recent example is the Computerized Customer Information System (CCIS), being tested at the Southern California's Rapid Transit District in the U.S. (Philips, 1984). In this system a transit information operator receives telephone inquiries from callers

314

and retrieves the desired information through the use of a remote computer terminal located in front of him or her. The results from this experiment so far are encouraging and, as it is noted in Philips (1984), this technology appears to have strong potential for assisting public transport agencies to provide information to the public in a timely and accurate manner, thus increasing the attractiveness of the whole system to potential users. A contemporary experiment in France with the minitel services gained world recognition (Dartou 1982). In its original form, the users could get information on the service of the railways and on the timetables of 1,500 trains, available for reservation between 1,000 French cities and 500 foreign cities. Moreover, it was possible to reserve seating and sleeping accommodation. The interactive communication was extended by the opportunity to pay with electronic currency and to use the system for electronic post. This trial by SNCF formed a part of a telematic experiment with interactive videotext that was started by various transport undertakings in France. Similar experiments and applications of interactive videotext in the United States are described in Behnke (1984).

Finally, a number of current applications concern the flow of information and other services to bus passengers exclusively during their trip. One such application is described by Yanata (1983) and concerns the introduction in Akita city in Japan of a "bus location" system that tracks the movement of up to 1000 buses on the network and informs passengers at the bus stops about the approaching bus, while a central control station can monitor the whole system at a glance. Similar experiments are in operation or planning in other European and North American cities (for example the AISY system being installed in Brussels and other Belgian cities and so on).

A major effort in the field of telecommunications and computer application (expressed usually with the abbreviation "telematics") to all transport operations is currently under way in Europe. Although far from an exhaustive review of these efforts, the following give a concise account of the efforts so far (summer 1988) and are meant to demonstrate the extent of the effort.

Personnel Assisted Systems

Even if one goes at great lengths to provide good signs and printed matter, there is always a need for direct oral information from the transportation company's personnel. The possibility of the direct, personal information is important for many groups of the society, for example, those with visual defects and elderly people. It has also been shown that many people prefer to confirm their own knowledge of the transport system even though they have access to printed material (TFB, 1984).

The category of personnel having most contact with the passengers is the drivers, who must often answer questions to the public. It is therefore important that they are trained for this purpose and that driving times take into account some time for answering inquiries. The conflict between driving times and service to the passengers is most often felt in the largest cities. The drivers are often obliged to listen to complaints about conditions which they themselves cannot influence, for example about increases of fares. It is therefore important that the company's internal information network functions well and that the personnel involved in direct contact with the passengers is prepared to answer such questions and, in general, to give information to the public.

Some International Innovative Research Programmes

In the European Economic Community a Council Regulation that was adopted in June 1988 established the EEC's initiative in the framework of project DRIVE (Dedicated Road Infrastructure for Vehicle Safety in Europe). The overall goal of this project is "to make a major contribution to the introduction of an Integrated Road Transport Environment, offering by 1995 improved transport efficiency and a breakthrough in road safety". Actual work on this project should start by January 1989.

Another major European effort, in the wider fields of interest of the EUREKA framework, is the PROMETHEUS program of research, which is jointly run by fourteen European automotive manufacturers. This program is not only concerned with developments of systems which are contained within the vehicle, but it has also initiated sub-programs concerned with communication between vehicles (PRO-NET) and between vehicles and roadside infrastructure (PRO-ROAD). PRONET is more specifically concerned with collision avoidance techniques and maximizing fuel efficiency and road capacity by means of such concepts as road-trains etc. PRO-ROAD is more concerned with route guidance and driver information systems. A third sub-program, PRO-GENERAL, is concerned with the traffic engineering effects of the systems developed and the framework for their possible implementation.

Two other EUREKA programs, EUROPOLIS and CARMINAT, are concerned with the application of modern technology to improving the general field of driver information and traffic management.

The OECD in Paris, has also carried some major studies in the field within the EURO- COST program. Similarly the European Conference of Ministers of Transport (ECMT) has established a Committee to derive standards for road/vehicle communication systems. Its first task was to define a standard for the traffic information component of the recently agreed European Broadcasting Union Radio Data System (RDS). The Council of Ministers in its May 1987 meeting has adopted a resolution on this standard.

Initiatives in Individual Countries.

USA

Despite early investigations of infrastructure based driver information systems, recent work has tended to concentrate upon autonomous systems of route guidance such as the ETAK navigation system, developed, marketed and for the time being exclusively used in California. The major US car manufacturers notably Ford and General Motors are vigorously continuing research work in applications of advanced electronics and telecommunications to vehicle design and driver information and guidance. The M.I.T. has initiated its second international study on the future of the motor vehicles, where a substantial part of the work will evolve around the issues discussed here.

Federal Republic of Germany

In Berlin a major trial of a route guidance system called ALI-SCOUT (an expansion of the ARI system introduced in 1974), which is based on infra-red technology, is currently under way. This system, consisting of about 240 beacons and 1000 equipped vehicles, is operational since the beginning of 1988. Pilot versions of the ARIAM radio based driver information system are in operation. The autonomous navigation system EVA has been under development for some years, and it is planned to incorporate real time updating of the in-vehicle information by means of RDS (Radio Data Systems) when it becomes available. All major German car manufacturers are participating in the PROMETHEUS project mentioned earlier.

United Kingdom

A route guidance system (AUTOGUIDE) similar in scope to the Berlin trial is under way in London. Bilateral discussions are currently under way between the British and German governments aiming at arriving at a draft standard for road to vehicle communications based on infra-red technology, and it is planned that the London system should incorporate this standard.

In the field of Urban Traffic Control SCOOT is the current traffic responsive system developed and implemented in the UK for deriving maximum efficiency from urban networks based on actual traffic conditions.

In the field of route guidance and navigation, two systems have been developed. The PINPOINT, a vehicle location system finally withdrawn, and DATATRAK and AUTOTRAC. PACE is another autonomous navigation device which uses sophisticated compass equipment and map-matching techniques to enable the driver of a vehicle to keep track of his position.

France

In France too, several attempts have been made to develop systems utilizing the capabilities of informatics in the road transport sector. Navigation systems such as the Dutch TELE-ATLAS have been used in the Greater Paris area. Also, improved driver information techniques have been developed, in particular by using the TELETEL viewdata system and the ANTIOPE teletex system.

Particular research is being conducted into advanced traffic control techniques, including the application of expert systems.

Besides the above, France participates in both the CARMINAT and EUROPOLIS programs, while its car manufacturers participate in the PROMETHEUS program.

The Netherlands

The CARIN in-vehicle information system for freight transport based upon compact disc technology is being developed by Philips and forms part of the Netherlands involvement in the CARMINAT, EUREKA programme now going on in Europe.

Other motorway control and communication systems have been developed and applied in the Netherlands, especially in the Rotterdam and the Hague areas.

Japan

At least three of the major Japanese manufacturers have already developed autonomous navigation systems.

A major research project is being conducted in Japan, funded by the Ministry of Communications, to investigate a network of beacons for route guidance using microwave technology. Even greater rates of data than with infra-red technology, may be possible from this work. This project builds upon earlier work done in the CACS loop-based trial.

ANNEX 1
AN EXAMPLE OF
URBAN TRANSPORT
ORGANIZATION: THE
CASE OF FRANCE

ANNEX 1

INTRODUCTION

The present organization of bus and urban transport in France represents the cumulative effect of the following four laws and related decrees passed since 1973:

1.   Law No.73-640 of 11 July 1973, which allowed local governments to levy the "Versement des Transports" (VT), a tax dedicated to transit, which was to provide a major funding source to fuel the resurrection of public transport in French cities (originally in Paris).

2.   Law No.79-475 of 19 June 1979 (Loi relative aux Transports Publics d' Interet Local), which clarified the relative roles of local and central authorities in connection with transit and established specific constraints with respect to the types of contract for transit operation (though these constraints have since been removed).

3.   Law No.82-1153 of 30 December 1982 (Loi d' Orientation des Transports Interieurs), which established basic principles of transport sector management, e.g. defined the social character of urban transport services, confirmed the supremacy of local authorities in matters concerning public transport, stressed contractual relationships between various actors in the sector, guaranteed fair enumeration of transport operators for services provided etc. and;

4.   Law No.83-8 of 7 January 1983 (Repartition des Competences entre les Communes, les Departements, les Regions et l' Etat), which established the principles and procedures for transfer of authority, property and means of finance from central to local/regional authorities.

These fundamental laws have established an organizational framework [a] which is described in more detail in the following.

---

[a].   Most of the information in this Annex comes from Mitric, (1987).

THE ROLE OF LOCAL GOVERNMENTS

The local governments in France have complete jurisdiction over public transport services and dispose of financial means for fulfilling this role. The most typical institutional form is that of an **Association of Communes (AC)**. These are one or more administrative units making up an urban area. From the ACs, an **Organizing Authority** (Autorite Organisatrice - AO) for transit (and/or other functions) is formed. An AO consists of elected officials from its constituent communes. Occasionally, a city is "governed" by one single commune (Marseille), or several small cities in a region may associate themselves to form a single AO, with the number of communes reaching several dozen. The geographical limits within which an AO exercises its powers, called "le perimetre des transports urbains", do not have to coincide with territorial limits of the associated communes and serve purely to divide urban from interurban transport links. Once several communes form an AO, they give up their power to make unilateral decisions concerning transit (except in matters related to traffic regulations, for which the jurisdiction is kept by individual communes).

The AOs can take several forms with the corresponding names:

a. An **Inter-communal Syndicate**: this is the simplest form, specifically for managing transit and possibly other urban services.
b. An **Urban District**: this is responsible by statute for fire services and housing, to which other responsibilities (including transit) can be added on an elective basis.
c. An **Urban Community** (Communaute Urbaine), which is the highest level of all, responsible by statute for the whole of the urban public infrastructure and services, including transit, parking, streets, traffic signals etc. Other responsibilities can be added on an elective basis by decision of the relevant commune councils.

The AOs are legal owners of all transit vehicles, facilities and equipment and are empowered to:

-    impose the local tax earmarked exclusively for transit finance known as "Versement des Transports" (VT)
-    make all the investment decisions

- define transit policies, including all
  service specifications and tariffs
- organize transit services whether by force-
  account ("en regie") or through a contract
  with a private transit operator
- enter into contract with the central government for the purpose of getting grants
  for transit system development ("contrats
  de development") in exchange for diverse
  conditionalities related to transit policies, services offered and the program execution.

The only means, by which the central government
can interfere, are by setting the overall framework
of organization through laws and decrees, by giving
some technical assistance to the AOs and through "development contracts" and public loans. It also sets
the maximum <u>annual rates</u> of tariff changes and the
maximum rates of VT tax.

FINANCING

Transit revenues (from fares) in France covered
in 1985-1986 in average only about 50% of direct operating costs (for individual transit properties).
This varied from close to 20% to exceeding 90%.

What is not covered by tariffs is made up by
subsidies, the key source being the local transport
tax "versement transport" (VT).[a]

The VT has proved to be the engine that powered
the development of transit in France over the last 15
years. In the early 1980s, it provided the finance

---

[a]. Instituted in 1971 for the Paris region, VT
was extended (at the discretion of the local AO) to
cities of 300,000 and more. This threshold has been
reduced twice more: to 100,000 inhabitants in 1974
and to 30,000 in 1983. The tax is levied on all
enterprises within the "transport perimeter", employing more than 9 people. The maximum rates were in
1986: 2% in Paris and nearby suburbs; 1.2% in outer
Paris ("grande couronne"); 1% for provincial cities
above 100,000 people, but this is increased to 1.5%
if the AO decides to invest in a large-scale project,
e.g. tramway or metro; 0.5% for cities between 30,000
and 100,000 people. The VT tax base is the total sal-
aries paid by the company up to a ceiling established
for social security payments.

(around 2 billion FF) to cover about one third of combined operating and investment costs of transit companies in 50 provincial cities.

In addition to traffic revenues and the VT, other sources of transit finance are:

    a.   "normal" fiscal resources of the local community,

    b.   loans from a special fund for Economic and Social Development (Fonds de Developpement Economique et Sociale) and

    c.   central government grants for large-scale investments (40% for metros, 50% for tramways); in some cities, these grants are given through a system of development contracts signed between the Ministry of Transport and AOs for a period of 2-3 years (renewable), with a conditionality referring to the extent and pace of transit development in the agglomeration.

For 100 provincial networks, the sources of finance for aggregated operating and investment costs were:[a]

Fare revenues	32%	(FF 1,859 million)
VT tax	33%	(1,925 million)
Local fiscal sources	15%	(863 million)
Loans	15%	(885 million)
Central gov. grants	5%	(324 million)
	100%	(FF 5,856 million)

Since the setting up of this system of financing, certain problems have arisen, which are worth mentioning, if nothing else, in order to show that each particular case is a separate case that could only be adopted after a careful study of the local conditions and constraints. In France the last 5-6 years the financial system of urban transit is starting to feel a financial "pinch". This is the combined effect of substantial investments in capacity over the past 10 years (i.e., increased loan repayments), of the decline in the proportion of costs financed through the fare revenue (although actual fares may be climbing a bit higher than inflation), of a steady

---

[a]. Data from ETUR published in Mitric (1987). The date of reference for these data is not precise but is placed by the author in the beginning of '80s.

increase in the operating costs and the stagnation of the yield of the VT tax (in turn due to the general economic stagnation). The root causes may lie in having pursued a subsidy approach without sufficient controls to maintain efficiency and financial discipline; the key examples cited by the critics include irresponsible, politically motivated tariff policies (imposed by the central or local governments), unbridled investments spent by AOs for the development of new lines, as well as padded labour contracts. A debate is under way, to select new sources of finance and/or find areas where economies of spending could be pursued.

Transit Operators

Among more than 100 transit networks in France (for cities above 30,000 inhabitants) about 20% are operated by the AOs themselves (force account); the largest of these public companies is <u>Regie Autonome des Transports Parisiens (RATP)</u> for the Paris region. The remaining 80% are operated by private companies on contract with AOs. The contracts are usually for a five-year period and are awarded only following competitive bidding.

A large part of the market is divided among three private companies:
- TRANSEXEL, which operates some 30 networks (including subways in Lille and Lyon)
- SCET with 15 networks
- CGFTE with 8 networks

Each of the three key operators has a somewhat different organizational approach. The TRANSEXEL typically sets up subsidiary companies in individual cities; these companies then enter into contract with AOs. The CGFTE uses a more centralized approach, involving the head office and branch offices. The SCET introduced a system of mixed-economy (public/private) companies for each network; the share holders include the AOs, chambers of commerce, banks and (through a symbolic contribution to capital) the SCET itself. Each of these city-based companies signs a service contract with an appropriate AO, as well as a technical assistance contract with the SCET. The main advantage of this approach is that it involves direct participation("contact organique") of the elected officials (AOs) in the management of transit, while the private nature of the company permits it to operate in ways normally not open to public enterprises.

The above three main operators show other differences as well: for example, the TRANSEXEL is very keen on marketing, the GFTE stresses engineering skills and, generally, the supply side of the operation, while the SCET has an integrative, urban management-type of orientation. In either case, the engineering and managerial know-how amassed by these operators is considerable and its vertical integration through mother-daughter firms is a grand achievement. Another type of integration of all private operators is achieved through membership in the Union des Transports Publics, which acts as an information clearing house, a lobbying spearhead, as well as a body for collective bargaining with workers' unions.

Contracts between AOs and operators specify the services to be provided and divide the responsibilities and risks with regard to investments, operating costs and receipts. This involves the listing of:

a. Route network to be served, as well as quantitative and qualitative description of services.

b. Rules for adjusting service specifications in the course of period of the contract.

c. Tariffs to be charged.

d. Means to be provided by each party (in parallel with the contract, a program of investments and other actions may be, but is not always, developed).

e. Enumeration for services and rules for adjusting these services (whether to respond to inflation, or to adjust for marginal changes in the services offered).

f. Details of contract supervision, arbitration, start and end of contract period etc.

Though four contract types were prescribed by law in 1979, only two types have taken root:

1. Fixed-ceiling ("prix forfaitaire") contract: an agreement to pay the operator a fee based on unit cost (per bus-km) and the amount of bus-km of service to be supplied; risks on the cost side are thus borne by the operator, but all investment and commercial risks are taken by the AO; in practice, such contracts also include marginal fees to pay for changes in supply demanded by the AO, as well as incentive formulae meant to increase revenues.

2. **Management Contracts** ("contrat de gerance"): this has been the most popular con-

328

tract type; the AO takes all the risks, paying the operator his actual expenses, based on a provisional budget which can be revised in the course of the year; in addition, there is a bonus for good management.

Since the above contracts have not been conducive to increased productivity of operations, new types of contract are being sought, with a goal of more balanced risk sharing between the two parties. So far, this search has not produced any substantial innovation. In some smaller cities, contracts have been signed, in which operators have undertaken both cost and revenue risks but within a very narrow band, based on inflexible service specifications and numerous safeguard clauses for the operator (including renegotiating before the expiration of the normal period for the contract).

Integration of Urban Transport

Traffic circulation plans carried out in numerous cities in the 1970s with state subsidies (about 50%) had integrative elements, but on a minor scale. The division of jurisdictions (AOs responsible for transit, communes for urban streets and traffic, the state for national roads) made it difficult to deal with inter-modal relations, essentially on a case-by-case basis.

The law of 30 December 1982 created a tool meant to fill this void. This was a new type of urban transport plan, "Plan des Deplacements Urbains" (PDU), with the following main features:

a. PDUs are multi-modal (including walking) and consist of general principles, policies, management programs and development plans for the agglomeration in question.

b. A PDU applies to the territory within the transport perimeter (or its part).

c. PDUs must be accompanied by an implementation plan including the financing of investments and operating costs (a major advance relative to past practices).

d. The authority for developing a PDU is given to AOs.

e. PDUs must be subjected to public inquiry; they are adopted by the AO, following the approval by the member-communes and

f. the implementing authority remains with traditional agencies.

It should be noted that PDUs have been defined as studies, and no legal power has been assigned to them. The state has refrained, both on paper and in practice, from using its subsidies (notably through the development contracts for transit) to enforce integration. Finally, no relationship has been defined between PDUs and urban development plans.

ANNEX 2
THE USE OF SERVICE STANDARDS AND PERFORMANCE INDICATORS AROUND THE WORLD

The Background

The elaboration of the subject of standards of service and performance evaluation, in Chapter 4, including a worldwide survey of the use of such standards and procedures. This survey was done by mailing a simple questionnaire to some 200 public transport agencies from the UITP's 1985 list, This questionnaire consisted of a general introduction and definition of the terms used, and 5 simple questions concerning the use of standards and/or performance indicators, their typ and the type of evaluation procedures used, if any.

A relatively small number of answers were received, totalling 59, i.e. a percentage of approximately 30%. The relatively small number of answers precluded any form of meaningful statistical analysis and, for this reason, what will be done in this annex is to simply give in a concise form the information gathered from this survey, as an example of current practice in some major public transport agencies around the world.

The agencies that have finally sent answers are shown in Table B.1 together with their size in terms of the number of buses.

The geographical distribution of these agencies is as follows:

Europe :	35
North America:	17
South America:	1
Africa:	1
Australia:	2
South East Asia:	1
Rest of the world:	2

By size, in terms of the number of buses, the distribution of the agencies that participated in this survey, is as follows:

Small (up to 100 buses):	8
Medium (100 - 500):	26
Large (more than 500):	25

Use of Standards and/or Performance Indicators

Agencies were asked to state whether they use any standards or performance indicators. The service standards were distinguished in two categories: Formal (i.e. statutory or officially approved and established) and Informal (i.e. set and used by the agency itself). The results of the replies are as follows :

333

Type of standard used:	No. of agencies
Formal	13
Informal	22
Indicator of Performance	26
No standards or PIs used	2

Finally, 82% of the answers indicated that there is some sort of a service evaluation procedure followed (see next section).

Table B.1

Name and Size of Public Transport Agencies participating in the survey (in alphabetical order of the city).

Serial No.	City-Country	Name of Agency	No. of buses
1	Athens-Greece	Urban Transport Agency (EAS)	1900
2	Bologna-Italy	Aziende Trasporti	430
3	Brisbane-Australia	Brisbane City Council Depart.of Transport	567
4	Bruxelles-Belgium	Societe Nationale des Chemins de Fer Vicinaux (SNCV)	2416
5	Calgary-Canada	Calgary Transit	N/A
6	Cincinnati-(Ohio)-U.S.A.	Southwest Ohio Regional Transit Authority	379
7	Copenhagen, Denmark	Hovedstadsomrodets Trafikselske	1460
8	Denver-U.S.A.	Regional Transportation District	760
9	Dortmund-FRG	Dortmunder Stadtwerke AG,Verkehrsbetriebe	144
10	Dublin-Ireland	Dublin Bus	814

Serial No.	City-Country	Name of Agency	No. of buses
11	Essen-FRG	Essener Verkehrs-Aktiengessellschaft	230
12	Geneve-Swiss	Transports publics Genevois	N/A
13	Genova-Italy	Azienda Municipalizzata Trasporti-AMT	1051
14	Glasgow-G.Britain	Strathclyde Passenger Transport Executive	N/A
15	Grenoble-France	Transports de l' agglomeration Greno-bloise (TAG)	N/A
16	Hague-Netherlands	N.V.Gemengd Bedrijf HTM	194
17	Hamburg-FRG	Hamburger Hochbahn AG	1200
18	Helsinki-Finland	Helsinki City Transport	437
19	Hong Kong	3 franchised compa-nies monitored by Transport Dept. Hong Kong Government	4000
20	Honolulu-U.S.A.	MTL	440
21	Huston - U.S.A.	Metropolitan Transit	1020
22	Istanbul-Turkey	I.E.T.T.	1449
23	Johannesburg-S.Africa	Johannesburg Transport Dept.	449
24	Leicester-G.Britain	Leicester City Bus Ltd	N/A

Serial No.	City-Country	Name of Agency	No. of buses
25	Lille-France	Les Transports en Commun de la Communaute-tcc	335
26	G.Britain	National Bus Company	14512
27	Louisville-U.S.A.	Transit authority of River city	318
28	Madison-U.S.A.	Madison Metro	200
29	Madrid-Spain	Empresa Municipal de Transportes de Madrid S.A.	N/A
30	Mainz - FRG	Stadtwerke-Mainz AG	145
31	Malmo-Sweden	Malmo Lokaltrafik	250
32	Massachusetts-U.S.A.	Massachusetts Bay Transp.Authority	374
33	Milano-Italy	Aziende Trasporti Municipali	1500
34	Montreal-Canada	Societe des transports de la Communaute urbaine de Montreal	2066
35	Munster-Germany	Westfalishe Verkehrs-gesellscchaft mbH	912
36	Napoli-Italy	Azienda Tranvie Autofilovie Napoli	1115
37	Newcastle-G.Britain	Tyne and Wear Passenger Transport Executive	N/A
38	Newport-G.Britain	Newport Transport Limited	93
39	New York-U.S.A.	New York City Transit Authority (NYCTA)	1077

Serial No.	City-Country	Name of Agency	No. of buses
40	Nottingham-G.Britain	Nottingham City Transport Ltd	N/A
41	Paris-France	Regie Autonome des Transports Parisiens	4000
42	Philadelphia-U.S.A.	Southeastern Pennsylvania Transportation Authority	1112
43	Pittsburg-USA	Port Authority of Allegheny	N/A
44	Quebec-Canada	CTCU2	475
45	Quebland-Australia	Quebland Regional Authority, Bus Transport Agency	543 / N/A
46	Riyad,Saudi-Arabia	Saudi Public Transport CO	N/A
47	Rouen-France	T.C.A.R./SIVOM	179
48	Sacramento-USA	Sacramento Regional Transit	207
49	Salzburg-Austria	Salzburger Stadtwerke Verkehrsbetriebe	130
50	San Diego-U.S.A.	San Diego Transit Corporation	485
51	Sao Paulo-South America	Companhia Municipal de Transportes Colectivos-CMTC	3313
52	Stuttgart-Germany	Stuttgarter Strassenbahnen AG	N/A
53	Thessaloniki-Greece	Organization for Urban Transport in Thessaloniki (OASTh)	450

Table B.1 (Continued)

Serial No.	City-Country	Name of Agency	No. of buses
54	Toronto-Canada	Toronto Transit	
55	Ulm,Germany	Stadtwerke Ulm Neu-Ulm Commission	1370
56	Warsaw-Poland	Miejskie Zaltady Komunikecyjne	1882
57	Wien-Austria	Aktiengesellschaft der Wiener	43
58	Yorkshire,West-G.Britain	West Yorkshire Passenger Transport Executive.	N/A

Types and Values of Standards Used

The types of standards that are used by the agencies surveyed vary substantially. Of the Formal standards used, there was no uniformity and practically each agency had its own different standards. Of the Informal ones the peak headway, load factors, and schedule adherence were the most usually stated. Several standards could be said to be similar or able to coincide with one another with proper modifications and convertions. These modifications could not be made here because they have to be based on information on the background data, types of surveys used for their calculation etc. So it is not possible or advisable to make comparisons between the agencies based on the values of the standards shown in the following Tables.

The types of standards used, as well as their values, are shown in Tables B.2 for the Formal, and B.3 for the Informal standards.

Table B.2

Formal Standards used by the agencies surveyed.

Name of Standard	No.of agencies	Serial no.of agency from Table B.1	Stated max or min values (if given)
Max distance to a stop	1	16	500m
Max headway	2	16	10 mins (peak) 15 mins (off-peak)
		3	30 mins
Max bus age	1	3	
Direct connection	1	15	City centre-railway stn.
Drivers' hours of work	3	46 1 31	11h/day (max) 10.5h/day(max) max no.of hours/week
Ratio of maintenance personnel per vehicle	1	36	0.6-0.7 pers/veh.
Fare box recovery rate	1	50	31% (min)
Cleanliness	1	39	-
Pull-outs	1	39	
Bus Loading	1	39	
Signs used	1	39	-
Trip "completions"	1	39	
Public information	1	39	
Climate control	1	39	-
On time performance	1	39	-

Name of Standard	No.of gencies	Serial no.of agency from Table B.1	Stated max or min values (if given)
Mean distance between failures	1	39	-
Preventive maintenance	1	39	-

Table B.3

Types of Informal standards used by the agencies surveyed

Name of Standard	No.of agencies	Serial no.of agency from Table B.1	Stated max or min values (if given)
Max walking distance to a stop	4	16	300m
		46	200-500m
		20	max 5mins for 70% of dwellings
		3	200-400m
Min Bus stop distance	1	20	300m
Bus stop design standards	2	20	1sq.m/25 pass
		16	L=15m,W=2.05m Shelter: 40pass sign standards
Running speed (min)	4	35	
		4	15-20 km/h
		16	23 km/h
		23	17km/h (peak)

Name of Standard	No.of agencies	Serial no.of agency from Table B.1	Stated max or min values (if given)
Frequency (headway)	10	33	6-10 min (peak)
		23	5 min (peak) 30min (off-
		46	30 min
		8	30 min
		27	30 min
		18	5-10min (peak)
		16	1 bus/70 pass (peak) 1 bus/55 pass (off-peak)
		4	10-20 mins
		21	According to demand (peak)
		29	10mins (peak) 20mins (off-peak)
Spare time buses	2	3	15%
		8	20%
Choice of mode	1	16	>3000 pass/km: tram opera-tion >700 pass/h: tram opera-tion
Fixed timetables	2	4 35	
Waiting time runs	1	3	5%
Bus maintenance	2	45	97.5%
		42	97.5%
On time performance	1	21	98%
Route performance	1	16	Ridership>59% of average occupancy

Table B.3 (continued)

Name of Standard	No.of agencies	Serial no.of agency from Table B.1	Stated max or min values (if given)
Bus Retirement policy revenue values	1	8	12 years or 500,000 miles
No standing passengers on long distance buses	1	45	30 kms
Fare revenue to bus operating cost ratio	1	45	50-60%
Ratio of maintenance personnel to buses	2	22	max 0.5 pers/veh.
		18	max 0.5 pers/veh.
Ratio of drivers in operation to buses	1	22	2.37/bus
Max load levels	3	21	130% (peak)
		27	135% max
		28	15 standing pass (max)

Types and Values of Indicators of Performance

Our remarks for the standards (see above) apply to the Indicators of Performance as well. Here, however, a somewhat greater "clustering" can be observed, as there are a number of Indicators that can be found to be used by several agencies.

The names of the Indicators and the numbers of agencies using them, as well as the names of these agencies can be found in Table B.4.

Types of Performance Indicators used by the agencies surveyed.

Indicator	No.of agencies	Serial no.of agency from Table B.1	Stated max or min values (if given)
A. Service inputs			
Employees/veh-km	1	33	
Operating cost	5	8	
		28	
		46	
		19	
		3	
Maintenance cost	4	47	
		19	
		28	
		8	
Staff cost	1	19	
Subsidy/passenger	3	28	
		48	
		20	
Total cost/veh-hour	1	6	
Operating ratio	2	20	
		28	
Maintenance empl/veh.	1	13	0.8-0.9
Average fleet age	1	13	9 years
Fuel consumption per 100 kms	3	50	48 lt.
		13	
		47	
Oil consumption per 100 kms	2	13	0.45 kg
		47	
Subsidy/hour	1	28	
Maintenance hours/ 1000 miles	1	28	

Table B.4 (continued)

Indicator	No.of agencies	Serial no.of agency from Table B.1	Stated max or min values (if given)
B. Service outputs			
Veh-kms	1	50	
Veh-kms/no.of empl.	1	2	
Veh-kms/veh in operation	4	22	
		19	
		33	
		37	
Veh-kms/hour of maintenance	4	47	
		8	
		3	
		13	
Miles between maintenance road calls	8	50	
		42	
		21	
		46	
		13	
		6	
		28	
		8	
Bus defects at spot checks	2	19	
		10	
No.of complaints per month	6	10	
		19	
		28	
		6	
		23	
		8	
Bus accidents/ veh-km	6	10	
		8	
		46	
		21	2.1-2.2 (1987)
		19	
		28	
Vehs in peak hour/total	1	13	90%
Waiting buses/ all buses	1	47	
Annual no.of bus journeys	1	22	
% lost kms/ scheduled km	3	46	

344

Table 5.4 (Continued)

Indicator	No.of agencies	Serial no.of agency from Table B.1	Stated max or min values (if given)
		19	
		10	
Commercial speed	1	36	
Peak load factors	1	20	
Average waiting time at stops	1	19	

C. Service Consumption

Passengers carried	10	36	
		37	
		8	
		20	
		22	
		35	
		3	
		23	
		31	
		10	
Pass/revenue mile	5	21	33.51
		46	(1987)
		8	
		2	
		44	
Pass/veh-km	3	19	
		2	
		3	
Pass revenue/ service hour	2	48	
		46	
Passenger/hour/week	3	5	
		28	
		6	
Revenue/bus-km	5	46	
		8	
		3	
		19	
		23	
Revenue/revenue hour	1	46	
Revenue/passenger	1	50	

Table 5.4 (Continued)

Indicator	No. of agencies	Serial no. of agency from Table B.1	Stated max or min values (if given)
Total revenue/ total cost	1	6	
Cost return	5	21	40% (1987)
		46	
		8	
		5	
		38	
Vehicle occupancy in peak hour	1	19	

Procedures for Evaluating Bus services

A final question was whether the agency had a standard procedure for evaluating the service and what this procedure entailed. In this question, only 82% of the agencies that answered the questionnaire gave a positive answer. A brief description of the procedures followed by each of the various agencies is given below.

Bologna, Italy

The most important parameters that are taken into account are: the number of passengers per veh-km, the number of passengers per line, the commercial speed, and the coefficient of utilization. According to these parameters, an evaluation and a proposal are made to the appropriate authorities for service changes as necessary.

Brussels, Belgium

The results of the exploitation are established for each line monthly. These include the total costs of operation and the receipts. The lines that present very low a coefficient of exploitation (defined as the ratio of receipts to costs) are subject to an in-depth study. According to the results of this study, a decision is taken as to whether the line will be dropped or changed.

346

Boston, Mass, USA

The agency (MBTA) has well established service evaluation and modification procedures. Most of them are similar to the ones described for Toronto in Chapter 4, and will not be described here in greater detail.

Brisbane, Australia

Patronage and cost recovery are the main criteria used in evaluating existing services. Routes for evaluation are chosen through experience and monitoring. Average patronage per bus of less than 5 (depending on route length) and fare box cost recoveries of less than 20% are considered poor. Services with these factors would seriously be considered for termination, depending on the social welfare aspects of the service catchment.

Recommendations for terminating a service must be approved by the Council's Establishment and Co-ordination Committee (the equivalent of a Council Cabinet). The State Commissioner for Transport should also be advised. Both these procedures are statutory.

Services showing signs of overcrowding are considered for increase in frequency. The frequency increase will depend on the severity of overcrowding.

Calgary, Canada

An integrated set of Council approved policies stipulate the goals established for transit service in Calgary. Route evaluation relates directly to these goals. Routes must also meet acceptable operating standards (e.g. safety concerns). Finally, all route revisions to existing services are discussed with the public, prior to presentation to the City Council for approval. Discussion of route proposals with the public allows direct individual comment on the perceived effectiveness of the proposed service revisions. It is acknowledged that policies, operating constraints and community desires are not always compatible. However, maximization of the area of overlap between the three basic components: Policies, Operating constraints, Public concerns, will produce the most successful route.

The route proposal review process is designed to accommodate a suggestion or inquiry from virtually any source (a citizen, a community organization, City Council, private industry etc). Additionally, the

347

existing bus network is continually reviewed to identify areas for service improvements (e.g. route ex-
tentions or revisions). Suggestions which appear to
have merit are processed in the following manner.

Prior to formal public consultation, all route
proposals (new routes and route revisions) are reviewed within the Transportation Department at two
levels.

The Current Transit Planning Team is a multidis-
ciplinary working group with representatives from all
areas of the Transportation Department (Calgary Transit, Traffic Operations, Finance, Safety and Transportation Planning). Proposals which are recommended
by this group are presented to the Senior Transit
Planning Team for senior management review. If approved by this senior group, proposals are presented
to the public as proposed revisions. This step in
route planning allows for public comment regarding
design effectiveness and desired levels of service.

Route and service evaluation is divided into two
major categories:
1. evaluation of new and/or revised services
2. monitoring of existing service.

Dortmund, FR Germany.

The main Town Planning regulations, especially
through the exclusion of residential areas to through
traffic, together with the further development of
housing estates result in the routing/structuring of
bus services. These have then to be adjusted to the
conditions of traffic on fixed tracks. The provision-
/operation of a bus service has to be permitted/ap-
proved by the local authorities in Arnsberg.

Mainz, FR Germany.

Changes in the urban transport services, concerning e.g. bus stops, the lines, vehicle provision
etc, are discussed internally at a technical level
and with the supervisory and policy making bodies of
the agency.

This may be followed, if necessary, by a further
discussion among the communal bodies/organizations
(county council and its committees).

In special cases the approval of the technical
supervising authority at city level is required.

Dublin, Ireland

Aggregate revenue and expenditure data are submitted to Government for assessment and comparison with present targets. Dublin Bus internally monitor the standard and quality of service offered. Proposed changes in service levels are not assessed in detail by any outside agency on a formal basis.

Denver, Colorado

Evaluation by the performance indicators shown in Table B.4, accountable to board of directors, who are in turn accountable to public (electorate).

Utilize a set of route service standards that accounts for ridership in quartiles. The lowest quartile routes are reviewed, revised if warranted and reevaluated.

Genova, Italy

Periodical surveys are carried out about the number of trips made for work and by students. According to the different lines loads, a decision is reached annualy, about the revision or not of the service on a particular line.

Hong - Kong

There are 3 levels of monitoring or evaluation of bus services by the Transport Department:

a. Franchise extension

Under the terms of the Public Bus Services Ordinance and the franchises granted to the three bus companies, franchises may be granted for a maximum period of ten years. Provided that the government is satisfied that the grantee is capable of maintaining a proper and efficient service, the franchises may be extended for a maximum period of two years at any time during a franchise period. In considering whether an extension should be granted, the Transport Department would make an assessment of the bus company's performance against the criteria given in Table B.4, and an extension would only be granted if the grantee's performance is found to be satisfactory.

b. Day-to-day monitoring

Under the Public Bus Services Ordinance, the Transport Department is authorized to specify the level of service (e.g. frequencies, vehicle types etc) on specific bus routes; any new routes and alterations to existing routes are also subject to the Department's approval. It is the Department's practice to issue "schedules of services" laying down the required level of service to the franchised bus companies for each of the bus routes. The Department makes use of traffic returns submitted by the companies, surveys conducted by the Department's staff, and complaints and suggestions from the public to monitor the performance of the companies against the schedules of service. Where there is a discrepancy between actual performance and the schedule of service, the cause will be investigated and remedial action will be taken. This may be in the form of the bus companies improving their performance to match with the scheduled requirements, or the schedules of services being adjusted to reflect actual demand where they have become out-of-date.

c. Forward planning

Under the Public Bus Services Ordinance, the franchised bus companies are required to submit to the Transport Department each year a forward planning programme covering their operations for the following five years. All proposals for new routes, route cancellations and alterations should be included in this programme. Upon receipt of the submission, the Transport Department will consult the District Boards, other transport operators and the Transport Advisory Committee on the programme; it will then evaluate it in the light of comments received from the parties consulted, policy guidelines laid down by the Transport Branch, surveys and studies conducted by the Department and suggestions and complaints from the public. Negotiations will then be held between the Transport Department and the bus companies with a view to agreeing on a programme. The agreed item will be implemented as far as possible.

350

Honolulu, Hawai, U.S.A.

A. System Performance Evaluation

Service level standards for the transit system as a whole have been established on the basis of the temporary service guidelines previously prepared by the Department of Transportation Services and the experiences of properties in other cities. These standards have been grouped as shown below and are discussed in a comprehensive reference manual by the agency.

1. System Access and Route Structure
2. Bus Stops, Benches, Shelters
3. Hours of Operation
4. Service Frequency
5. System Dependability
6. Loading Standards and Riding Conditions
7. Street Supervision and Traffic Checking
8. Bus Condition and Maintenance
9. User Information Services
10. Safety
11. Community and Social Concerns

B. Selected Route Evaluation Procedure

As a result of the review of practices elsewhere and the anticipated current and future availability of data, the evaluation measures and methods of comparison shown below were selected for evaluations of bus route performance in Honolulu.

Operations
1. Peak load factors
2. "Pass-ups"

Patronage
3. Peak load factors
4. Average total passengers per scheduled bus hour

Economic
5. Operating ratio
6. Average deficit per passenger

Other Considerations
a. Route history and trends
b. Support of transit goals, objectives not related to operations, patronage or finance.

The basic evaluation is done using weekday data. Where necessary and appropriate, supplementary analyses for weekends, holidays and portions of the weekday (peak period, eaarly morning, evening and night), using available data for the corresponding period or periods, is possible.

The standards used in a first study by the same agency are as follows (see also Tables B.2 and B.3).

Measure	Value

Operations

| 1. | Peak Load Factors | 100-150% |
| 2. | "Pass-Ups" | Zero |

Patronage

3. Average Total Daily Passengers 70% (System Average)

4. Average Total Passengers per
   Revenue Hour   20 (1)

Economic

5.	Operating Ratio	30% (2)
6.	Average Deficit per Total
	Passengers	(Not Applicable)

Other Considerations

a.	Route History and Trends	(Not Applicable)
b.	Support of Transit Goals,
	Objectives and Community	(Not Applicable)
	Concerns

Notes
(1) Applies to weekdays only. Use 10 for weekends, early morning, evening or night service evaluations.
(2) For fixed route local bus service. Use 50% for limited stop or express service.

Houston, Texas, U.S.A.

The data used in the evaluation of service come from the following sources:

352

1) Load checks taken at maximum loading points approximately at eight time intervals in a year. Used in adjusting service to ridership.
2) Ride checks on-board the bus. Taken at least once a year on every trip. Used for running time and boarding and alighting information.
3) Origin/Destination surveys conducted about every four years.
4) Census data taken from 10-year U.S. Census and updated regularly by State and Regional Planning agencies. Used for route planning.

Istanbul, Turkey

In evaluating the services, the most important factor is the demand of passengers for bus trips with the buses. In morning and evening peak hours bus services given to operation at maximum number; at off-peak the number of buses are reduced. Also express bus services are operated at peak hours. Changes to services may be made in order to meet weather conditions (snow, fog.etc.) New routes or changes to existing ones are made according to operational analysis and examination of passenger requests. All the changes regarding to services are done by the Directorate of exploitation of the municipality of Istanbul.

Johannesburg, S.Africa

Evaluating in case of a proposed change in the service characteristics, is based on passenger demand and revenue and expenditure indications.

Milan, Italy

The performance of the service is evaluated by systematic surveys on passengers traffic along the maximum load sections of the lines. The passengers are counted by the agency's (the ATM) staff waiting at stations.

The experimentation of a new automatic monitoring system along two lines is starting in a short time and will probably be introduced on the whole network. This system enables the supply of information on the bus position in real time, the possible "aheads" or "delays" with respect to the timetable, the number of passengers on the trains, the state of

the equipment on board and the communication by dig-
ital code device or by two-way radio.

As concerns urban bus lines, the service organization is planned by the agency upon authorization given by the Province and the Region to the Municipality. This authorization enables the agency to
establish the total number of kilometres for which a
subsidy on production costs is granted to it.

The changing of line routes, on the contrary,
must be decided and approved by the Municipality of
Milan.

As far as surburban bus lines are concerned both
the operation programme of the lines and the changing
of routes must be authorized by the Municipality and
approved by the Province and the Region.

Naples, Italy

A new service or a change to an existing one is
usually originated by a social request. The agency
answers after careful consideration. The considerations are of economic -administrative nature and of
mobility for the users too.

The agency (ATAN) of the Napoli Administrative
Commission, by proper resolution, submits the service
- programme to the town council, which takes the
final decision.

New York, USA

Evaluations are conducted through field surveys
and audits of company records.

Regular performance reports are submitted to the
NYC Board of Estimate. The bus companies are under
the jurisdiction of the Bureau of Franchises. Specific standards were and are still being settled. These
standards are mandated by a resolution of the Board
of Estimate.

River city, USA

Route Performance can be evaluated by either
revenue or ridership measures. However, since there
are a variety of fare classifications (regular,elder-
ly and handicapped, commuter, student and transfer),
revenue alone cannot adequately reflect a route's
performance.

Ridership measurements (passengers per hour,
passengers per trip) present a more accurate method
of judging a route's service to the community and

354

enable valid comparisons to be made among routes that provide similar service.

Since coaches on local routes pick up and discharge passengers anywhere along the entire length of the route, the number of passengers carried per hour is virtually unlimited. Because of this, comparisons of passengers per trip will yield the most valid measure of express route performance.

The resulting comparisons are evaluated as follows:

If ridership exceeds 80% of the likely service average, the route should be considered worthy of continuation and no action should be taken.

If ridership falls between 60% and 79% of likely service average, the route should be reviewed to determine if there are any segments of service for which corrective action could be taken.

If ridership falls below 59% of the likely service average, the route should be reviewed to determine if there are any segments of service for which corrective action could be taken. After corrective action, the route should be reviewed again in 6 months. If after 6 months the ridership level has not increased, then two actions can be considered.

If it is judged that the service requires minimal resources or provides a special service, then it may be continued on a trial basis.

If continuation would require a significant allocation of the system's resources, and alternative service is available, then the provision of the route should be terminated.

Ridership for new service should be reviewed 6 months after institution. If ridership falls below 59% of the likely service average, the route should be reviewed again in 6 months. If after the second review, ridership has not increased, then the actions indicated for existing service will be taken.

Route performance is monitored by both the Schedule and Planning Departments. The Schedule Department takes periodic ridership counts throughout the year, with each route being checked independently and separately from all others.

On a regular basis, the Planning Department will conduct on-board ridership counts for each route in the system, presenting both a route and a system profile.

Riyadh, Saudi Arabia

The agency (SAPTCO) carries monthly, quarterly, half yearly and annual evaluations. Each evaluation comprises of operational and financial aspects, along with recommendations for further improving the service.

Performance of each Evaluation period is compared with the performance of the preceding similar period and with that of the same period in the previous year. The service performance of November 1987, for instance, will be compared with that of October 1987 and also with the performance of November 1986.

This evaluation procedure is part of SAPTCO's Management Information System (M.I.S.); so results are consequently channelled up to the Company's top management to take part in the decision making process.

This information is analysed and tabulated by a computer in the department of Statistics and Information. This department is accountable to the Manager of Corporate Planning and Followup who reports directly to the General Director.

For the evaluation of service characteristics (parameters) field surveys become necessary.

The following surveys are the most common:
- Maximum Load point survey.
- Running time survey.
- Passenger boarding and alighting survey.
- Passenger Origin/Destination survey.

References

Abkowitz,M. (1983), <u>The Transit Service Reliability Problem and Potential Solutions</u>, UMTA Report No.NY-06-0097-83-01.

AC Transit (1983), <u>Transit Facilities Standards Manual</u>, Alameda Contra Costa Transit District, California, USA.

Ampt.E.S., Richardson, A.J., Brog, W. - editors, (1983), <u>New Survey Methods in Transport,</u> 2nd International Conference, Hugerford Hill, Australia, NVU Science Press publishers.

Anderson, P., Austin, M., Becker, A., Krumke, J. and Talley, W.(1981). <u>Prototype Bus Service Evaluation System.</u> Washington, D.C.: U.S. Government Printing Office.

Attannccii, J., Wilson, No., MC.Collom, B. and Burns, I. (1982), <u>Design of Bus Transit Monitoring Programs,</u> Transportation Research Record 857.

Babbie, E.R. (1979), <u>The Practice of Social Research,</u> Wadsworth publishers, Belmont, CA.

Barbour, L.C. and Zerrillo, R.J. (1982), Transit Performance in New York State, Transportation Research Record 857.

Bayliss, D., (1986) Technology Bus Services in London, a paper gives to the university of Newcastle upon Tyne, annual public Transport Symosium, February 1986.

BC Transit (1987), Service Planning Program, British Columbia Transit, Vancouver, Canada.

Behnke R.W., (1984), Videotex - Transportation Information Systems, Proc. Governor's Conference on Videotex, Transportation and Energy Conservation, Honolulu, Hawaii, pp.36-44.

Buckley, Ed. (1987), Elements of the Service Planning Process at the Orange County Transit District, APTA Western Conference, Phoenix, Arizona, USA.

German Promotion Group for Public Transportation Systems (1985), The Bus System, Studiengesellschaft Nahverkehr mBH, Berlin.

Boston Redevelopment Authority (1973), City Signs and Lights: A Policy Study, The MIT Press, Massachusetts, USA.

Brown,S.J. (1986), Buses to Match Needs of the World's Cities, City Transport, May/July 1986.

Cameron, J.C.F., Management of Firms to Satisfy Transport Needs: Urban and Regional Passenger Transport, ECMT 9th International Symposium, Madrid, 1982.

Carter, D.W., Mundle, S.R., and McCollom, B.E. (1984), Comparative Evaluation of Bus Route Costing Procedures, Transportation Research Record 994.

Ceder, A. (1987), Methods for Creating Bus Timetables, Transportation Research A, Vol.21A, No.1, 1987.

CPT (1981), Urban Planning and Design for Road Public Transport, the Confederation of British Road Passenger Transport (Bus & Coach Council), London, UK.

358

Cray, G.E. and Hoel, L.A. (1979), Public Transportation: Planning Operations and Management, Prentice-Hall, New Jersey.

CUTA (1985), Canadian Transit Handbook, Second Edition, Canadian Urban Transit Association and Roads and Transportation Association of Canada, Toronto, Canada.

Dartou, M. (1982), SNCF "trial" commercial services offered by telematics to the public at large: Design, Implementation, Initial results, Prospects, Rail International, May 1982, pp.99-104.

Daskin M.S., Schoter J.L. , Haghani A.E. (1988), A Quadratic Programming model for Designing and Evaluating Distance based and zone fares for Urban Tansit, Transportation Research B, Vol. 22B, No.1, pp.25-44.

De Leuw, Cather and associates (1983), Bus Terminals and Bus Stations - Planning and Design Guidelines, Report PG 2/83, South African Dept. of Transport.

Drosdat, H.A. (1977), Transit Performance Measures: The Significance in Local Funding Allocation, Seattle, Washington:Urban Transportation Program, University of Washington.

ECMT (1981), "Report on the transport of handicapped persons in wheelchairs", Paris 21/4/81, OECD.

Fielding, G.J., Glauthier, R.E. and Lave, C.A. (1977), Development of Performance Indicators for Transit, Washington, DC: U.S. Government Printing Office.

Fielding, G.J. and Glauthier, R.E. (1976), Distribution and Allocation of Transit Subsidies in California. Irvine, California: Institute of Transportation Studies, University of California, Irvine.

Fielding, G.J. et al (1984), Indicators and Peer Groups for Transit Performance Analysis, Urban Mass Transportation Administration, U.S.Department of Transport, Report No. CA-11-0026-2.

Fielding,G.J. (1987), <u>Managing Public Transit Strat-</u>
<u>egically</u>, Jossey-Bass Inc,San Fransisco, 300 pp.

Fitch, L.C., et al (1981), <u>Service Levels of Urban</u>
<u>Public Transport in the Netherlands</u>, a report of
a Study by the Institute of Public Administration, Washington DC, and the Netherland's Economic Institute.

Fruin J.J. (1971), <u>"Pedestrian Planning and Design"</u>
<u>Metropolitan Association</u> of Urban Designers and
Environmental Planners Inc., New York.

Giannopoulos, G.A. (1980), <u>Fare-free Public Transit</u>
<u>Potential in Athens, Greece</u>, Traffic Quarterly,
Vol. 34, No.2 ENO Foundation.

Giannopoulos, G.A, Zekkos K. (1980), <u>Transportation</u>
<u>for Brega-New Town in Libya,</u> McGaughy-Marshall-
McMillan (Consultants), Athens 1980.

Giannopoulos, G.A. (1985), <u>Financing Urban Public</u>
<u>Transport: Some Issues and Prospects for the Fu-</u>
<u>ture</u>, proceedings of a Seminar on the Economics
of Transport in the 1980's Organised by the Italian Center for Transport Studies (ICT's) in
Amalfi, Italy, October 1984.

Giannopoulos,G.A.,et al (1986), <u>Functional Standards</u>
<u>and Current Situation in Urban Bus Transport in</u>
<u>Greece</u>, Vols 1 & 2 (in Greek), prepared for the
Hellenic Organisation for Local Government and
Development (EETAA) by Kykloforiaki Consultants,
Thessaloniki, Greece.

Giannopoulos,G.A., (1988), <u>The influence of Telecom-</u>
<u>munications on Transport Operations,</u> Transport
Reviews, forthcoming.

Habricht, A.T., et al (1984), <u>Effective Width of Ped-</u>
<u>estrian Corridors</u>, Transportation Engineering
Journal of ASCE, Vol. 110 No.1, January 1984.

Haritos Z.J. (1987), <u>Public Transport Enterprises in</u>
<u>Transition,</u> Transportation, Vol.14, pp.193-207

Hartley, T. (1981), <u>A Glossary of Terms in Bus and</u>
<u>Crew Scheduling,</u> in Computer Scheduling of Pub-
lic Transport, A.Wren (ed.), North-Holland Publishing.

Institute for Urban Transportation (1971), Mass Transit Management: A Handbook for Small Cities, Graduate School of Business, Indiana University.

ITE (1976a) Manual of Traffic Engineering Studies, Institute of Transportation Engineers, Arlington Virginia USA.

ITE (1976b),"Characteristics and Service Requirements of Pedestrians and Pedestrian Facilities", Report of Technical Committee 5-R, Traffic Engineering, May 1976.

Keefer, L.E. (1984), Innovative Financing of Urban Transportation in the United States, paper in LET (1984).

LET (1984), Financing Urban Transportation, Proceedings of an International Colloqium organised by the Laboratoire d' Economie Societe Lyonnaise de Transports en Commun, Lyon, September 1984.

Levinson H.S.,Adams C.L., & Hoey,W.F. (1975), Bus Use of Highways - Planning and Design Guidelines, NCHRP Report 155.

M.A.N. (1985), Development for a Future Bus Transport System, M.A.N. (1985), Development for a Future Bus Transport System, M.A.N. Commercial Vehicle division, March 1985.

MBTA (1977), Service Policy for Surface Public Transportation, Massachusetts Bay Transportation Authority, Boston, MA.

McCrosson, D.F. (1978), Choosing Performance Indicators for Small Transit Systems, Transportation Engineering 26-30.

Metropolitan Washington Council of Governments (1984), Surface Transit Alternatives Study, Phase III: User's Guide for the Evaluation of Local vs. Regional Transit Service Provision, prepared by JHK Associates, National Transit Services & Econometrics, USA.

Mitric S. (1987), Organization of Urban Public Transport in France: Lessons for Developing Countries, Paper presented at the 66th Annual meeting of the TRB, Washington DC.

Talley,W.K. (1986), A Comparison of two Methodologies for Selecting Transit Performance Indicators, Transportation , No.13, 1986.

Nash, C.A., (1982), Economics of Public Transport, Waltham Cross, London.

Navin, F.P.D., et al (1975), Urban Bus Design. The University of British Columbia Dept.of Civil Engineering and the Engineering Undergraduate Society, Transportation Research Series, Report No.9, February 1975

OAS (1984), The 1983 O-D Athens household survey: Survey Methodology and Procedures, (in Greek), Organisation of Urban Transport (OAS), Athens, April 1984.

OECD (1980), Urban Public Transport: Evaluation of Performance, a report by a Road Research Group.

Oldfield, R.H., and Bly, P.H. (1985), Using Smaller Buses in Central London, TRRL Research Report No.31.

Pajonk,E., Walkenhorst,R. (1981), Research Project-Telebus, Studiengesellschaft Nahverkehr mBH, Berlin.

Parten M. (1966), Surveys, Polls and Samples: Practical Procedures, Cooper Square Publishers, New York.

Perry J.L., Baditsky, J., Gregersen H. (1988), Organizational, Form and Performance in Urban Mass Transit, Transport Reviews, Vol.8, No.2

Philips, R.O. (1984), The CCIS Experiment : Comparing Transit Information Retrieval Modes at the Southern California Rapid Transit District,US-DOT/UMTA Report no.UMTA-MA-06-0126-84-4.

RATP (1977), Autobus en Site Propre, report of a study commissioned by the Regie Autonome des Transports Parisiens (RATP) and conducted by the Societe Generale de Techniques et d' Etudes, the Societe Civile Freeman Fox, and the Centre d' Etudes Techniques de l' Equipement d' Aix-en-Provence, with Peter Midgley consultant.

362

Rensselaer Research Corporation (1970). Bus design Concepts and Evaluation, Troy, New York.

Talley W.K. (1988), An Economic Theory of the Public Transit Firm, Transportation Research B, Vol.22B, No.1, pp.45-54.

Talley, W.K. and Anderson, P.P. (1979), "Effectiveness and Efficiency in Transit Performance: A Theoretical Perspective", Transportation Research 15A: 431-436

Taylor,D.H. (1977), Bus Terminal Studies, Working Paper 36, Urban Transport Research Group, University of Warwick, Coventry.

TFB (1984), Information on Public Transport, (Summary in English) Transport Forsknings Bereduingen, Stockholm-Sweden.

TRB (1985), The 1985 Highway Capacity Manual, Transportation Research Board / National Research Council, Washington DC.

TRB (1981), "Transportation for Elderly, Handicapped and Economically Disadvantaged Persons", Transport Research Record No.660.

Tri-Met (1986), Planning with Transit, Tri-County Metropolitan Transportation District of Oregon, Portland, Oregon.

TRRL (1976) Bus Priority Systems, by a NATO Committee on the Challenges of Modern Society (CCMS), report no.45, published by TRRL of Great Britain, 1976.

TTC (1980-84) Survey manuals on: Cordon Count Program, Modal Split Count Program, Riding Count Program, Toronto Transit Commission, Service Planning Department.

TTC (1985a), The Service Standards Process, Toronto Transit Commission, Service Planning Department, August 1985.

TTC (1985b), Service Standards Application Report, Toronto Transit Commission, Service Planning Department, August 1985

Turner, R.P., and White P.R. (1986), **Recent UK Experience of the influence of Regulation on Performance**, Paper presented at the World Conference on Transport research, Vancouver, Canada, May 1986.

U.S.Department of Transportation (1978), **Proceedings of the First National Conference on Transit Performance**. Washington, D,C : U.S. Government Printing Office.

UITP (1985) **Handbook of Public Transport, 1985-86**, Vols 1,2 and 3 International Union of Public Transport, Brussels.

UMTA (1977), **Low-Fare, Fare-Free Transit: Some Recent Application by US Transit Systems**, Us DoT Urban Mass Transportation Administration.

UMTA (1984a), **Bus Route Costing Procedures: Final Report**, U.S.Department of Transport, Urban Mass Transportation Administration, Report no. DOT-I-84-24.

UMTA (1984b), **Bus Service Evaluation Methods: A Review**, Urban Mass Transportation Administration, U.S.Department of Transport, report no. DOT-I-84-49.

UMTA, (1985), **Transit Data Collection Design**, Urban Mass Transit Association (US Department of Transport), report DOT-I-85-38, June 1985.

UMTA (1982), **Route Level Demand Models: A Review**, U.S.Department of Transportation, Urban Mass Transportation Administration, Report No. DOT-I-82-6.

UMTA (1977), **Low-Fare, Fare-Free Transit: some recent applications by US Transit Systems**, UsDoT Urban Mass Transportation Administration.

US DOT (1983), **Bus Route Demand Models: Cleveland Prototype Study**, prepared for the UMTA Technology sharing Programme by D.Krechmer, G.Lanton, and M. Golenberg, S.G. Associates., Inc.

US, DOT (1981), Bus Route Costing Procedures: A Review, prepared for the UMTA Technology Sharing programme by Simpson and Curtin Division of Boss, Allen and Hamilton Inc.

Utah Transit Authority (1986), Transit Development Program, Wasatch Front Regional Council, Bountiful, Utah, USA.

VOV (1983), Unverbindliche Typen-und Konditionempfehlung fur den Standard-Linienbus SLIi, VOV, Koln.

VOV/VDA (1979), Bus - Verkehrssystem: Fahrzeug,Fahrweg,Betrieb , Verband Offentlicher Verkehrsbetriebe / Verband der Automobilindustrie e.V. , Frankfurt.

White,P. (1986), Public Transport: its Management and Operation, Hutchinson Publishing Co.

Wilson,N.H.M., et al (1984), Short Range Transit Planning: Current Practice and a Proposed Framework, prepared for UMTA Office of Technical Assistance, report No. MA-11-0035.

Yanata, R.(1983), The New Public Transportation Systems - Bus System in Akita City, IATSS Research Vol.7.

Index